# EAR ON WASHINGTON

# EAR
## ON
## WASHINGTON
### BY
# DIANA
# McLELLAN

**ARBOR HOUSE**
New York

Library of Congress Catalogue Card Number: 81-71683

ISBN: 0-87795-394-5

Manufactured in the United States of America

10 9 8 7 6 5 4 3 2 1

FOR DICK, FIONA AND THE TAR-BABY, WITH LOVE

# Acknowledgments

With special thanks to all my gallant former colleagues of the late *Washington Star*—they made churning out seven columns a week a delight; to my friend and sidekick Poppy, a.k.a. Caroline Stewart, without whom I could not have written this book; to Secret Sources, fine-feathered friends, the mighty, the flighty, my new friends at the *Post,* and all who call, on a whim, to share a laugh; to Debbie Young and Cosette Saslaw; to Audrey Adler and Eden Collinsworth, who made me stir my stumps and my editor, Arnold Ehrlich; to Jim Bellows, who had this screwball idea about a daily gossip column so very long ago; and to my parents, Harold and Phyllis Dicken—a retired Air Commodore and his wife, who brought me to Washington at an impressionable age but now, far away, cannot imagine what I do for a living. Oh, dear, mum. It's this sort of thing.

# Contents

9

## TROOP MORALE

## FURLOUGH

## SHINING THE BRASS

## TAPS

# WELCOME TO WASHINGTON

# It's No Place
# Like Home

*"I stand behind any statement I have made—if I fail to withdraw it within 24 hours!"*
— PATRICIA HARRIS, FORMER SECRETARY OF
HOUSING AND URBAN DEVELOPMENT

YES, IT'S a screwy town.

Politics snake through the city like the Potomac River—shiny on top, murky underneath, swift, cold, and sometimes kind of fishy-smelling.

You come here with clear eyes and see it all: blossoms blowing around the Tidal Basin, marble monuments to men and ideas, handsome formal vistas that fill the eye and stretch the spirit.

You catch the political sideshows: a Senate staffer paints her toenails to look like her candidate's campaign buttons. Greasy-spoon restaurants replace a mint dish with a jelly-bean jar—we're-in-it-too homage to Ronald Reagan. A gay disco plays "The Star-Spangled Banner" at evening's end during a national crisis, then its world-weary sin-seekers, eyes still moist with patriotism, pile into their Rollses and tumble home to Lord-knows-what.

What you don't see, at first, is that Washington is a small town, a really small town. So small that Kay Graham, the chairman of the Washington *Post* lives in the same house where the mother of G.

Gordon Liddy, the Watergate burglar, grew up.

After you've been here a while, something small-town happens to you. You go native. You begin to see the city, not as it is, but as reflected in the River of Politics. It's still grand, but your perspective is turned on its head.

Maybe it's something in the water. So deeply does Politics drench the Washingtonian's consciousness that pre-election polls taken at the D.C. jail reflect probabilities better than national polls or journalists.

In a variable town, you discover small constants, from the best rush-hour route home to what happens to your paycheck after you cash it. (If you're a federal worker, it gets stashed away for seven years by the Treasury, then is recycled into federal toilet paper). You read as many papers as you can lay your hands on. You cheer on your side in the spectator sport of politics.

Larger immutables seep into your bloodstream unawares, like triglycerides. They include the realities of power, the fallibility of the media and, still shining through the occasional patches of tarnish, the glow of ideals that, after all, remain the sterling basis of it all.

Other towns recede like distant planets.

Washington thinks big—huge, because of the great tasks that confront the city—but it must see small too, because of the daily exigencies.

"What Washington needs is more statesmen!" cried Ronald Reagan at a Washington dinner party in 1980, before he moved in.

"No, you're completely wrong," shot back millionaire Joe Allbritton, once owner of the ill-fated *Star,* after five years of listening to statesmen. "What Washington really needs is a decent carpenter and cook."

It takes about six months in Washington to know that most people only mean "We must get together for lunch" if they write down the date that very minute. ("Do you do breakfast?" is, on the other hand, a very sincere question.)

For about the first year, when out-of-town visitors arrive, the new Washingtonian shows them his city's graces—the view from the Monument, the Air and Space Museum, the National Gallery. Later,

he begins to pepper his tour with tales of scapegraces. There's the
choice spot on the Capitol steps where Abscammed Rep. John Jenrette and his fair Rita surrendered to Venus. See the Tidal Basin by
moonlight, as it was the night Rep. Wilbur Mills was stopped by the
cops and Fanne Foxe took a splash? Over here, the Watergate, where
Nixon met his Waterloo, but where many of the Reagan people live
in luxe; the now-changed bar where Hamilton Jordan just possibly
spat Amaretto-and-cream down the bosom of a young woman, and
created a trinity with Jimmy Carter and Fritz Mondale: Grits, Fritz
and Spits; the door at the Kennedy Center where Frank Sinatra was
barred from the Reagan inaugural ball.

By now, our local is a full-blooded Washingtonian. He is also, alas,
a trained consumer of the city's first product: gossip.

"Washington's the only town in the world where sound travels
faster than light," remarked Wade McCree, when he was the solicitor general.

Everybody gossips, high and low. Nowhere else is the pleasure of
knowing what you're not supposed to know more keen.

Aware of the city's fatal flaw, secretive people are flummoxed.
When Joe Califano reorganized the Department of Health, Education and Welfare, he decided he had better send his secret plans over
to the Pentagon to be typed. There, at least, he supposed, gossip had
been neutroned to the Stone Age. For double safety, he swore all who
saw the plans to secrecy. Of course they were the hottest gossip in
Washington.

Some people think they just can't take it any more. They clam up
and withdraw from the fray. Young Sen. Larry Pressler proclaimed
he would drop out completely one spring—a capital offense for a
much-needed bachelor on the social circuit—and devote himself to
a course in classical-music appreciation.

"A senator without gossip's like a pig without slop," grumbled one
disappointed host as Pressler emerged, maddeningly whistling Beethoven, from seclusion.

The most an elected official can do to stem the gossip tide is whip
his own staff up to a frenzy of loyal circumspection. One senator,
powerful Strom Thurmond, took his entire office in hand. He

dragged experts to the Russell Senate Office Building to hold seminars on morals, drugs, alcohol, sex and nutrition. "Nutrition" was
the last straw. The senator had to lurk outside the classroom to herd
rebellious staffers in again as they tiptoed off to a nearby bar to
indulge in the only vice they really enjoyed anyway—gossip.

Feudal concern with morals and digestion of underlings is nothing
new in Washington. It has always provided some of the town's juicier
morsels. Lyndon Johnson, according to excellent gossip, lost Pierre
Salinger as his press secretary at a small luncheon where diet was the
issue.

"Pierre," LBJ supposedly called down the table. "You haven't
eaten your beans."

"Mr. President, I happen not to care for this variety of beans."

"Pierre, eat your beans."

A hush fell. Other guests fidgeted.

"Pierre, I said to eat your beans," boomed LBJ. Rigid with embarrassment, the company watched. Pierre, the story goes, ate every
bean on his plate. And that was the day he resigned.

Gossip and food are inseparable in Washington. That is why journalists are such popular dinner guests, in spite of their table manners.
A good Washington dinner party is a covered-dish supper of gossip.
You bring your tastiest offerings to table, and share generously but
selectively. In return, you walk off with a well-stuffed doggie bag of
fresh gossip, ready for your next foray.

Of course, there's a disadvantage. Most gossip, like homemade
fruitcake that you give a friend for Christmas, is bound to turn up
a few days later squatting on the buffet of someone you both know.
It's still tasty, but no longer appetizing.

This works to the disadvantage of the gossip, but to the benefit of
the nation as a whole. This, you see, is the stage at which gossip goes
public. Not in the press, of course—after all, Washington journalists
must take along their bread-and-butter gossip to eat out, and even
a journalist's mother doesn't want to hear a lot of warmed-over stuff
she read in the paper two days ago.

No. Serious columnists lovingly collect the plumpest raisins from
the Washington fruitcake. Then they scatter them, not on skeptical

editors and carping readers, but on the good citizens of the nation. They go, in short, on the lecture circuit.

In godforsaken convention halls across the land, roundly deploring demon gossip as part of their show, the serious columnists spread the wealth. This system has the wholesome effect of keeping earnest coventioneers from all over the country, meeting in South Bend or Paducah, often far better informed on what's really going on at the White House than Joe Blow who lives ten blocks away from it. It is also what makes columnists rich, since they may get between five thousand and ten thousand dollars a pop.

Meanwhile, back on the Georgetown dinner circuit, little bits of information collect like dustballs under sofas: who hates whom and why; who is pushing what bill or cause; who is using sex for what; the lengths people will go to protect their image; how power alters and consumes; why Washingtonians worship information; whose money comes from where; the extraordinary underpinnings of a successful Washington marriage.

These are not what Washington is all about, any more than dustballs are part of the decor. But there they lie, beneath all the brocade and big talk.

In the same way, the Washington the gossip columnist sees every day is not the one you read about in civics class.

It's not the one you think about with hand over heart when the national anthem plays; it's not, of course, the important one.

But its inhabitants are those same men and women who guide the destiny of a great nation. To be where they are, they must be superhuman. They must also be cruel and compassionate, vain and humble, greedy and self-sacrificing, strong and flexible, pushy and self-effacing, hopelessly provincial and consummately worldly.

In this book I try to give a clue as to why all the Mr. and Ms. Smiths who go to Washington from all over the county will be different when—and if—they go home again.

While they're filling their roles in the capital—on this perverse, provincial, isolated feudal stage—they must dance as fast as they can, under a relentless spotlight.

A small-time vaudevillian may end up playing Hamlet. A passionate idealist may find himself playing the clown.

The great show rolls on. The players make us mad, they make us laugh, they make us cheer and cringe and blow razzberries and pay taxes.

They've got an awful lot of guts.

I salute them.

# FALL IN

# The Status Chase:
# Of Turks, Perks and Jerks
# in Washington

*"On all correspondence over the signature of the Secretary, between the word 'Sincerely' and the Secretary's typed name, please leave a space of eight lines. The Secretary has recently enlarged his signature."*
   —MEMO TO TYPISTS IN A CABINET OFFICE

THE PHONE rang in Henry Kissinger's downtown office. It was Gretchen Poston, the White House social secretary. Would Henry be coming to President Carter's treaty-signing party?

"Vell," said Henry, "I haf not received an invitation."

Gretchen was aghast. Surely she'd sent him a Mailgram? Oh, said Henry. *A Mailgram.* He'd never been invited to the White House by *Mailgram* before. Was that an invitation?

Gretchen sat down and hand-wrote a formal invitation on cream-colored White House stationery, put it in a stiff gold-embossed White House envelope, and summoned a limousine. The invitation was delivered into Henry's hands.

That is status.

The boast of heraldry, the pomp of power. In the democratic capital of the most egalitarian of nations, status is worth definitely fighting for.

It cannot be faked; it is clearly measurable.

Are you worth preserving? Then you will be surrounded by body-guards. Do you have a lot on your mind? An entourage will trail in your wake, to supply whatever is needed at short notice. Is your time valuable? Then you shall be whisked about in an other-driven car, with a small light focused over your shoulder on your important papers. Are you desirable? Then you will be invited, properly, to everything. Might the president require your advice at any moment? Then you need a little beeper about your person. Is your comfort important to the comfort of the Republic? Then you shall fly first class at all times.

"Ah shall stop flying first class," Robert Strauss told a "little twerp" at Jimmy Carter's White House who had tried to book him in tourist, "when they invent something better."

That is what status is about.

*"Washington is the only town in the world where status and power bear no relationship at all to wealth."*
   —AL EISELE, FORMER VICE-PRESIDENT FRITZ
   MONDALE'S PRESS SECRETARY

Remember, you are dealing with a city where the small son of a Mr. Everyman columnist opens his lunch box at kindergarten and wails, "Oh, no! Not pâté again!"

Status permeates Washington from the cradle—pervasive as pollen, subliminal as microwaves, inescapable as skin color.

If everyone doesn't recognize it immediately, somebody takes steps to make them. Admiral Stansfield Turner, when head of the CIA, instructed an aide to issue an order: "Nobody must barge past the director when he is walking in the hallways." Instead, foot traffic slowed to his pace. This gave him the air of the lead craft in an armada as he strode or dawdled down the corridors of power: there was no mistaking his status.

Once you possess your status, of course, you may ignore it. Robert

Strauss, who understands the symbolic importance of the chauffeur-driven limousine, also knows well the virtue of a democratic image: as Carter's special envoy for trade, he rode in the front seat with his chauffeur. Henry Kissinger's greatest ambition at the height of his glory was to be a spear carrier in a show at the Kennedy Center. (Unfortunately, the Center at the time was casting for *Caesar and Cleopatra*. Spear carriers had to tower between 5'11" and 6'3".)

Status is a non-transferable commodity. You cannot bring it with you to Washington. Charlton Heston could not get in the northwest gate at the White House when his name was accidentally left off a Reagan guest list; Frank Sinatra, although he had contributed hundreds of thousands of dollars to the Reagan inaugural festivities, was barred from the inaugural ball he was supposed to attend by a fire marshal, because the building was too crowded.

The most gratifying sign of status in Washington is the evidence of desire in high places that you stay alive. That is why you have Secret Service men swarming around you. That is why members of the Cabinet must submit to tiresome but prestigious nuclear attack drills periodically, during which they are whisked away by helicopter to the bowels of a nearby mountain. These are sometimes called off on account of rain.

The second most gratifying sign is the way you get around. Absolutely A-status, of course, is the motorcade. You cannot beat howling sirens, uniformed outriders, a dignified line of limos nosing down the wide avenues like great black beetles, the security and press wagons, the gapers on the sidewalk, the stopped traffic at every intersection.

Carter's efforts to de-imperialize the presidency shrank Washington's motorcades depressingly. But as the election drew nigh, and the importance of status, particularly as perceived abroad, dawned on his staff, the motorcade made a halfhearted comeback. Advance staffers for the Carter trip to Italy wired a consul there: "Arrange good motorcade for presidential arrival in Venice."

The consul protested. Venice was built on canals, he pointed out. How about a gondolacade instead? Furious word came back: Stop trying to be smart. This is an election year. Get cracking on that motorcade.

The incredible roaring-siren motorcade adopted this year by the vice-president, justified by "the threat of Libyan hit squads," is splendid for the status of the office that John Nance Garner, FDR's veep, described as "not worth a bucket of warm spit."

A little digression, now, on that office. The vice-presidency, though the second-highest office in the land, is in no-man's-land, status-wise.

There's an odd reason for this. Affection for the man who holds it inevitably implies a desire that he become president. Because that often happens in an unpleasant way, the office bears a sort of superstitious, bad-mojo stamp. Its occupant—who, ultimately, has bet his wad on the demise of the president and is an uncomfortable *memento mori* every time he winks—must be insignificant and good-humored.

Thus, his status is in a twilight zone in Washington. This carries over to the country as a whole.

Former Vice-President Fritz Mondale tells about the large crowd that turned out to see him off when he was campaigning in Lewiston, Maine.

"I'm really very, very flattered," he told one of the locals, just before hopping aboard. "There must be about two thousand people here!"

"Well, yes," said his host. "But to be perfectly truthful, we've never had a 747 land or take off at our airport before. Everyone turned out to see if it'll take off okay, or crash."


*"Vice-President Walter Mondale, right, inspects a turkey, left."*
   —EXPLANATORY CAPTION BENEATH A
   PHOTOGRAPH IN THE WASHINGTON POST, JUST
   BEFORE THANKSGIVING


*"I was really reassured about leaving my house near Three Mile Island, after Jimmy Carter went there. After*

*all, if there's been any real danger, I'm sure he would
have sent Fritz Mondale."*
—OVERHEARD IN PALM BEACH, AFTER THE
NUCLEAR POWER PLANT SCARE

George Bush's advance team, in Las Vegas to lay out a trip,
thought they had done far better than their predecessors in enhanc-
ing their vice-president's status there. They decided on a little test.

"Do you know the name of the vice-president of the United
States?" one of the team asked a waitress in a steak house, settling
back rather smugly.

"No, I don't," she said, "But I'll sure find out for you." She
bustled off, and was gone for some time.

"I got it from the chef!" she cried triumphantly when she returned.
"Walter Mondale!"

The little group packed its bags and returned glumly to Washington; the vice-presidential trip to Vegas did not come off.

Well, the motorcade must make up for some of that. Directly
under the motorcade in the status chase comes, of course, the limousine, back in full purr.

During the Carter era, the humbler the car, the higher the status.

Neighbors of Ray Marshall noted that he began his career as
Carter's Labor secretary being driven in a Lincoln limo. Then his
cars began to dwindle, through a Ford LTD all the way down to a
Plymouth Valiant.

This was comical because practically the only people tactless
enough to bowl up to Carter's White House in Cadillac limousines
were labor leaders, in town to plead for fatter federal funding for
New York.

With the Reagan election, the writing was on the wall. The very
first thing Chief Justice Warren Burger did—even before the inauguration—was to acquire the longest gray Cadillac limo anyone
remembers seeing in Washington.

"Bought secondhand, of course," a press secretary hastily pointed
out.

The number of White House cars with drivers has more than doubled since the Carters left. It has gone from fourteen to twenty-nine.

"Our staff has more important things to do than wait around for taxis," is the explanation.

Nobody likes to admit that status means a lot. If you cannot have a car and driver, you can at least attend to your license tags. Nowhere else do they mean as much.

The senior senator from each state generally has Number 1 from that state; the junior, often, Number 2. High-powered Sen. Strom Thurmond and his wife Nancy trundle around in an old Chrysler station wagon with South Carolina plates modestly emblazoned "US 1." Nancy used to ride everywhere in taxis; it became too expensive and risky.

"Oh, please be careful," she cried to one cab driver darting at breakneck speed from National Airport one day, "I'm the mother of four small children!"

"Lady, you're the one who should be careful," he said, passing on a curve and narrowly missing a moving van. Shortly after, the Thurmonds rented a bus.

Of course there are "Member of Congress" tags. Some congressmen prefer not to use them. Unfortunate Rep. Bob Bauman, whose clearly tagged car sat outside when he was cavorting in local gay bars, provided a lesson in discretion not lost on his peers. Neighbors of young women who entertain married congressmen at home frequently call gossip columnists to report the guilty license numbers.

Washingtonians, of course, are trained from birth to recognize the tags on a rented limousine, as opposed to a higher-status private one. Rented limousines are better than none; but they have a disadvantage. Zsa Zsa Gabor, shopping in Washington, whirled out of Saks to find that her chauffeur had vanished. She jumped into the limo to wait. A few minutes' elegant fidgeting and finger-tapping, before the admiring eyes of fans. Then, Zsa Zsa jumped out to peer around. No sign of the man in the hat. Then in. Then out. Then in. Then the scowl. The sublime posterior raised, the dainty diamond-plastered hand pressing for a good long, loud, impatient honk on the horn.

Bleeeeep-beeeeeep. *Beep.* BLEEEEEEEEP. A large crowd gathered. And then, around the corner smoothly nosed her real rented limo, with her very own rented chauffeur at the wheel.

Low D.C. license tag numbers are jealously vied for by Washington city-dwellers. Like limos, they are presumed to have some sort of immunity from the predatory police, who spare almost no one. (Even Ethel Kennedy's white convertible is not sacred. It has had the immobilizing iron "Denver boot" attached to it, as she sat giggling at the Maison Blanche with Art Buchwald.) When the precious numbers are assigned, a list is printed in the newspaper—perhaps the most avidly read tiny type in town, apart from White House dinner guest lists.

Fashions in out-of-town tags change with administrations. A young Georgian woman editor who coincidentally arrived in town at the same time as the Carter administration was approached by a complete stranger on the street, with a question now heard by Californians: "Will you sell me your tags?"

The quadrennial scrum for inaugural tags, temporary tags made at the D.C. jail especially for each inauguration, is a lesson in status.

They cost $35 a set, and may be emblazoned with a name of five letters or fewer.

An ordinary guy who worked for the Department of the Army, a man named Jim O'Rourke, was told that he could not get his surname on his tags: it had too many letters. Besides that, D.C. Jail could under no circumstances handle an apostrophe. Why, even Johnny Carson had to have his tags stamped simply "HERES" on the front and "JOHNY" on the back.

So Mr. O'Rourke asked for his second choice: "USA 1." Nobody else had asked for it. He got it. Content, he attached his tags to his little Honda. As he drove on his daily rounds, cops saluted, mothers held up their babies to see him, cars honked, strangers waved and small dogs barked.

The day before the inauguration, he got a frantic call. The two men who had organized the inaugural balls, Charles Wick and Robert Gray, wanted tags USA 1 and USA 2 respectively. Mr. O'Rourke was persuaded to surrender his tags. In exchange, he became the only man in Washington history to have seven letters and an apostrophe on his inaugural tag.

Of course, he was no longer saluted.

Charles Wick—USA 1—is now head of the United States Information Agency; Robert Gray—USA 2—is the best-connected lobbyist in town.

There is a moral to this story.

Apart from Mr. O'Rourke, no man abandons status gladly.

Ron Nessen kept his White House identifying tags dangling on his briefcase for several years after his departure as Jerry Ford's press secretary. Mieke Tunney, ex-wife of ex-Sen. John Tunney, kept the meter maids at bay long after her divorce and her husband's loss of an election: she simply propped his old Senate tags on her dashboard when interestingly parked.

Elliot Richardson left his status with grace. After all, he had held almost every post in the Cabinet. Oddly, people spoke of him in even more reverent tones when he was appointed ambassador to the Law of the Sea Conference—a job negotiating for manganese nodules and cod. No wonder. All his friends were under the delightful impression that his title was "Lord of the Sea."

Status is also habit-forming.

The first time Henry Kissinger went back into the State Department after his exit from office, he arrived at a party there both late and flushed. "I vas lost!" he explained. Never before had he been in the building without bodyguards or entourage; alone, he found himself wandering around the seventh-floor kitchen.

Years before, when a reporter had asked him his street address in Georgetown, he simply didn't know. Nancy had picked out the house, he said. Henry just got out of his limousine when it stopped; the Secret Service took him from there. And when he walked Tyler, the dog led him back without fail.

*"Hello, I'm Rose Kennedy. Will you drive me home?"*
—ROSE KENNEDY, HAILING A STATION WAGON
FULL OF NUNS (THEY DID.)

If status on wheels is vital, how very much more so, in the eyes of one's staff and visitors, is the throne of status: the executive toilet. After the last major upheaval in the Seante, several senior senators lost their status, and their seats. Also, alas, their status seats. Some of the very high-status offices vacated by the defeated solons were swiftly divided up into two offices. In some cases, private johns were annexed by neighbors. The result: some senators suddenly possessed two thrones. The new boys, slow to nail down their interests, found themselves with none at all. Swiftly, a class system was born. "He's a no-johnny man," it has been said of one who lost out.

The executive john is the first thought of those coming to government directly from private industry or the military. One of Reagan's top military men is said to have pondered turning down a State Department job because a private john did not come with the office.

The secretary of Commerce's office boasts not only a lavish bathroom but a sauna, a notorious setting in an earlier administration for romantic encounters. Energy czar Jim Schlesinger demanded that each executive's office in the Forrestal Building have not only a john but a shower. Robert McKinney, when chairman of the Federal Home Loan Bank Board, had a very fine toilet installed at a cost of $60,766. When Marjorie Fine Knowles, as inspector general at the Labor Department, had her throne room custom-installed smack next door to her office, as befit a presidential appointee, several investigators were swept from their offices to allow room for the plumbing. Several handmade buttons: "I was moved for the appointment."

Toilet status was particularly ironic during the Carter energy crisis, because, in government washrooms, hot water was banned to save energy. Even in the old Executive Office Building, where most White House staffers toil in the lap of luxe, the "H" tap ran a chilly dribble. The only hot water pocket remained in a portion of the West Wing of the White House where the very senior staffers still splashed in comfort.

Status is in the flush of health for the Reagan Administration. Within the White House itself, nowadays, the highest status belongs to those who may use the White House gym. They have dwindled down to a precious few. Two women, Karna Small and Elizabeth Hanford Dole, are theoretically allowed to use it during certain hours. One story says that one of the above, arriving during the women's hour, found top presidential aide Michael Deaver using the gym, and threw his clothing from the changing room; the other story has her clothing being thrown out. Now, the women do not seem to use the gym.

The White House mess, or dining room, was open to most of the White House staff during the Carter years. It has become a high-status retreat with the Reagan crowd.

It is no longer dry, as it was before. Highest status is the senior-senior staffers' section, on the right as you go in, by the Situation Room. It holds about thirty high-powered diners. Even the ordinary senior staffers' mess offers lunchers a tasteful blue, gold-embossed wine list, touting California vintages. Beer is served every day. Each Thursday, with the Mexican lunch, ice-cold Margaritas are served. (Sophisticated supplicants always plot their pleas for Thursday afternoons, of course.) Both sections boast Princess phones. These do not ring. When a status person is wanted on the horn, a Filipino steward bustles over and plugs in the phone next to his table, rather like at "21."

Presidential matchbooks, banned as pretentious during the Carter Era, perch proudly next to the After Eight mints and cashews. They say "Ronald Wilson Reagan" and sport a white-on-white picture of the White House. It is all very country-club.

(Reagan, by the way, also keeps cards in his Oval Office desk drawer. They are simply engraved: "Ronald Wilson Reagan, President, The United States of America.")

Two brand-new status dining rooms were quietly added under the Reagans so that even more status-aware White House staffers could exclude those beneath them.

The most status-y White House staffers return from lunch to offices decorated with large model ships borrowed from the Navy. Ed Meese, for example, picked a neatly rigged frigate, the U.S.S. *Ohio;* George Bush has two preppy war ships, the sloop *Enterprise* and the privateer *Fair American.*

The dashing globe-trotting aura of these ships is not lost on Washington. One of the most envied perks in the city is its leaders apparently endless and offhand flittings overseas.

Much is made of congressional junkets abroad. These "fact-finding and diplomatic missions" are usually planned for comfort as well as close-up views of the real world: Paris in the spring, to semitropical climes in mid-winter, to temperate but gay capitals as the summer heat seeps over D.C. like a steambath.

The Congress is furious at their esteemed colleague Rep. Ron Mottl. Quite out of the blue, Representative Mottl introduced a House resolution forbidding junkets—which cost $7.5 million in 1979 and 1980—unless three-fourths of the House okayed each single junket. It seems to have been buried.

Often, congressional travel is not as glamorous as it seems. Official jets do have beds for VIPs—but they're fold-down slumber bunks, like luggage racks. These are not perfect. When a Korean premier died, the U.S. delegation flown to the funeral included Cy Vance, then the secretary of state, Chip Carter, the president's son, and Sen. S.I. Hayakawa. Halfway through the flight back, Hayakawa, perhaps dreaming of a recently mastered tap-dance routine, jolted suddenly in his sleep. He tumbled from his narrow bunk onto one of Cy Vance's guards. Blinking but unhurt, he took advantage of the interruption to totter sleepily to the lavatory. A stewardess, passing the vacant VIP bunk, slammed it shut. Returning, as he thought, to his roost, the unfortunate senator clambered into another, on top of Chip Carter. Both almost plunged to their dooms in shock. Apologizing profusely, the senator debunked and wandered off to hunt his lost bed. It was a wearying eleven-hour flight. Upon his return, he snoozed soundly on the Senate floor.

Quite apart from the inconvenience of travel, there is the unpleasant fact that foreigners do not properly appreciate Washington status.

Nancy Reagan decided to go without her husband to the wedding of Prince Charles and Lady Di. When she heard how lowly would be her seat at Saint Paul's Cathedral among the foreign heads of state, she almost changed her mind about going. Her escorts—Peter

McCoy and Joe Canzeri, both of whom have since left the White House—made up for it by ensuring the most dazzling status symbols they could think of parading around London—the largest limos, an entourage of attendants and hairdressers beyond anything the English, including the queen, had imagined. The queen drove her own small car to a race meet; Nancy arrived in state like a Mafia empress; the status did not translate successfully (See chapter, "Nancy Through the Looking Glass").

The Eastern shuttle to New York is the longest trip status Washingtonians undergo by choice. (Excepting, of course, their annual pilgrimages to Martha's Vineyard, the Hamptons or Rehoboth, and obligatory visits to newly fashionable countries.)

Elizabeth Taylor even tired of the shuttle. When *The Little Foxes* moved to New York, she hired an Amtrak club car. The car was loaded with fresh flowers, champagne, a French accordionist singing the street songs of Paris, caviar, pepper steaks, creamed spinach, and Dominique, her favorite Washington restaurateur, in a Maurice Chevalier hat. She had a cast party all the way there.

*"Got my tickets?" "Any I.D., sir?" "Gee, no. I left it in the car. But I've got my initials embroidered on my shirt cuffs. Will that do?" "Of course, sir."*
　　—CONVERSATION AT THE BOX OFFICE AT
　　CONSTITUTION HALL

Perhaps it's time to pause now for a quick checklist of current status symbols in Washington.

　• If you are in the public employ: a bodyguard, a chef, a chauffeur, at the taxpayers' expense.
　• Having your phone bugged. In 1979, a Harris poll showed that four out of ten members of Congress believed theirs were. The number has probably increased.

• The Presidential Box at the Kennedy Center. (This is quite often used by senators, Cabinet members and their staffs. It has a small red-plush anteroom behind it, with a bucket of champagne provided and, of course, a private john.)
• Being invited to Edward Bennett Williams' brunches at the Redskins games.
• Catching the president's cold.
• *Women's Wear Daily* and *W* cover your party.
• Not having your parties covered at all.
• Harvard. The more than forty Harvard hotshots in the Reagan Administration include Caspar Weinberger, the secretary of Defense; David Stockman, architect of the Reagan budget; the attorney general; the secretary of Transportation; the chairman of the Federal Reserve Board, the NASA administrator; White House Communications Chief David Gergen. In the Carter Administration, the lone three—Schlesinger, Adams, Califano—were purged.
• For men: squash.
• For wives: Savitri's yoga classes.
• A silver Concorde bag.
• Having a baby animal at the National Zoo named after you.
• A Top Secret security clearance. (While he was still National Security Council chief, Dick Allen ordered Henry Kissinger's security clearance upgraded and updated, so they could chat.)
• Yes, a limo. Don't be shy. Even Ralph Nader, when asked to appear on a television show, has said yes, "if you send a limo."
• Having a dish named after you, or adapted to your name. (The Steak Oregano at the Intrigue became Steak O-Reagan-O after the election.)
• Sidesaddle riding in hunt country.
• Exotic trees in your office, courtesy of the National Arboretum. (Members of Congress and other certain high officials may cultivate these.)

• Happy Hour in the Embassy Row Hotel. (It is coyly
called the Negotiation Hour.)
• Living quarters: the Watergate, with all the Reaganists;
Georgetown, with the Washington immortals; Capitol Hill,
with the Congress; Cleveland Park, with Art Buchwald;
Potomac, with the horsey set; McLean, with the Kennedys;
Kalorama, with Justice Sandra Day O'Connor and Diane
Sawyer, when she's in town.
• Your hairdresser comes to you.
• An elevator in your house.
• A summer retreat on Martha's Vineyard. Jackie Onassis is
a shell's toss away. Lillian Hellman won't let Art Buchwald
walk across her property. Walter Cronkite and Kay Graham
retreat there. Lawyer Frank Ikard has rented one of his
houses there to the queen of Sikkim. Robert McNamara sold
a place there because of the nude bathers. Carly Simon goes
because Washington people don't know who she is. And
once, when the airline service failed, the late John Belushi
chartered a thirty-two-seat plane and flew everybody home.)
• Your house displayed on the Georgetown House Tour, for
charity. (This is for status, not ego-reinforcement. One
couple put their historic house on the tour, and tramped
after the visitors, pretending to be tourists too. "I don't
understand why *anybody* wants to live here. Do you?" one
tourist asked them.)
• An entourage. This is helpful in case you are stuck in an
elevator, or suddenly need sex or a Coca-Cola.
• Sheets designed by Jane Wilner. (The Georgetown shop
did Ethel Kennedy's bed in multicolored Porthault floral
bouquets; White Houser Jim Baker in tailored
beige-and-green; best-dressed lister Deeda Blair in French
country check; and Jack Valenti, of the Motion Picture
Association, in green-and-white striations. The shop is
part-owned by Susan Brinkley, wife of David.)
• Silly macho dinners: the Gridiron Dinner, where silly
songs are sung by media people in white tie. The Alfalfa

Dinner, where a silly speech is given to the powerful by one
they nominate for president.
• Administration piano players at your parties. (Charlie
Wick, Michael Deaver and other Reagan biggies play.)
• Home computers.
• Media fame.

*In Washington, do not expect status from:*

• Cocaine. Slightly risky. Comedian Mark Russell, at a party
he gave for Mort Sahl, used as his centerpiece a large pile of
white powder with straws stuck into it. It was flour.
• The Lacoste alligator. This is so clichéd that beefcakey
beaux on the gay beach at nearby Rehoboth often have them
tattooed on their chests.
• A pool. "For God's sake, why have a pool? How middle
class! People rich enough to afford a pool are *never* in town
to use it!" The status builder who said this put a fountain in
the middle of *his* pool, to prove he didn't use it.
• Perrier. Last time I looked, Georgetown mailmen had the
coolers in their jeeps packed with it. They are probably on
to San Pellegrino now.
• Going to every party and event. Garry Trudeau, who
draws Doonesbury, summed up what most status
Washingtonians feel after their first two years on the town:
"I've been trying for some time now to develop a lifestyle
that doesn't require my presence."
• Long titles. High-status in most world capitals, they are
not envied in Washington. A pity. The National Oceanic and
Atmospheric Administration at Commerce boasted one
staffer called the administrative assistant to the assistant
administrator for administration. Finally, he got his own
administrative assistant, and had to change his title.

A friend of powerful Sen. Russell Long tells of driving past the
White House with him in 1979.

"You're still pretty young, at sixty," said the friend. "Why don't *you* run for that spot?"

"Nah," mused Big Russ, chairman of the Senate Finance Committee. "I don't want to take the step down."

For a powerful and entrenched member, that's what it would be.

There is no questioning the status on Capitol Hill. Perks include splendid dining rooms and cafeterias, at very low prices; mail-franking privileges; low-rate barbershop and hair salon, very important in these days of gavel-to-gavel cable television coverage.

A senator never has to push his own buttons in the elevator; to make up for that, there are special buttons outside the Senate elevators that only he may push. They take him where he's going, fast. Other low-status occupants of the elevator go up and down until he gets there.

As well as his large office in the Senate building, a powerful senator will have a private office in the Capitol, with easy access to the floor and more privacy for whatever. There is much whatever.

Senators may take a great deal of luggage at no cost on frequent, free plane trips to and from their home states. Once, on a trip back from South Carolina, a large, very heavy box labelled "Official Luggage" belonging to Sen. Strom Thurmond burst open on the conveyor belt. A gigantic watermelon rolled out.

House and senate staffers often take members' shirts to the laundry, ferry his kids, argue with his wife, and fill his car with gas.

Both the House and the Senate offer excellent gyms, pools and paddleboard courts.

The athletic life is not without danger. In the pool one day wallowed enormous Sen. Lawton Chiles, the Florida Democrat, contemplating eternal verities and serenely performing his famous dead man's float. Suddenly, a terrible splash. Commotion. Somebody grappling for his neck, ducking him, dragging him, spluttering and half-drowning, toward shore. Senator Chuck Percy, who had taken out his hearing aid and perhaps imagined Chiles gurgling his last, had dived to his rescue.

Access to the paddleball courts in the Rayburn Building is very sought after. Representative Sonny Montgomery, the urbane Mississippian, worked out a successful method of clearing the court at noon for his own game: he would ask for a quorum call on the House floor. It would be broadcast over speakers in the gym. As congressmen on the court fled to answer the call, Sonny and his playmates would simply bound on to the empty court, paddles in hand.

You must not presume that every congressman spends his days and nights in luxury. Status is not evenly spread around. Hawaii's Rep. Cecil Heftel's office was so tiny that he installed a phone booth in the middle of it just to speak privately without his entire staff overhearing every word.

A congressman's $60,663 annual salary does not go far in Washington.

Some congressmen, strapped by alimony payments or unable to meet the expense of keeping a house both here and in their home districts, actually sleep in their offices. Some sleep on cots in the gymnasium, convenient to the showers. Some live on hors d'oeuvres and catch-as-catch-can dinners.

"I cook on a hot plate," Vermont's Rep. Jim Jeffords, who has a foldaway bed in his office, told *U.S. News & World Report.* "More often, I bum meals. Almost every night some reception is going on. Saves a lot of money."

At least three parties are thrown each weeknight evening in the House and Senate office buildings. Often, these are hosted by lobbyists. They provide excellent food. One congressional wife, Mrs. Philip Crane, who now works as a private detective, was spotted in leaner times stuffing several pounds of sausage and fruit into her capacious tote bag. It was at a reception given by a meat-packing lobby. Nobody minded a bit.

Should they overindulge and get stomach trouble, all members of Congress can have free surgery at Walter Reed Army Hospital. (Unlucky Rep. Walter Jones, went in twice—once for surgery; the second time, for more surgery to take out the sponge left in there during the previous round.)

Of course some are millionaires. But when *People* magazine did a roundup of the really rich in Congress, the proudest member was Sen. Paul Tsongas. With a net worth of $49,104.23, he declared himself the Senate's poorest man. Immediately the scramble was on. The feistiest contender was Sen. Larry Pressler, who proudly declared his net worth the lowest: $25,000.

*"GIFTS: From Southwestern Baptist Seminary in Fort Worth, Texas: one pair lizard skin cowboy boots, still in box. Value unknown but perhaps over 100 dollars. Of no use to me. Will consign to government. No place of consignment to date."*
    —FROM THE FINANCIAL DISCLOSURE OF GRIFFIN BELL, THEN ATTORNEY GENERAL.

The Senate and House perks are standard. Men approach Cabinet office with different expectations. James Watt, Reagan's interior secretary, was so overwhelmed by the scale and splendor of his office that he crept off to a smaller, undersecretary's office, down the hall. He frequently eats in the cafeteria.

Joe Califano, when secretary of Health, Education and Welfare, asked to have a tennis court laid on its roof. He maintained a $17,000-a-year chef, a chauffeur and a bodyguard, and there was a great deal of fuss. But hardly anyone noticed when Pat Harris, head of Health and Human Resources, and Shirley Hufstedler, who ran the Education Department, hired cooks. Both were classified as stewards, government graded GS-9 through GS-11. (Bottom pay: $17,035. Top: $26,794.)

"A steward saves a lot of time. People who eat here will pay $3.50 per head, and the secretary or undersecretaries pay for guests," Education said. Cried Health and Human Resources, "Having someone here to cook works out far cheaper than going out or having working luncheons catered."

Cabinet members, of course, have cars and drivers. Some secretaries now sport their department flags, flying on the front of their limousines. Alexander Haig says he has so many security guards that he must kiss them good-night before his wife.

Cabinet members have gigantic offices with large anterooms and several layers of staffers and secretaries; they have access to the Presidential Box at the theater, and, of course, the ardent attention of city hosts and hostesses. The higher up one is, the less often one has to pay for one's food.

It is no wonder that, after a couple of years in Washington, even the least status-aware Congressman displays a smooth, well-fed, pampered, first-class air.

First-class plane travel is a perk of most Washington offices.

To a few, of course, there is a sort of counterstatus status in flying tourist.

When Robert McNamara headed the World Bank in the Carter years, he made his underlings flit the world in tourist class. The idea was not to offend the class sensibilities of developing nations. He himself flew tourist, he pointed out. The fact was, his staff always tactfully phoned ahead and arranged to have the seats on either side of him left empty. That way, he could nap crossways. "There's tourist class, and then there's tourist, class," grumbled one staffer.

As long as anyone can remember, it has been one of the most vital components of status to leave in your wake, after departure from office, an oil painting of yourself, for history.

Jimmy Carter, horrified by the cost, ordered his Cabinet members to submit instead to photographers. Some hired high-priced lenspersons who charged more than the painters, like Jill Krementz. Those who did not had friends pay for oil paintings. Many people suspect that Michael Blumenthal, for one, paid for his own.

Because of the apparently inexhaustible generosity of taxpayers, some of the most conspicuous symbols of status are taken for granted while insignificant gadgets take on ponderous status weight.

Beepers, sported at dinner parties, are such gadgets. The Supreme buttons are others.

At the Supreme Court, each justice has a button in his lair—a discreet electric gadget close to his desk, for emergencies. After all, many are well along in years. Should life be threatened from within or without, a simple push on the button sends an end-of-the-world alarm blaring out downstairs, and a flying wedge of cops streaking into the chambers.

A fury of status jealousy exploded when a court flack got a button installed too. "Why does a flack need a button? In case of sudden leaks?"

Of what use is the status chase? Basically, little.

Status simply provides a buffer zone between you and life's nasty little encounters. You do not have to deal with rude bus drivers, disrespectful underlings or unpleasant strangers. You do not have to stand in line. (Although one of Washingtons most charming sights at the King Tut exhibition black-tie opening was a queue of several hundred people—ambassadors, Cabinet members, senators, the extremely rich, all shivering democratically together in the chill night air in the pursuit of art.) The more inferiors you have on the status scale, the less likely to are to find yourself screamed at, insulted, or facing hard truths from unwelcome sources. You will always be able to get a hotel suite, a restaurant reservation, a ticket. You are able to cast the charitable, warming beam of your status on family and friends. Sometimes, you may even do it without knowing it.

Two young women, spurned at the door of the fancy restaurant at the Kennedy Center, went to a cheaper eating spot and decided to test status ploys.

They telephoned the restaurant that had excluded them. "Hello, Act III? This is Senator Warner's office. Two of our staffers are down at the Kennedy Center today. They'd love to eat lunch there."

"But of course," came the answer. "Just have them ask for me."

In Washington, love still means never having to say you're sorry. Status means never, ever, having to say "please."

# Sex and Sensibility:
# How They Think about
# Romance in the Capital

*"Before you meet the handsome prince, you have to kiss a lot of toads."*
—ETHEL KENNEDY'S T-SHIRT

"THE ONLY romance in town is the one with power," whined the wife of an undersecretary of state in a magazine piece about why she hated Washington. "It's like an Ivy League university during a never-ending week of finals."

Romance there is not. Washington romance in high places means one thing: trouble. Romantic people don't get the job done. They run away with each others' mates. There are tears and fights and division of friends. Divorces must be carefully planned for August, when the House and Senate are out and everybody who'll notice is away.

Love affairs, as known in other capitals of the world, have a high casualty rate in this nosiest of cities.

Extramarital sex among the powerful is snatched on the wing, often in depressing and cramped quarters—in cars, in executive toilets, on sticky black leather sofas in offices, even, on one memorable occasion, in the private sauna of a Cabinet officer. (It was switched off at the time, which detracts somewhat from the daring of the undertaking. But the happy high-ranking couple caught *in flagrante delicto* went on to divorce their respective spouses and live happily ever after.) The pursuit of romance can be both exhausting and risky.

Wedlock is not only an honorable state; it's almost obligatory.

Cher once said in Hollywood, "When you're married, you become safe, no matter what. Man, you could've been a hooker your whole life, but once you're married, you're dignified and respectable. No one says ill about the dead, the old and the married ladies, right?"

This is triply true in Washington, for reasons that will become clear. Luckily for the balance of power, Washington men need wives too. They need them for at least two reasons: first, so that everybody doesn't automatically assume that they are gay; and second, to save hosts the trouble of finding a spare woman for the city's Serious Dinner Parties.

Any wife won't do. When Carter aide Greg Schneiders' star was on the rise, columnist Rowland Evans called him on the phone. (This is done before all Serious Dinner Parties, to drop the names of other guests. Nobody must feel as though he's wasting his time at what is unfortunately called a Chicken-Shit Event. (See chapter, "Some Enchanted Evenings.")

After the great roll of the mighty was called, Rowly asked Schneiders, "So, would you like to come?"

"Sure," said Greg," an unspoiled soul. Inquired Rowly, "By the way, do you have a wife?"

"Well, yes. As a matter of fact I do."

"And is she presentable?" asked Evans, quite unself-consciously.

Jimmy Carter, who did not understand what Washington wives are for at all—he'd eschewed the pleasures of the Georgetown dinner party from the beginning—proceeded to encourage all his aides marry, rather than enjoy happy and convenient live-in relationships with what some gracelessly called their "stuff." Several, like Tim Kraft, blame their subsequent divorces on the pointless flurry of better-wed-than-bed hitchings.

Marriage was an obsession with Carter. When his Federal Trade Commissioner, Mike Pertshuk, came for his first interview at the

White House, Carter asked him "Well. Mike. When are you planning on getting married?"

"I was thinking of waiting until the azaleas are in bloom," said
Mike.

"Where I come from, Mike," said Jimmy Carter softly, "the azaleas are in bloom right now."

The azaleas are always in bloom at a certain level in every administration. The wise woman who happens to be living with a man
suddenly elevated to high office moves out immediately, as did the
girlfriend of Reagan's budget director, David Stockman. And the
thinking woman does not take up with a Washington name lightly.
She knows she will be defined later as "the girl who used to screw
So-and-So" if the affair does not end in marriage. (If she doesn't
mind, of course, this may work to her advantage. That depends on
So-and-So's current standing.)

Officially, for a Washington woman, sex does not exist. Witticisms
a worldly woman might make about her own sex life in Los Angeles,
New York or London, or hints that more than one beau is being
strung along, no matter how talented and liberated the woman, mark
her as a trollop. The successful Washington single woman acts, at
least superficially, like a character in *The Scarlet Letter*. If you plan
to be a trollop, you can probably have a very pleasant time indeed
—chuckling with girlfriends over your favorite congressman, whom
you may call "my member," knowing incredibly private things about
incredibly public people, and basking in the sunny greetings of the
best maîtres d'hotel for some time.

You will certainly have a better time, on the whole, than a Washington wife.

*"Tell her you love her, but you love your country more."*
    —ADVICE FROM THE LATE PANAMANIAN
    DICTATOR, OMAR TORRIJOS, TO HAMILTON
    JORDAN, PRESIDENT CARTER'S AIDE, ON THE
    WIFE QUESTION

Washington marriages of long standing are unique. In the most successful, teamwork is more important than fidelity. The long-term Washington couple slides through the city like a SWAT team. Ideally, each partner has a Special Weapon and Tactic that complements the other's.

As administrations change, the cast of characters at center stage switches. The SWAT teams, mostly media people and lobbyists, linger on the outskirts weighing their chances, taking the measure of the main cast. Then they move in.

The powerful gossip columnist is invited to parties at the top level; her lobbyist husband gets access to the ears he needs.

The diplomat who hopes to rule his country one day offers a former "model" security and status; she gives him beauty; together they wow the city and push his career.

The political columnist's wife gives parties in a wine-soaked, candlelit setting that makes the powerful feel loved for themselves—a most unusual feeling in Washington. He gets something to write in his column. His guests get the kind of ink they want. His wife, if she is so inclined, gets the satisfaction of a job well done, possible romance, Washington-style, and, if she fishes for it, a fat job offer.

Washington wonders what on earth is going on if a marriage is not of this ilk. Nobody can understand what appears to be an extremely happy marriage between Nancy Reagan's press secretary, Sheila Tate, and her husband, an insurance man; his income, after he married and moved his business to Washington, plummeted. "Where's the synergy?" shrugged one old hand.

Sexual fidelity is not important in the classic Washington marriage. It is, in fact, peculiar enough for one columnist to blame the breakup of a television newsman's marriage on the fact that the latter's wife was "a fidelity queen."

At 60, Joan Braden, wife of columnist Tom Braden, longtime good and dear friend of Nelson Rockefeller, mother of eight and just settling into another well-paying lobbying job, talked to a reporter: "It's not necessary for a man and woman to be monogamous," she said. "But there's no sense in hurting or embarrassing [your husband either]. The prerequisites for a happy marriage are not monogamy, but respect, trust and love."

Embarrassing a mate with a show of infidelity is far more wicked, in Washington eyes, than infidelity itself.

Loyalty counts for more: before you marry a Washingtonian, or one who aspires to be one, forget the roses. The objective is pushing each other's causes, carrying each other's crosses, biting the bullet in the tough times, putting on a good front. Joan Kennedy earned the plaudits of all until she just couldn't hack it any longer.

Meanwhile, at least in theory and to the public eye, every Washington marriage is seamless, perfect, exemplary, monogamous, with dippy Dagwood-and-Blondie underpinnings.

On the surface, you see, Washington is a strangely prudish city. When a radio station here advertises the popular *The Best Little Whorehouse in Texas*, the title becomes *The Best Little Bleephouse*. The Greek Embassy gives its bronze statue of Poseidon, god of the sea, to the Kennedy Center to see if they can handle it; Washingtonians visiting the embassy had habitually covered the deity's endowments with leaves from nearby flower arrangements. Carpeaux's statue of a nude fisherboy, displayed in a shop window, coyly sports a loincloth.

A modest decolletage on a Washington woman draws stares like a topless whore of Babylon with her cymbals in full tinkle. An upper-crust local horsewoman, handing out trophies at the Horse Show in a dress that wouldn't draw a wink from a French waiter, is described grinningly as "presenting the cups" for years after. When the wife of OAS Ambassador Alejandro Orfila wore a very chic number cut down to there for the signing of the Panama Canal Treaty, jokes about the Darien Gap, the Culebra Cut and the Big Breakthrough were traded by State Department wiseguys for weeks.

On the other side of the coin, quite without warning, the mayor of Washington will suddenly declare to the astonished populace that it is "National Condom Week." ("I'd rather have a co-op, thanks, with a nice view of the river," said one wag.)

Regular and inexplicable waves of nudity wash over the city into the strangest places. It is now a tradition to have a mounted streaker at the very Horse Show where a spare inch of the female form divine draws such smirks. The first year, wearing a Halloween pumpkin over his head, he sailed over four jumps in fine style; more than a dozen outragees called the police. The next year, although he offered only a canter across the show floor with a simple brown paper bag over his head, he drew more applause than the Gentleman's Hunting, Hat Class, event.

At the fashionable Arlington Y tennis courts in Virginia—you can see Ethel Kennedy's convertible parked outside right in the ivy, or watch ABC newsman John Scali's ace serve on the courts—mixed doubles will suddenly appear skillfully volleying in the nude. "I see you're not wearing your whites," the pro, Don Floyd, chided one group primly. "It says here in the regulations that you must. Therefore, you must leave." They did.

Symptoms of strange hypocritical counterpoints co-exist at every level in the Washington mind. A big and active block of naughty peep-show houses and adult Swedish gadgetry is a few steps from the terrifying concrete confines of the FBI building. Maureen Dean, wife of Nixon aide John Dean, swore that porno movies were shown at Camp David, the president's retreat, during the Nixon years. (The Carter White House had Bo Derek's *10* sent out there, and felt quite wicked.)

One problem is that everyone's too busy for ordinary, affectionate, Cleveland-style sex with all the trimmings—unless they really, really need it, or, God forbid, they're in love.

*"My idea of a good time with a woman is to hole up for three days, watch old movies, make pizza, be silly, act like children and get the giggles."*
    —BURT REYNOLDS (NOT A WASHINGTONIAN.)

*"Are you interested?"*
    HAMILTON JORDAN, TO THE FAIR HELGA, IN
    BONN, SUMMER OF 1978

Busyness is the reason undemanding young women are so important in the sex lives of many male politicians. The gentleman doesn't
want a lot of scenes, thank you. He can enjoy those quite privately
at home, with the daughter whose birth control pills fell out of her
purse at the breakfast table, or his son whose pupils look wacky when
he wafts home from a pricey private school.

On top of that, his wife is beginning to get that weary, caged air
that all politicians' wives get in Washington, sooner or later.

If he seeks dalliance, he doesn't want somebody ratting to his
constituents or wife, and in that order. He wants what he wants when
he wants it, and he's got an awful lot on his mind. To ensure that
the right thing stays on his mind and the wrong thing remains inside
his trousers, a few politicians' staffs loyally shoulder duties as "the
Members' Zipper Patrol."

Bottle-blondes are still the preferred trollop type among politicians with zipper problems. (Even Ronald Reagan, talking about
screen kissing, once said that in a pinch he preferred kissing blondes:
"When you kiss even the most frozen blondes, they seem to, well, uh,
glow.") Their allure on Capitol Hill is timeless. Chilling fallout from
tumble-and-tattle Hill blondes like lobbyist Paula Parkinson and
non-typist Liz Ray does not dim their appeal. Pretty Republican Rita
Carpenter, who switched politics when she married Democratic Rep.
John Jenrette, kept that old blonde magic even after leaving him high
and dry. Some time after their marriage was ended, betrayal complete, and the $20,000 cash in his brown suede shoes just a memory,
John asked Rita to autograph a copy of *Playboy* in which she starred
in *déshabille,* just for him.

Perhaps, like bright birds courting, Hill blondes are simply designed to be instantly recognizable to potential mates. That saves a
lot of time. Congressmen are always in a hurry. Besides, other politicians understand the blonde syndrome.

When Paula Parkinson threatened to unveil two hitherto-
unrevealed congressional beaux to the world—one of whom she had
naughtily videotaped at play—the unhappy duo trudged over to the
White House Political Affairs Office to confess their sins to Lyn

Nofziger, then President Reagan's chief adviser on such delicate matters. Neither was excommunicated.

*"I come to Washington to get screwed. I'm a taxpayer, aren't I?"*
—ROBERT MITCHUM

A bachelor congressman or senator can lead a happy and discreet life with consenting adults from his own or others' staffs. There are risks. Although surely his constituents don't expect monkish chastity from a single, healthy man, neither is he supposed to be observed flitting from a night of joy straight to the arms of his country's business. Therefore, it is convenient for a congressman's girlfriend to live close to his office on Capitol Hill. The member may thus leave the bed of his beloved at dawn, when snoopers from the *National Enquirer* are still nursing hangovers in lavishly appointed apartments on the city's best outskirts.

One Midwestern congressman who spent such a night awoke, gratefully gulped the glass of water his charmer had thoughtfully placed beside the bed, showered and left for his office before sunup, in the approved manner. At 8:30 his phone rang: "You have drunk my contact lenses," she said. He had.

Bachelor congressmen's apartments are the most popular retreats for the adventures of his married friends. Two or three well-known congressmen are deeply admired as absentee hosts. Several lobbyists maintain corporate suites in apartment buildings or hotels; some congressmen have keys to these. "Courtesy suites" donated by hotels to powerful Washington figures are not new. The smart pol avoids them; the almost-smart chooses one in a large, convention-type hotel, with garage access to avoid awkward encounters and unnecessary explanations.

If espied, he makes much bustle about "these damned conventions" or mentions a visiting constituent. One distinguished gentleman was actually spotted slithering into a suite by a journalist coincidentally doing the same thing. He made a point of saying sternly to the angel-faced slip of a girl preceding him, "Now, Miss Thompson, did you remember the Detweiler report? We must mark that up first."

"Marking up the Detweiler" became the standard phrase at one Washington news bureau for the getaway act of love.

Press-shy Carterites preferred to take their quest for romance to other cities. Hamilton Jordan took his love to his friend Nate Landow's beachside retreat on Maryland's Eastern Shore. He may have been spurred to absent himself by frosty remarks from his estranged then-wife, Nan, who toiled for Rosalynn Carter in the White House's East Wing. Before going over to the West Wing, where he worked, she always phoned ahead. She would explain, sweetly and loudly, "I don't plan to walk in on anything."

Geography solves some problems. Others then arise. One married Lothario sought consolation in the arms of a good Catholic girl. Though still a virgin, she was determined to do things the right way. She had memorized the rhythm system of birth control. She was an artiste, thus slightly fuzzy on the side of the brain which deals with time and numbers. Being a Washingtonian, though, she could recall with pinpoint precision that her last period had coincided exactly with the day the American mission to rescue the hostages in Iran was aborted. It was late at night. The pair telephoned the international desk of a local newspaper. I'm calling for Congressman So-and-So, she said, using the name of a different member, and what was the precise date of that event? The answer came. *Amour* bloomed; the earth moved. Unfortunately, the international desk was off by two weeks, and she became pregnant. Could they sue? she wondered.

Probably not. Love, you see, is not built into the system. Long articles have been written about Why Washington Men Are Such Lousy Lovers. The true answer is, they are tired. Lord, they are tired. How many times can they be expected to go through the demanding motions of courtship—wooing, wining, flowers, walks in the light rain by the blossoms, firelit flattery—when it's all most can do to jolt down a couple of drinks and struggle out of their BVDs at night?

For a busy man, there is nothing like a worshipful, fresh-faced staffer (his own, or someone else's), a charming girl who knows the trouble he's seen, and is happy, as a gift of womanly charity, to perform comforting sexual services for her hero. And to be quick about it. There is a certain virtue in being the hasty handmaiden of one who has the woes of the world on his mind.

Loyal staffers will not comment on office affairs. Disloyal ones, or Women Staffers Scorned, can be dodged. One Western congressman avoided the icy eyes of a former love by meeting his new sweetie regularly in dangerous territory—halfway between the House press gallery and the House television and radio gallery. Both galleries were swarming with reporters from his home state. Quite plainly, he could not be up to anything in so visible a spot; the pair—arranging assignations—passed unnoticed, until he dumped his wife.

Often, it's congressmen with the most straitlaced constituencies who shed wives as snakes shed skin. Mickey Edwards of Oklahoma, at this writing, is on number four: Lisa is a former Miss Oklahoma, first noticed in Washington three months before the marriage, warbling "America the Beautiful" to President Reagan and the Conservative Political Action Caucus. Mickey's latest discard fumed silently in Oklahoma, filing for divorce.

Not so the ex of former Texan Rep. Bob Eckhardt. When he took his third wife, Celia Morris—incidentally the ex of writer Willie Morris—the pending event was noted by the *Washingtonian* magazine. Eckhardt's second wife, Nadine, wrote the editor. Thank you for the announcement, she wrote. It had alerted her that she should hasten home to get a fair property settlement as quickly as possible. "The Texans got what they wanted, I got the land and she got the, uh, well, she got what she wanted." Her neatly poisonous P.S. was omitted when the magazine printed the letter: "Ex-wife No. 1 committed suicide."

Generally speaking, it is considered good manners for couples who settle in Washington and then split to omit mention of each other from their respective biographies. This was done by Sen. Don Reigle and his wife Meredith, now editor of *California* magazine. It is not to keep a big secret; it is to avoid confusion.

One rare and happy exception was Rep. Dick Ottinger, the New York Democrat. A year after his divorce, colleagues on the Hill were charmed to receive letters from him advising them that his ex, Betty Ann, had set up an office for psychotherapy and counseling, conveniently located near the Capitol itself. "She does individual and group therapy and marriage counseling," he enthused, after listing her qualifications. "She is a very caring, sensible and able person. I would appreciate it if you would let your staff and friends know of her availability should any of them be interested in counseling services . . ."

On the whole, Capitol Hill wives are not supposed to have biographies at all, with a few rare exceptions like Sen. Bob Dole's wife Liddy Dole, the highest-placed woman in the Reagan White House. Ex-wives are supposed to become non-persons. Senator Dole's first wife, quietly divorced by a Kansas judge when nobody was watching, has vanished from the pages of history.

In the heady ether of the Capitol itself, love with an equal is almost unthinkable.

With a superior, it's totally unthinkable.

Clare Boothe Luce, once a congresswoman herself, would not have been a good political wife or mistress. "Politics is a terribly non-creative thing," she once sighed, "a scrimmage and a place for second-rate talents."

That is not the sort of stuff a congressman wants to hear after a hard day doubting his own wits.

"A woman who's smart as me is usually busy looking for her space. A woman who's smart and really beautiful wants all the consideration I don't have time to give," confides one solon, whose own romantic life is limited to young and low-ranking staffers.

One exception was the amour that blossomed between Representatives Martha Keyes and Andy Jacobs. Their eyes met at a November Democratic Caucus. They learned to love over the ledgers of the House Ways and Means Committee. In the Washington tradition, Representative Keyes shed her first husband during the summer recess; Representative Jacobs popped the question the following fall. It was all very beautiful. Neither was re-elected.

The reason for planning your divorce in August—the most important month in Washington serial polygamy—is that August is a non-month in Washington. It is a sort of lonesome Mardi Gras, when anything goes. It is so hot that everyone vanishes. As mentioned, the House and Senate are out. Slumlords go condo in August; porn shops open in chic Georgetown; people make conspicuous architectural additions to their houses, which will spoil the neighbors' view. Of course it is the ideal month for a politician to trade in his wife for a newer model. Even the gossip columns close down; theoretically, nobody is left in town to gossip about. It cannot be said strongly enough that any major changes in social or sexual status must always be undertaken in August in Washington.

It is quite common for congressmen and women—Rep. Shirley Chisholm leaps to mind—to vanish in the early summer with no announcement of a divorce and reappear in the fall with completely different mates. It is standard for Washington friends to pretend not to notice the change when they get back.

Supreme Court Justice John Paul Stevens made the mistake of fleeing his nuptial nest when he wed in the spring—completely out of season—to wed a woman who also had a tiresome legal entanglement. He was furious that anybody noticed.

"If he'd been a truck driver I would have punched his lights out a long time ago," his intended's ex-husband angrily told a newsman. Had the justice chosen the correct month, all the newspapers would have been concentrating on chicken salad recipes and cold punch refreshers for the dog days.

For some, despite all seasonable precautions, the outcry at a change of wife would throw the voters back home into an uproar.

Some powerful men remain faithful.

Others launch comfortable traditional mistress relationships with younger women. These have few disadvantages, if discreetly handled. Still, a lot of gloomy soul-searching went on in Washington after Nelson Rockefeller, who had been well-liked here, gallantly went to his reward in the midst of toiling on his Great Work, with young aide Megan Marshak.

"What would you do if I kicked the bucket at your apartment?"

one elder statesman anxiously asked a staffer. "I'd drag you into the elevator, push the Lobby button, and jump out before it went down," she replied. He seemed perfectly satisfied with her response.

One couple of disparate ages seriously sought a love nest in a building with a large laundry chute, just in case.

As president of the American Federation of State, County and Municipal Employees, the late Jerry Wurf offered to have a legend tattoed across his chest: "In case of emergency, phone 911. Not afraid of scandal."

Indeed, some Washingtonians would be rather proud of the right kind of scandal. The wrong kind, which upsets everyone from mothers to voters, is homosexual.

Just after unfortunate Rep. John Hinson was caught by Capitol policemen in a gents' room at the Longworth House Office Building in a compromising posture with a swart young man, the telephone began jangling at the home of Washingtonian Dick Munn. (He was then the writer of a column called "The Gay Life" in a small local newspaper.)

"Was he in the fourth floor or the sixth floor tearoom?" inquired the callers anxiously. The sixth floor convenience was where fans of gay bathroom sex could be expected to meet for chance encounters or hurried ones, spiced with the added risk of discovery. The fourth, being less accessible and guarded by two sets of squeaky doors on either side of the vestibule—a sort of early-warning signal—was for more leisurely observances; its atmosphere and lighting were also considered more agreeable by connoisseurs.

A certain triumph was detectable in the gay community over Mr. Hinson's political party—as it was also in the case of Moral Majorityish Bob Bauman, the Maryland congressman who walked on the wild side at Ninth Street bars.

"Republicans are far more in the closet than Democrats," says Munn. "When I first came here, I was amazed at how many there were. You just don't expect it; as you don't expect Republicans to be health-food nuts."

Some people, of course, don't expect any congressman at all to be gay. Others are even more outraged that they should be revealed. But what shocked the Hill more than the revelation of goings-on in the various gentses was the fact that House speaker Tip O'Neill had known that the Capitol cops planned their raid in advance. The police had offered three options to the Speaker: they could post a warning sign outside the men's room; they could stand an officer in full regalia outside the door, as a discouraging gesture; or, they could simply pounce, without warning.

No warning, was the decision. It had apparently never crossed the mind of the Speaker that a congressman—even a Republican—might be surprised at his pleasures, along with the lowlife. Perhaps he had not dwelt on the topic.

Odd. Politically minded Washingtonians are ordinarily keenly aware of gay political strength. Anyone hoping to be mayor of Washington, for example, had better woo the powerful and active local gay groups.

Woe betide the Democrat who forgets them on a national level. Even Jimmy Carter sent his son Chip to the Los Angeles Gay Community Services Center for their fundraising fiesta. Someone who sat close to Chip at the head table found him most refreshing: "Chip said yes, his mom and pop knew where he was. Much nicer than Miss Lillian, who came last year and kept pretending she didn't know where she was herself."

*"Who knows? Perhaps homosexuality is nature's way of keeping the population down?"*
     —THE LATE ALICE ROOSEVELT LONGWORTH

The show of political support for gays is a shallow one. In the summer of 1981, as the San Francisco Gay Men's Chorus boomed "Give Me Some Men, Who Are Stout-Hearted Men" in concert on the Capitol steps, a Georgia Democrat was amending a bill to prevent Legal Services funds from going to "defend, promote or protect homosexuality."

Meanwhile, the capital's gay life burgeons. Gay marriages, or blessings, are frequent. (Popular wedding present: "His" and "His" towels.)

It may be the ultimate democracy. It transcends conventional class and race lines more than any other facet of Washington life. Behind the glossy facade of Washington society, totally different lines are drawn—lines based on preference for different types of sexual activity. Thus you have the Moral Majority congressman and the busboy meeting in the Longworth Building's men's room for activities the former's voters have never heard of; the administrative assistant dancing with the hairdresser at a disco in Southwest Washington; the millionaire and the housepainter kissing at a bar on P Street; the highly paid lobbyist and the drag queen putting on a show at small private beach parties in Rehoboth, the fashionable Delaware beach resort; the White House staffer and the passing stranger making fleeting contact in the YMCA; the respected journalist and the wan blue-collar youth in grimy expense-account motels.

This means that beneath the ordinary web of crossconnections that exist in everyday life, a totally different web of connections, social, sexual and secret, is spun. The secret reality would come as a vast surprise to the majority of family-oriented Washingtonians, who have no idea it exists. The most surprising thing of all, ultimately, is that it is such a secret.

*"You want romance? You've got the wrong Washington. Try Spokane."*
   —VOICE IN CLYDE'S, A GEORGETOWN BAR

Probably the most romantic thing that ever happened to Washington D.C. was Elizabeth Taylor.

At the time, it must have seemed deliciously romantic even to her: meeting the queen at the British Embassy, on the arm of handsome John Warner, when he was running the whole Bicentennial.

"He looks like he has combat fatigue," one of John's friends confided after two weeks of love and Bicentennial fever.

"John's overmounted again," nudged a member of the Warrenton Hunt. (John is famed for choosing horses used to better equestrians.) The original challenge of helping him become elected senator must have been dazzling, although after it was all over Liz swore never to do it again. Certainly, she refused to grant a single interview to the Washington *Star* after it ran the Oliphant cartoon showing him riding Liz, à la National Velvet, to victory. So romantic a figure was she to worshipping, star-starved Washingtonians that even her X-rays were stolen from a local hospital.

John was swept away too.

"What's it like being married to Elizabeth Taylor?" a child asked him.

"Well, it's like this," he said. "Ben Franklin was walking down a street in Philadelphia and met a pretty lady. Immediately, he fell in love. And, my dear, it was only after he fell in love that he discovered: electricity!"

Right about then, Elizabeth was discovering more than electricity; she discovered what a Washington marriage means to the wife of a politician: playing a thankless supporting role with minimal applause and low billing.

"You're gonna have to learn to change in gas-station restrooms, if you're going campaigning with John," she was told by a pol's wife at a ball in Richmond. She had been so mobbed by the romance-crazed crowd that she had had to wriggle away and hide in the ladies'. For someone accustomed to having the decor of her dressing room—including white shag carpet, lavender-lace walls, floor-to-ceiling mirrors and an aquarium full of soothing tropical fish—written into her contract, it must have seemed a strange state of affairs.

As the political noose tightened around her neck and the horrors of campaigning sank in, romance died. She began to tell friends in Europe that she'd had it up to here with the goddamn chicken dinners.

It finally became clear that Washington's notion of Romance might not fit Elizabeth at all at the gala she chaired for the Wolf Trap Center for the Performing Arts, a favorite Washington recreational

spot and charity. This affair, out in the countryside of nearby Virginia, was the most bizarre social event of the summer of 1980. It was
memorable only because Rod McKuen and Burt Reynolds sang
"Baby, It's Cold Outside" to each other. Most of its weary patrons
left aching with boredom before Liza Minnelli finally got onstage
after midnight; and Johnny Cash got into a hellacious fight with Park
Service security because they wouldn't let him escape from the melee
early.

Dizzy with the freedom and camaraderie of showbiz people after
the strangling restrictions of politics, Liz greeted John's arrival
backstage with a merry "Well, well! Here comes Senator Asshole!"

Soon afterward, plans were laid for her performance in *The Little
Foxes*—her declaration of independence from her Bicentennial beau.
It was after *The Little Foxes* premiere in Washington that John said,
"There are three things in my life—my marriage, the senate, and
squash."

Squash! What had happened to electricity? The rest is history; we
just don't know it yet.

We do know that the whole mess will serve as a dire warning to
Washington politicians who think that romance can be part of their
lives, too.

"Of course it would have been different if John had been a Democrat," several Democrats still say smugly.

Capital wisdom has always said that the parties have divergent
sexual characters. Former Irish Ambassador Sean Donlon used to
give a little speech, particularly around Kennedys, pointing out the
differences:

"Republican boys date Democratic girls; they plan to marry
Republicans, but want fun first. Republicans sleep in twin beds, even
separate rooms. That's why, in the last analysis, there will always be
more Democrats."

At least one Republican congressman has banished all ideas of
romantic foolishness from his head: Rep. Mark Siljander of Michigan. A quiet mention to his hometown pastor that he was looking
for a "good Christian girl" to marry led to a media flurry in his
hometown and nearby cities. At least two hundred would-be brides

answered his plaintive mating call. One proud papa, impressed with the congressman's simple request, informed him that in addition to the required qualification, "my daughter has been artfully arranged by the Lord." A very keen young woman thoughtfully enclosed a sample of her wedding dress material; and a letter came from a four-times-wed woman who wrote that she could cook, sew and clean, and would love to be his wife as soon as she got out of prison.

The congressman is still single.

Perhaps he will vanish one August and come back with the lady when she gets out.

Who understands Washington sex? Planned Parenthood does. When Jimmy Carter asked Americans to lower their winter thermostats to sixty-five degrees, the pro-birth control group sent out an alarm: Washingtonians would go to bed earlier to stay warm, it said. Watch out. Here come the babies.

Anywhere else, no one would take it seriously. But Washington gave it at least a passing thought before dismissing it. Planned Parenthood brought up the topic of the last baby boom—exactly nine months after the televising of the Watergate hearings.

Most of those new babies were Democrats.

There's your sex in Washington.

# THE BEACHHEAD

# Some Enchanted Evenings: RSVPing on the Party Circuit

*"At any given party it's hard to know who's paying the bill,
and for what motive you happen to be invited."*
   —AUSTIN KIPLINGER, FOUNDER OF THE
   KIPLINGER REPORT

IN WASHINGTON a lot of parties are paid for by the taxpayers.

For most White House receptions, the White House, using taxpayers' money, pays the bill. For state dinners at the White House, the State Department, also using taxpayers' money, pays the bill.

Gerald Ford's dinner in honor of the queen of England, it was reckoned, cost $150 per head. (For comparison: to fête the chancellor of West Germany cost $170 per head. The Australian prime minister, $149. The Finnish, $144.)

Salaries and time of White House staff, aides, protocol personnel and so on must must be added to current State Department estimates; these put the food-flowers-booze expense for a Carter Era state dinner for about two hundred diners at around $12,000.

For a Reagan Era state dinner, with fewer than a hundred guests, the current estimate is $15,000. Estimates do not include Park Service support personnel. These people work on high overtime salaries to trundle the tables to and from the East Room before and after dinner.

(The rooms must be cleared for tourists during the day.) If there is to be a tent on the lawn, as there was for the queen of England's dinner, that means an especially laid floor, special wiring for air conditioners and blowers, and unusual decorating expenses.

What do White House state diners eat? So far, none has sampled the president's favorite food, macaroni and cheese.

The menu for the White House dinner honoring President and Mrs. Herrera of Venezuela, November 17, 1981, is more typical.

It started with fruits of the sea in a golden crust with sauce *Américaine.* Next came roast saddle of lamb, braised hearts of celery, tomatoes florentine; green beans *amandine;* then a romaine lettuce and grapefruit salad with Bel Paese cheese, followed by hazelnut bombe with almond brittle *sabayon* and petits fours. The U.S. Air Force Strolling Strings played during the dessert course. The seafood was washed down with a Kenwood 1980 Dry Chenin Blanc; the lamb with a Simi 1974 Cabernet Sauvignon Reserve; and Papagni Vineyards' Spumante d'Angelo sparkled compatibly with the hazelnut bombe.

King Hussein of Jordan and Queen Noor had a royal change of pace: dinner began with poached halibut in dill sauce with fleurons, served along with President Reagan's favorite wine, a Chateau Montelena Chardonnay 1979. (Actually, 1977 is Reagan's very favorite year, but Hussein was threatening to buy his military hardware from the Soviets at the time.) This was followed by sliced tenderloin of beef with sauce *Choron,* soufflé potatoes, broiled tiny tomatoes, artichokes *St. Germain,* served with a Jordan Cabernet Sauvignon 1976. (A little pun to compliment the guest, there.) Then came bibb lettuce salad and Brie cheese. A Schramsberg Cremant Demi-Sec 1979 was poured to liven up the chestnut bombe and acorn petits fours; but this time—now came our side's hint of military might—the U.S. *Army*'s Strings strolled and played.

It was all very elegant and one can see why it cost twice as much per head as the previous administration's *soirées.* But variables besides mere elegance and inflation change costs from administration to administration.

Lyndon Johnson's overall dinner costs, for example, came out higher on White House accountings than John Kennedy's, although Kennedy's dinners were the more elegant. The reason was that Kennedy unashamedly used military aircraft to fly in his entertainers; Johnson, who had other plans for the military, paid from the White House and State Department funds.

The White House aside, some Washington parties at government departments, art galleries, museums and libraries are paid for with tax dollars.

Most Cabinet officers' entertainments are paid for with "special donated funds," tax-deductible dollars contributed by private individuals or corporations. Purposes for "special donated funds," of course, include throwing parties for the donors of those funds. The liquor that is served at Cabinet officers' receptions is actually contraband booze, confiscated by the U.S. Customs service, a fact that might add a merry-smuggler note to the festivities if only it were advertised more widely.

Parties to celebrate the openings of grand shows at the National Gallery of Art are occasionally paid for by a special fund created by museum founder Andrew Mellon for that purpose. More often, corporations pick up the tab for both the parties and the shows they celebrate. The corporations can then invite Washingtonians they wish to impress, and write it off on their taxes. So, although the "Board of Trustees of the National Gallery of Art" invited you to the affair, that lavish dinner for the opening of the show of Chinese art was on IBM. United Technologies whooped it up for the Old Masters from the collection of Baron Thyssen-Bornemisza; and General Telephone and Electronics, the benign muse suffusing its wire-and-computer-chip heart, hailed Post-Impressionism with a splash.

Even some members of Congress seem unaware of such arrangements throughout the government.

*"I find it hard to believe that people and corporations who made contributions intended them to be used for*

*the private entertainment of James Watt and his friends."*

—REPRESENTATIVE EDWARD MARKEY, UPSET
OVER INTERIOR SECRETARY JAMES WATT'S
PARTY AT THE LEE MANSION

That very elegant private reception in a new friend's elegant house or apartment might be subsidized by a corporation, lobby, promoter, publisher, foreign businessman or private individual in search of access. The late Washington hostess-with-the-mostes', Perle Mesta, often had the mostes' because someone else was paying.

Long-standing Washingtonians are not astonished to find out that quite a lot of Washington parties "in honor of" somebody are paid for by the honoree.

On the whole, if one is a persistent host in Washington without apparent motives, one's guests conclude that one is either simpleminded or up to something so sinister that it is not immediately clear. The preferred host has glaringly obvious motives, a genial manner, a lot of money and a large house. The motives are then politely ignored, like a pegleg.

Korean wheeler-dealer Tongsun Park's parties for people like House Speaker Tip O'Neill were models of their kind, before his little scandal broke.

"What a nice fellow," everyone said, proud of the evident virtue in such lack of prejudice. (Tongsun, in fact, is still popular in Washington. He makes frequent forays to town to clear up small legal problems. These days, he just gives his friends expensive eelskin wallets. "They smell funny when wet," complains one recipient. Gratitude is not a Washingtonian trait.)

A large house helps every host. The Averell Harrimans frequently lend their names and house to Democratic fundraising events, large and small. At large garden parties, people like Robert Redford will turn out to support their favored pols. I asked Redford once if the whole scene didn't remind him exactly of his political movie, *The Candidate.* He giggled and said, "Exactly." (I like to think that was the very moment he decided to run for sewer commissioner in Provo, Utah.)

The small Harriman parties are the most interesting. That became clear when a tape recorder ran, unbeknownst to most of the guests, during a September 1981 gathering. On it, Clark Clifford, the Washington super-lawyer, was heard to call Ronald Reagan "an amiable dunce" whose policies would be "a hopeless failure"; and Felix Rohatyn, the New York financier, was heard to say that if something wasn't done "society's going to blow up."

The guests, although all Democrats, almost fainted with horror when a transcript of the tape leaked out. Only the worldly Robert Strauss sighed, "Hell, I wouldn't say anything in a room with more than two people in it."

Some people quite openly rent their homes to party-givers. The genteel John Sherman Coopers annually slip away from their large Georgetown house for a week or so, and rent it—for several thousand dollars a pop—to convening World Bank or International Monetary Fund officials for entertaining.

Several Washingtonians buy mansions and then, by using them a certain number of times a year for charity or political fundraising parties, can write much of their upkeep off on taxes. Liz Taylor and John Warner would lend their Georgetown house and themselves to groups like the Republican Senatorial Trust Committee—a secret club of Republican millionaires like insurance mogul Clement Stone and Donald Hall, the Hallmark Card man. All were flattered silly to eat *chez* Liz and John.

Certain officials without glamorous houses, and those who do not wish to use them, can arrange parties in government-owned buildings.

A Washingtonian on the party circuit or a reporter covering it can expect to go to dinners at the National Gallery of Art, Blair House, the Smithsonian Institution's Museums of History and Technology, Air and Space, Natural History (dancing around the stuffed elephant is particularly popular) the Hirschhorn art gallery, the Woodrow Wilson House, the seventh floor of the State Department, the Organization of American States' handsome building, most government departments, and several historic houses in the care of the National Trust for Historic Preservation.

Right after one election, a top-level White House staffer wished to throw a party at Blair House for his friends, before the incoming president's inauguration. He invited his guests. To his horror, the incoming First Lady announced that she wished to stay at Blair House on the very night he had chosen for his social swan song.

A terrible flap ensued. The incoming First Lady was persuaded to come a day later; a government plane was sent to pick her up, at considerable expense.

*"I want to tear off my clothes and jump into bed. It's been heaven, but I've had enough."*
—JERRY ZIPKIN, AFTER THE FIRST SOCIAL WEEK OF THE REAGAN ERA

*"I love the administration. They're working hard. And it's good to celebrate a little bit, before the bombs fly. Who knows?"*
—BANDLEADER LESTER LANIN, DECEMBER 1981

The art of entertaining in Washington takes more than money and a house, of course. It takes a guest list.

Look at your classic Washington entertainment—your Little Georgetown Dinner. This is classic because everybody there can use everybody else there to advantage, and no jaw motions are wasted. The usual form is one White House person, one senator, one congressman, one journalist, and one embassy or State Department official, each with his respective partner.

Mix briefly with martinis or sherry, arrange around table (putting prettiest wife next to most important man and then ignoring her), pour on wine, fill stomachs and brew briefly in drawing room with coffee. Dinner party will be over at 11 P.M., which is Washington curfew.

Your guests let you go to bed at curfew, because they must do it all again tomorrow night.

"If they stay 'til 11:30, it means they're having the kind of time that will go in their memoirs," explains an ambassador. "If they stay 'til 12, they're bombed."

### "WHEN ARE THE GUESTS LEAVING? ISN'T ANYBODY GOING HOME?"
—SIGN BORNE HIGH BY THE CHILDREN OF
CLOVER GRAHAM AT HER PARTY IN HONOR OF
HOPE COOKE NAMGYAL, FORMER QUEEN OF
SIKKIM

For receptions in your house or extravagant Watergate apartment to honor, salute, say hello, say goodbye, celebrate the appointment of and so on, your purpose is to mix a superior people cocktail—stirred, not shaken.

Your guest list is not so stringently cast as the Little Georgetown Dinner's. Of course you will graciously omit those who might push each other downstairs, steal your silver or hurl piña coladas at the guest of honor.

Some daring souls like to sprinkle in a few mild incompatibles. These lend verve and give guests something to gossip about later.

Lawyer-lobbyist Steve Martindale managed to invite to one party —in honor of Virginia Graham—both Sen. Don Reigle and Betty Jane Ackerman. Betty Jane had recently made public tapes of intimate interludes with Riegle. Everyone except the senator enjoyed the event thoroughly. ("My dear, it was *ghastly*. You could have cut the tension with a *knife.*")

The Washington host knows that timing is all. You probably want to catch important people at the end of their working day—just when they really need a drink, but before they go home and take off their clothes. That is why 5:30 or 6 P.M. to 8 or 9 P.M. works best for cocktails (at which people expect to nibble what amounts to dinner) If you want to catch them after that, dinner is at eight, and it had better be good.

A few clever hosts have found success with unusual hours, for special purposes. One hostess, Maria Fisher, kicked off a sudden and successful spate of midnight parties. These attracted television newscasters, who popped by for post-program drinks, and idle bigtimers who had attended classic end-at-eleven dinner parties and had nothing to get up for in the morning.

The embassy of Ireland, on the other hand, worried guests to distraction with invitations inviting them for "drinks at ten."

Lifelong Washington newspaperman Jeremiah O'Leary was observed staring perplexedly at his little square of pasteboard for some time. Then he picked up the phone.

"Is that ten in the morning, or ten at night?" he inquired softly.

"Why, ten at night of course," chortled the embassy's social colleen. She added reproachfully, "Sure, an' I can't think of any embassy that would be servin' drinks at ten in the mornin'."

O'Leary hung up.

"I could only think of one," he sighed.

*"I have all my guests change places between courses. It keeps things lively, doesn't it, True?"*
*"Frankly, Allison, I've always hated it."*
—CONVERSATION BETWEEN WASHINGTON
HOSTESS ALLISON LALAND AND SOCIAL BANKER
TRUE DAVIS

If you are not up to *frissons* and friction, there are two classic techniques for avoiding them.

One sneaky hostess who wishes to remain friendly with all sides mails her invitations out on time—except those addressed to the undesired. Theirs are mailed the day before the party. The recipients do not get them in time to attend. She calls them after the party to ask why they didn't come, takes them out to lunch, and moans about the mails.

The conventional method is the two-party, A-list and B-list maneuver.

This has several points. Its lesser purpose is to avoid overcrowding and mixing incompatibles. The greater purpose is to avoid the impression among the important that you have invited them to what is regrettably called a C.S.E. (for Chicken-Shit Event). You invite all your important people together, so that they may relish their importance properly.

Your not-so-fancy friends are graciously all asked together on the following night, or possibly the previous night, to an almost-identical party—well, perhaps just a *leetle* shorter on the caviar.

Only the Nelson Rockefellers, who gave nine sequential housewarming parties when they bought the vice-president's house for the nation, kept equal caviar for all. They were also the only people not suspected of A-and-B-listing, as they did not have to impress anybody.

Rockefellers aside, the Washington mind is exquisitely tuned to pick up vibrations indicating its spot on the lists.

Just how exquisitely was shown when the Reagans chose to divide their White House Christmas press party into two different evenings. (The Carters had simply slashed the guest list by 175 the year before "to avoid overcrowding." The cut media people were obviously delighted when the Reagans won.)

Invitations were mailed. Within two days, a feverish round of comparison and decoding analysis began among invitees. Were the two parties grouped by salary? Fame? Glamor? Age? Size of newspaper or television outlet? Past favors versus expected favors? Or *what?*

"I don't get the pattern," complained a New York *Times* man.

Nobody could figure it out. Finally, in despair, a little group called the White House press office.

"Okay. We give up. Which is A and which is B?"

The White House had taken an alphabetical list of names and

simply alternated them, inviting this one to party A and the next one to party B.

The press was dumbfounded. Those who believed themselves A-listers were enraged.

"There's no exclusivity any more," grumbled one at an excellent and lavish party that was, alas, maddeningly identical to the excellent and lavish party the night after.

Party exclusivity, you see, is the Washingtonian's nirvana—the craved, blissful state of sublime smugness.

If you are among the blessed, invited where others dare not hope to go, it behooves you to treat your good fortune with benign indifference. You must not rub it in to the unfortunate excluded, unless they *really* need whipping into line. The thoughtful invitee only name-drops a party in advance to friends who have done the same to him.

This delicacy sometimes backfires. It did one year at the drearily predictable annual dinner tossed by the White House for the Supreme Court justices and their spouses.

Just after Jimmy Carter's inauguration, a simple, charmingly personal invitation went out to each justice.

Each note gave, somehow, the breathtaking impression that just the recipient and his mate would be there. Alone with the First Pair. Perhaps later it would be "Jimmy" and "Rosalynn!" Supreme exclusivity, indeed. And wouldn't the others be furious?

Tactfully, none of the nine breathed a word to his peers about his upcoming tête-à-tête-à-tête-à-tête.

On the appointed eve, each crept from his chambers to prepare for the anticipated nouveau-simplicity event. Riding the wave of redneck chic, the Justice Brennans even dismissed their chauffeur for the evening and drove themselves. Dinner was served—plain fare of roast beef with gravy, cupcakes and ice cream. Over it, eighteen pairs of familiar eyes stared balefully at each other and their host. Certainly, it was A-list. But each had expected AA-exclusivity. The little cupcakes sat as ashes in the expensive bridgework of nine disappointed mouths. It isn't just exclusivity, you see. It's whom you're more exclusive *than.*

After attending an exclusive event to which, happily, his peers have not been invited, the experienced Washingtonian knows he gets super-smug points by not mentioning it at all for about a week. Then, the reference is tangential: "Well, the president mentioned at George's house the other day . . ."

*"You just can't have two meats at a dinner party, the way prices are today."*
    —THE LATE GRANDE DAME AND MILLIONAIRESS
    MRS. ROBERT LOW BACON. SO PREPARED A
    HOSTESS WAS SHE THAT SHE ORDERED STRAUSS
    WALTZES TO BE PLAYED AT HER FUNERAL.

If you hope to entertain the president or the First Lady, and thus set off a cycle of envy among your friends that will spin out for the entire administration and probably cause them all to vote against the incumbent, you must brace for an extraordinary going-over by the Secret Service before the happy event.

It's doubtful that you'll be sweating over the stove yourself. But if you were planning to, you should know that a White House steward will prepare the food the president and his wife are to actually eat. If it is being catered, Secret Service men will spend a merry day with the caterer and tag along with the food to your house, keeping their eyes upon it until it goes down the presidential hatch. (For the vice-president, there is no point in going overboard. They simply switch the filled plate that is intended for him with the plate of somebody else. At one Press Club function, observers grinned to note that the sole Democrat at the head table was the unwitting taster.)

Your background will have been cleared, to make sure you're not a hopeless dingbat or a Russian mole with a long-standing assassination plan. The Secret Service will very thoroughly pick through the contents of your house. In the kitchen, your rent-a-butler's long knives will probably be confiscated, along with any gadgets that look as though they might splatter projectiles into the dining room.

Secret Servicemen will block each possible entrance and exit of your house. The motorcade that draws up at your door will include outriders, sirens, and a car bearing Uzi submachine guns. A SWAT team will mount the roof of your house and case the neighborhood.

In large or public buildings or at your club, Secret Servicemen will crawl through the air vents running under and over where the president will sit. A man looking for his shorts outside his club's steamroom was slightly surprised when the ceiling above him collapsed. Tiles, beams, wires and huge quantities of soot poured upon the naked member, followed by a young Secret Service agent in a jumpsuit and with an earplug. The unlucky young man, tumbling with a thump onto the partitions between toilets, apologized but explained briefly: "President's coming. Secret Service."

The loving attention to detail is only slightly reduced for Nancy Reagan's down-home social lunches.

These are arranged for Nancy by Muffie Brandon, Nancy's social secretary, in order for Mrs. Reagan to meet Washington's female permanent villagers. (See chapter, "Nancy Through the Looking Glass.")

Tossers of Nancy Lunches range from Ambassador David Bruce's widow, Evangeline, to the beautiful Buffy Cafritz, wife of a rich builder.

The terrible thing about them is that they cannot be gossiped about by the hostess. Everything—the conversation, the machine guns tossed casually in the back seats of cars, the delightful, unspeaking, stone-faced, earplugged young Secret Servicemen, and Nancy's famed "puddling up" with tears over sentimental topics—is doomed to eternal oblivion.

The reason is not for Nancy's security; it is for the hostess's future. Each Nancy Lunch is, you see, restricted to about six women. Each luncheon therefore sows the seeds of a bitter falling-out between the hostess and all her intimate but uninvited women friends who will never feel the same about her afterward.

The idea of the luncheons is for Mrs. Reagan to "meet her kind of woman." Indeed she does. At one such lunch she met Lucky Roosevelt, her present protocol chief. Then, Lucky proceeded to give *her* Nancy Lunch, and failed to invite her original hostess. Another friendship withered.

Larger luncheons including Nancy are not envied as passionately as the smaller. These are therefore healthier for the subsequent social life of the hostess, and are called Safe Lunches.

Nancy attended a Safe Lunch just before President Reagan was shot at the Washington Hilton Hotel.

History might like to note that it was at Lucy and Michael Ainslie's Victorian house in Georgetown. (He is a preservationist, so the luncheon was Victorian too: turtle soup, shad roe with bacon, salad, and raspberry-sauced pears *Cardinale.*) Mrs. Reagan's forty fellow-lunchers included several Cabinet wives and a few neighbors. The ladies and a few *simpatico* gentlemen ate at four tables covered with silk moire—two in murky blue, two in rust—overlaid with antique lace. Each luncher got a small pottery pillbox shaped like a famous house as a favor, to which, though she didn't know it, she could point forevermore and describe The Day Reagan Was Shot.

The Ainslies are now even more popular than they were before the lunch.

*"How you're rated's how you're feted."*
    —OLD WASHINGTON SAYING

*"Well, she had very big feet and she ate all the olives in our dish."*
    —REPRESENTATIVE BARBER CONABLE, QUOTING
    HIS GRANDMOTHER REMINISCING ABOUT A VISIT
    FROM FEMINIST SUSAN B. ANTHONY

If you plan to make a social splash in Washington, it should be clear by now that you must keep one fact in mind: Washingtonians get just *ugly* if they're not fed. Everybody starves all day, or at least skips cheesecake at lunch, if they're rolling from work to a cocktail reception. They will never freeload off you again if you mention the word "buffet" and then give them a few measly bits of cheese and chips.

Marion Javits, the frightfully chic wife of New York's former Sen. Jacob Javits, did not grasp this at all. She once in New York threw a "cocktail buffet" birthday party for artist Robert Rauschenberg and invited Washington's arts Establishment for the event. The Washingtonians arrived ravenously sniffing the air for the filet.

"Not even a *peanut,* my dears," shuddered one *grande dame* upon her return explaining why she would never speak to Marion Javits again. "A ghastly homemade cake appeared, and then vanished forever after the candles were blown out. We were all reduced to scrabbling in the sangria for orange peel. If that's your New York, my dears, you can keep it."

As I've mentioned elsewhere, the Lucullian standards now expected by Washington are set by the vast buffets provided by lobbyists on Capitol Hill.

You may be sure that even Burger King, busily lobbying for lower minimum wages for young help, will not slam down its famed Double-Meat Whoppers with Onion Rings at Congressional receptions. It fetes senators and congressmen at a nearby high-toned restaurant like the Monocle, plying them with smoked salmon mousse, fine pâté and large, blushing shrimp.

Bigger lobbying associations of course use the reception and hearing rooms in the Senate and House buildings, piling tables with more of the same. Like locusts the great and near-great swarm over these at eventide.

Unfortunately, they can be unpredictable.

Off in search of the usual roast beef and ripe Brie in a House or Senate office building, hunters can stumble into specialized events like rabbit meat purveyors' conventions, the brandy producers' meeting with dry crackers provided for tasting, or the soybean fiesta.

At the last, now a regular event, the extruded soy industry plies astonished freeloaders with its wares. A cornucopia of soybean sausages, soybean shish-kebabs, fruit-flavored soy beverage, soy "clam" dips, mysterious Polynesian soy tidbits, soy bacon lookalike strips and extruded soy chicken roll greet the greedy eyes of the gatherers.

Upon this scene one day burst a well-known Washington feaster, who prowls the halls daily bearing in her purse an eleven-inch styrofoam plate. (This is a precaution against tricky hosts, who provide tiny, five-inch plates in a rude effort to control the starvelings' consumption.) She loaded up a heaping plateful of the soy provender, began wolfing away happily, and suddenly looked as though she had been poleaxed.

"What's with this stuff?" she asked of a grazing congressman from a soy state.

"Soy," he beamed.

Without a word, she spat out a mouthful into her soy-laden plate, slid the plate under the buffet table, and stalked from the room in search of greener pastures.

*"Peanuts will be served."*
—ADDENDUM TO INVITATIONS AT THE 1976
DEMOCRATIC CONVENTION

Hard liquor consumption in Washington has been for years the highest in the country. It averaged six gallons per capita in 1981, excluding wine and beer. (Statisticians pickily point out that people from Maryland and Virginia suburbs also buy liquor in the District; but they ignore thousands of gallons bought tax-free and drunk at embassies and for government, White House and military functions.)

Beer and Coke were the constant entertaining fluids of choice at the Carter White House. Carter had strong Coke connections. His attorney general's law firm handled Coke in Atlanta; his HEW Secretary Joe Califano had handled Coke in Washington; his Deputy Secretary of Defense, Charles Duncan, was a former Coke president. Visitors to the White House were not offered a cup of coffee, but pointed toward the Coke machine.

The Carter White House did not serve hard liquor to guests at all.

Suddenly, the booziest city of them all was drowned in beer.

For fancy Georgian parties, like Pat Caddell's poolside cookouts in Georgetown, it was Heineken's. For others, it was Pabst Blue Ribbon.

Billy Beer, the First Brother's own brand, made a dazzling debut, but quickly died. Miss Lillian complained that it gave her diarrhea; and Rep. Mo Udall grinned that he'd sent in a sample to a lab for testing.

"I just got back the report. It's very possible my horse has a bad case of diabetes."

Even at the party to celebrate the swearing-in of Joe Duffey, chairman of the National Endowment for the Humanities, upper-crust and literary Washington found itself munching peanuts, pop-corn, pretzels and apples—and, of course, guzzling beer.

Beer-and-Peanut Fever struck everywhere. The urbane New York *Times* Washington bureau threw a square dance featuring both of the above. A group of rich ladies from the Philadelphia Junior League, visiting the French Embassy for a little *salon* in the *après-midi*, were served Doritos, peanuts, Cheeze Doodles and Coca-Cola.

The Averell Harrimans' chef worked out a way to make peanut pâté. Betty Talmadge, the senator's ex-wife, threw a pig-picking. Peanut soup became a staple. Even John Warner and Liz Taylor served beer along with the predictable Perrier and champagne at their fundraisers.

Simplicity's coy mantle enfolded traditionally elaborate official functions, too. When finance ministers from 140 countries came to Washington for a World Bank convention, Paul Volcker, Carter's chairman of the Federal Reserve, and Bill Miller, his secretary of the Treasury, threw a party for them at the Corcoran Gallery.

Word apparently flew around about the probable provender, which turned out to be scraps of congealed chicken on sticks and some cheap Muenster cheese. Only two ministers turned up—the Mainland Chinese, who was flattered to be invited at all; and the one from Granada, which had just had a revolution and didn't know what was going on. All 138 of the missing ministers were at the

Egyptian Embassy, throwing down the finest America had to offer
—caviar, mysterious little packages made of grape leaves, pita and
couscous and whole roast baby lamb.

*"It's so boring. When I'm in Washington, I just feel like
I'm waiting for Amy to come home from school."*
—MISS LILLIAN

Back at the White House, carefully handled parties are still grand
ceremonial occasions. Even more, they are unbeatable public relations ploys. Wily Lyndon Johnson understood this.

LBJ began the tradition of dancing after state dinners. At these,
he tripped the toe with, buttered up and charmed the female press,
which had never been invited before. (The Kennedys only danced at
private parties. Before Kennedy, only journalists like the president
of the National Press Club and his wife were invited to White House
dinners at all. It was Betty Beale, of the Washington *Star*, who
suggested that the women who covered such affairs might occasionally catch a nibble at the tables.)

In the LBJ Era, too, an informal tradition began of inviting some
Washingtonians to the White House to watch the after-dinner entertainment; around the same time, for the visit of Princess Margaret
and her then-husband Lord Snowden, extra guests were invited to
dance and thus swell the gaiety of the occasion immediately after
dinner.

Soon the two ideas combined; people invited to the entertainments
could stay and dance until the small hours. Many of these were press.
They were profoundly flattered. Even the most sophisticated scribe
turned out with fluttering heart beneath rented tux to dance under
the chandeliers of the White House.

The Carters' kind invitations to the entertainment were still sent
out. Alas. The host thought that Washington's eleven o'clock curfew
applied to the White House, too.

He did not know that the reason people want to be in Washington is so that they can drag into the House, Senate, or wherever one morning, ashen and wrung-out and moaning to their envious peers and underlings: "Oh, God. I feel awful. We danced our legs off at the White House until 3 A.M."

Instead, guests were bundled home after the brief show. For the first time anyone could remember, people began to send regrets to the White House entertainment.

In dazzling contrast, from the public relations point of view, take the Easter Egg Roll on the White House lawn.

It has always been a vague, unstructured affair. Annually scores of children gathered, milled about and desultorily nudged their eggs around the lawn with their feet. Photographs of the event looked charming; the children knew they were having a horrible time.

The Reagan team looked at this unpromising scrum.

For their first Easter, hundreds of wooden eggs, painted pink, blue and yellow, were sent out to Hollywood for signing by the stars. Henry Winkler, Elke Sommer, Red Skelton, Burt Reynolds, Paul Newman, Jimmy Stewart, Johnny Carson, Charlton Heston, Bob Hope and Efrem Zimbalist Jr., were tickled to sign. Dinah Shore and Jaclyn Smith drew daisies on their eggs. Meanwhile, back in Washington, every Cabinet member soberly signed *his* pastel egg in felt-tip pen. The entire House and Senate did likewise—on the whole pleased to be asked. (The second year, major sports figures and astronauts were added to the list of egg people. Several football players complained about being asked to sign pink eggs.)

The eggs were hidden around the White House grounds for children to hunt, one egg per child. The whole strange affair found a focus. Newspapers found something to write about. Children found eggs, if not necessarily the one they were looking for. "I was looking for the Fonz," grumbled one tyke, scrambling back into the foliage to bury the egg he had just found. It was marked, "John Block, Secretary of Agriculture."

Even Dame Education polka'd in on winged feet for this affair: a hundred American artists received naked wooden eggs, and were asked to do something artistic on them. Blank eggs were delivered to embassies, who reproduced national crests upon them. A few painted theirs a defiant Communist red and sent them back for display. The whole event has now been buoyed to a mythic scale, like Macy's Thanksgiving Day Parade or the Rose Bowl game.

Apparently, it is what children want from their White House, parents want for their children, the television cameras want for their news. Clearly, it's what Washingtonians want from their parties: an occasion that does not close the door late that night, but flings it open again for business next morning.

*"Now, look. You've had me over for cocktails; I've had you over for dinner. Let's leave it at that, shall we?"*
    —BETTE DAVIS, TO HER NEW NEIGHBORS. NOT IN WASHINGTON, OF COURSE. IN CONNECTICUT.

# I Cannot Tell a Lie: Prayer and Propriety in Washington

*"The guy cheated!"*
> —RONALD REAGAN, EMERGING FROM HIS
> DEBATE WITH JOHN ANDERSON, AND NOTING
> THAT THE LATTER HAD USED NOTES

*"That man [Soviet Minister Andrei Gromyko] sat there
and lied to me! He lied to my face! I can't imagine an
American diplomat doing that sort of thing."*
> —PRESIDENT JIMMY CARTER

WASHINGTON IS, of course, a very pious city.

Politicians do a great deal of praying. Although public schools do not, the House and Senate open with a prayer each morning. (In the Senate, this is frequently followed by Sen. Howard Baker reading poetry aloud.)

Politicians maintain as intimate a relationship with the Almighty as possible. Even political crowds show a certain respect. John Kenneth Galbraith noticed this at one convention, when the band's repeated playing of a lively tune failed to hush the crowd.

"Try 'Faith of Our Fathers,' " he bawled to the bandleader. The

79

gloomy Episcopalian hymn blared out. It did the trick. The crowd was hushed.

There are prayer breakfasts almost every morning in Washington —for the Cabinet, the House, the Senate, various government departments, and the military. There are prayers before sporting events and after elections.

White House prayer breakfasts are enormously popular. They were even bigger during the Carter Administration. A hearty y'all-come Christian spirit reigned over these events. They were believed to bear considerable weight with the Heavenly Father, who was suspected of keeping track of attendance the way Washingtonians read State dinner guest lists.

One day, a gentleman named Thiounn Prasith, who for some reason still represented the ousted Cambodian government of Pol Pot at the United Nations, was carelessly invited to a White House prayer breakfast.

Luckily he was off lurking in the mountains outside Cambodia with Pol Pot at the time of the invitation itself.

But his New York staff jumped for joy. What a plain-writ sign of favor from the inscrutable American government! They set up an elaborate Washington whirl of pro-Pol Pot activities for their man's return, to surround the prayer breakfast. It included interviews with reporters, a seminar on Cambodia and more prayers—this time at a prayer luncheon with the vice-president.

A State Department official caught wind of the praying plans, and decided they might prove embarrassing.

"There's a lot of suspicion that we're in league with the Chinese in backing Pol Pot," he said. "We certainly don't want his ambassador praying with our people at a national prayer breakfast."

The State Department promptly clamped a stop order on Prasith's travel. Once back in New York, he was not allowed to go anywhere until all danger of praying in Washington was past.

*"If Moses had gone to Harvard Law School and spent three years working on the Hill, he would have written*

*the Ten Commandments with three exceptions and a*
*saving clause."*
—CHARLES MORGAN, FORMER HEAD OF THE
AMERICAN CIVIL LIBERTIES UNION


Washington's military prayer breakfasts are rather rough-and-tumble. As God is more accustomed to regular appeals from military men than from politicians, He probably does not require the same formalities.

At one typical local air force prayer breakfast, assembled top brass and chaplains were shaken from their meditations as the Singing Sergeants chorus, after several mellow hymns, suddenly rollicked their way into the drinking song from *The Student Prince.* ("Lips as red as fruit and soft arms . . . the priceless boon /Of her love beneath a sweet May moon . . .")

"It did not go down too well with the danish and devotion," opined one chaplain, "but I expect God was glad of a change of tune on His Washington channel."


*"Since Big Oilmen began holding regular prayer*
*breakfasts, oil's gone up from $3 to $34 a barrel."*
—A TEXAS CONGRESSMAN


Despite the local wisdom that Nancy Reagan's faith is "Christian Dior," prayer is extremely important to many of the Reagan team.

Interior Secretary James Watt is a profoundly religious man, given to glossolalia, or praying in tongues. (The story of his interviewing a stiffly preppy potential staffer from Geroge Bush's office, urging him to pray with him and then lapsing into tongues, is probably apocryphal; but in a previous job, he was known to have fired employees, then hastily suggested that they fall to their knees beside him in prayer.)

Top presidential aide James Baker stayed for several months at the

Christian Fellowship House before moving into the Foxhall Road mansion that once belonged to Adlai Stevenson. (All his friends, incidentally, envisioned him living in a sort of monkish cell. But the Fellowship House is actually a large embassylike house in a very fashionable part of town.)

Senator Mark Hatfield is a happy and popular host at Washington prayer breakfasts. He is renowned for rapport with his Maker. When forty senators and congressmen piled up to Camp David, milling around and moaning about the gas crisis, it was Hatfield whom President Jimmy Carter nudged for support.

"Mark, why don't you start with the prayer?" he murmured softly. In stentorian tones, Hatfield suddenly boomed heavenward over the babble: "Almighty Father . . ."

Louisiana's Sen. Bennett Johnston turned to him with concern.

"Say, Mark, aren't you taking this gas thing a bit seriously?"

*"Does the fact that you worked for the senator mean you would give more weight to his testimony if you were on the case?"*
*"As a matter of fact, I would give it less."*
   —FROM THE SCREENING OF A POTENTIAL JUROR
   WHO HAD ONCE WORKED FOR SEN. STROM
   THURMOND, AT JOHN JENRETTE'S ABSCAM TRIAL

In spite of the warm religious climate, people are not necessarily more truthful in Washington than they are elsewhere.

Of course, in a city of appointees who are constantly called to account, the truth has to stay—well, slippery on the outside. It is like a jellyfish—better not grapsed by those who will slap you with it while you are busy fighting sharks.

To cope with this, Washingtonians do not fib; they forget.

They forget the first two wives of a congressman, who suddenly vanish from his biography. They forget the $100,000 test car of the National Highway Traffic Safety Administration. (One day, it was accidentally towed away and dumped in a landfill, and simply never spoken of again.)

They forget old political alliances, now embarrassing; they forget old passions, now discredited.

Who—except Richard Nixon's first press secretary—remembers that Jack Kennedy once gave Richard Nixon $1,000 to boost his Senate campaign against Helen Gahagan Douglas?

Who remembers that the two major opponents to Lyndon Johnson's Vietnam War were Oregon's Sen. Wayne Morse and Alaska's Sen. Ernest Gruening? Both voted against his Tonkin Gulf resolution; were sneered to scorn and voted out. Columnist Walter Lippmann, who took a similar position, gave up his column in despair and shuffled off into premature exile.

*"I like the little guy. But that born-again Christian stuff!"*
   —BOB STRAUSS, OF JIMMY CARTER

Forgetting is Washington's protective coloring.

The present is making History. Time's a-wasting, the voters are watching; worse, the tides of trend are treacherous. Even the House and Senate barbershops know it's time to stock up on hair dye when a young president is elected, or when television cameras are installed in Capitol Hill hearing rooms.

Add to forgetfulness an irresistible tendency to take advantage of what might be called flattering misapprehensions. Cast your mind back to the Three Mile Island nuclear accident.

An editorial in the New York *Times* credited Connecticut's Sen. Lowell Weicker, then a presidential candidate, with the grand idea of forming a blue-ribbon commission to investigate the affair.

The senator's press secretary was delighted, but puzzled.

"When on earth did you say all that?" he asked the senator.

Well, Weicker admitted, actually he hadn't said it at all. It was Sen. Richard *Schweicker* of Pennsylvania who had said it. The *Times* had gotten it wrong. But it *was* a helluva good idea. So Weicker's press secretary quietly found a copy of Schweicker's press release and ringingly rewrote it. Then, Weicker grandly submitted it on the floor of the Senate. Now it is ensconced in the *Congressional Record* as the offering of Lowell Weicker himself. Nobody fibbed; the truth just sort of spun around on its hind legs and caught its tail between its teeth.

The most formalized form of Washington forgetfulness is the pointed memory lapse.

The Washington committee that puts on the annual Oxford and Cambridge Dinner at the International Club is a choice exemplar. This distinguished group, all of whom attended one of the English universities, gets together, as one member says, "to eat bland food and trifle and pretend we were all in *Brideshead Revisited,* but not queer."

One of the committee members, Daniel Minchew, formerly of Sen. Herman Talmadge's staff, had been very much in the news. He had recently spoken publicly of his senator; he had just as publicly failed a lie detector test.

What could they do? He was a committee member in good standing. Besides, nothing had been proved against him. But should the image of the entire committee suffer by having his name tacked on?

After hours of debate, they came up with the perfect Washington answer. Minchew would remain a member of the committee in good standing—but his name would not be printed on the program. All were satisfied.

This was acceptable only because this specific Washingtonian was not running for office.

For the office-seeker, you see, to be conspicuous by lying is better than being inconspicuous. This even applies in Philadelphia. There, a three-hour tape of Rep. Ozzie Myers was aired on television, showing him taking an Abscam bribe. Instantly, his opponent in the next election squawked. Unfair exposure for his rival! He wanted equal time on the air! A court conceded that he was right about the exposure, and proceeded to give him a chunk of prime television time.

A word of caution, here. Even the office-seeker cannot afford to be too conspicuous.

One particular congressman leaps to mind—a good, substantial, churchgoing Democratic congressman from an important district.

He had a son at Harvard and a wife who was very socially active in Washington. Quite unaccountably, this model family man and politician took up with a six-foot, red-haired transsexual halfway through a sex change. He met this unusual person frequently, and took him/her to his fashionable house for some of their liaisons.

Apparently he paid with a check. The person, discovering who he was, asked him for more money for more surgery. The congressman thought he smelled blackmail. The playmate held a news conference at which he/she revealed all. Washington reporters knew the sorry story, and pitied the man. Washington editors and newspaper owners, who had shared their social lives with the family, would not cover it. The city dropped the topic hastily. God knew who would be next.

The congressman dared not run again.

On the whole, omissions required for a pleasant life are pettier, their purposes simply mannerly.

The wise pol, like the wise mate, knows there's no point in stirring others' emotions up over nothing; you might want to stir them up for something later on.

Representative Sonny Montgomery, the smooth and civil Mississippian, stood one Sunday outside Saint John's Episcopal Church, waiting to glad-hand the approaching Jimmy and Rosalynn Carter. Something glinting in his own lapel caught Montgomery's eye—a "Save the Canal" button, left over from the last time he'd worn the suit. With one swift gesture he snatched it off, flung it into the bushes and stretched out the hand of Christian fellowship. Why be disagreeable?

A tactful silence is not a fib. Shortly after Israel bombed Iraq's nuclear reactor, Democratic Senator Robert Byrd was quite surprised to get a call from Reagan's CIA director, William Casey. "He thought he was talking to [Independent senator] Harry Byrd," the Democrat told friends. And of course, he politely let the CIA director think it for at least three minutes.

)ut in the world of the international arena, where honor stalks in hobnailed boots, even to hint of untruth is unthinkable.

At the State Department every day, for example, the Foreign Information Broadcast Service issues little background books specifically for journalists, telling them what is being said over the underground airwaves abroad. These are neatly laid out each day in the press area, labelled "Eastern Europe," "Western Europe" or whatever.

Regularly, for some time, the book tagged "Soviet Union" disappeared. Large signs were displayed in the press room: "ACCREDITED PRESS ONLY, PLEASE. NO DIPLOMATS."

Still the books vanished. One day, a suspicious Western journalist printed a sign in Russian: "HANDS OFF." The books stopped disappearing instantly. The Soviet Embassy filed a diplomatic protest. The State Department's Soviet Desk ripped down the sign. And then the books started disappearing again.

Another international vanishing act was handled with more delicacy. This one happened just before the Bicentennial. A group of English dukes came over on a goodwill visit, to try to patch up any bad impression left by King George III.

The Duke of Argyll had tucked into his luggage a lock of George Washington's hair, which an Englishman had happened to own.

Someone had told Argyll that the gift would please the Americans. When he arrived in Washington, he unpacked his own suitcase. He stashed the relic in a corner of his hotel closet. He promptly forgot about it. Several days after he had checked out of the hotel, just before the great Fourth of July celebration, someone reverently dropped the name of the father of the new country.

My God, thought the duke, turning ashen. I left the fellow's hair on the closet floor.

Rushing back to the hotel, he raced to the desk, and thence to the room. The hair had vanished. The hotel was turned upside down; its vacuum cleaner bags were emptied and its trash dumpsters picked through. Unhappily, the hair was gone. It had been sucked up the Hoover of history, dumped with the detritus of time.

The duke did not raise the topic of the hair to his hosts. His hosts, who must have caught wind of it, did not mention it either.

Truth is sometimes not only rude; it is the opposite of what Washingtonians really want to hear.

Even the media, hard-shelled arbiters of veracity, do not care for the unvarnished article on all occasions, even from their own kind. At the wake celebrating the closing of Duke Zeibert's restaurant, a pretty young woman reporter asked a dignified network newsman what he was thinking about.

"Your tits," he replied, probably truthfully. Gratitude was not forthcoming. Horrified, the young woman raced back to her newspaper, and complained long and loud to her editor. He, in turn, picked up the phone, called, and demanded an apology. And the newsman slammed down the phone.

On the other side of the coin, certain fibs are more than acceptable in Washington. If you are in the CIA, for example, you may pretend to be in wheat negotiations or pork belly futures.

This is balanced out by the number of Washingtonians who habitually hint that they are in the CIA.

To make this easier to understand, reflect on the tasks some Washingtonians perform all day. Some of these involve very little of anything except protecting bureaucratic territory. Others—well, take a look at any in-house government department newsletter. I am particularly attached to one put out by the Customs Service, which instructs its toilers on "How to Resuscitate Imported Lizards":

"1) Scoop lizard from pool. 2) Shake out lizard. 3) Massage lizard's torso, applying on-and-off pressure directly behind front legs. 4) Apply mouth-to-mouth resuscitation to lizard's mouth, breathing slowly and forcefully."

Will a young Customs hotshot, hoping for a good-night kiss at the very least, tell his girl what he's been up to all day?

Certainly not.

He says, "I'm in international work—you wouldn't want to hear about it," lets her guess the CIA, and reaps the reward of all mystery men.

Of course the CIA offers in-house psychiatrists; I do not know if the Customs Service has prayer breakfasts.

# Shall We Join the Ladies? Woman's Place on the Potomac

*"Do not keep a box of Kleenex on your desk. It will make the men in your office think you cry a lot."*
—INSTRUCTOR AT THE NATIONAL SECURITY
AGENCY'S MANAGEMENT COURSE FOR WOMEN

NEXT TO the Japanese cherry blossoms around the Tidal Basin, the prettiest show in Washington is the perennial eyeful provided by women's equality.

Just look around! The liberation of womankind seems to be in bloom everywhere.

Our first female Supreme Court justice is ensconced. In her first-day-in-court picture most often shown in the press, she even appears to be holding hands with Chief Justice Burger.

There are 250 Reagan women appointees to government posts. All were invited to a White House briefing and luncheon together in early 1982. "At that time, there will be full White House Press coverage, so wear your finest!" urged the memo they all received first.

Open University, Washington's own course-by-course school-on-the-run, was able to kill its class on Dealing with Sexual Harassment: out of 135,000 potential scholars, only one had signed up for training. Sighed the professor of counterharassment arts, "Either an era's ended, or they don't mind any more."

But wait. These dainty flowerings of woman's progress, like the cherry blossoms, are pure spectacle. Don't expect cherries, too. There will be no pit-spitting for some time.

An example.

After the 1980 election, Jimmy Carter summoned his top staffers into the Oval Office one by one. He wished to offer them help and counsel on their futures, he said. Sarah Weddington, his top woman for women's affairs, was among the gloomy supplicants. Tripping gracefully in, she revealed her ambitions. She hoped to remain in Washington, she said. Perhaps she could hit the speaking circuit and extol Carter's contributions to the lot of womankind? Perhaps a niche as a director might await her on the board of a corporation?

The president eyed her in silence. After a while, he leaned forward.

"Sarah," he inquired, "have you thought about getting married?"

"Why, no," said she, somewhat taken aback. "Of course I don't *completely* rule it out . . ."

"Well," said he, "do you have any prospects?"

It must have been then that Sarah realized that she had slipped through the wide mesh of the Good Ol' Boy Network.

Shortly after the Reagan inauguration, her friends and the press were awed to receive an inch-thick book entitled *Women* from the office of Sarah Weddington, Assistant to the President 1977–1981. (It immodestly, but probably usefully, included fifteen pictures of Sarah and forty-four mentions of her name.) It came with a poster showing 158 Carter female appointees.

"It's an ad. So we can all find husbands," grinned one of the women.

The fact is, the Establishment is snuggled into its settled, sexually determined ways—comfy as a fat clubman puffing a cigar in a well-stuffed leather chair.

One of the Establishment's handiest tools in this Southern town has always been gallantry.

Gallantry—not to be confused with good manners—puts Northern women at a tremendous disadvantage. They are not trained, as Southern women are, to be exceedingly agreeable to men and then do whatever they please. It is, to them, an unfair weapon in the war of the sexes. Yet it's one they are reluctant to outlaw. Oddly, it protects them from their own prejudices against their sex.

During the Carter Era, it extended to the the White House's memo to congressmen about Who was Who on its congressional liaison staff. With great delicacy, the biographies gave the ages of male professionals, but not of women.

What woman would complain? Youth is her traditional ally. But gallantry's secret function is simply to ensure that women are securely pigeonholed in second place. During the Carter campaign, someone asked Mary King, who was to become the top woman in ACTION, why all the Carter women seemed to be deputies and not chiefs.

She said, "I'll turn that question over to my husband." And she did.

The trouble with Southern gallantry is that when it's fired, it kicks like a .45.

In 1980, for example, Donald Blum, husband of Carter's deputy administrator for the EPA, Barbara Blum, filed for divorce in gallantry-drenched Atlanta. The grounds were peculiar enough: "meretricious cohabitation." Even odder for a Southern man, he wanted not only custody of the two children, but child support—and generous alimony.

*"As a woman, she is more motherly."*
　　—SENATOR HOWELL HEFLIN, A FORMER JUSTICE
　　IN ALABAMA, TELLING WHY HE APPROVED OF
　　THE CHOICE OF SUPREME COURT JUSTICE SANDRA
　　DAY O'CONNOR.

In Washington, the *intentions* of both Northerners and Southerners are irreproachable.

The reality is, simply, the reality of the schoolyard: Washington boys don't *want* to play with Washington girls.

They'll put up with them on the job. Just like in school, they have no choice. They'll tolerate them at home, where they come with the furniture and help out with the chores.

But they don't *want* them in the treehouse. They don't *want* them in the clubhouse. They don't *want* them playing in the power structure. And they sure as hell don't want their cold, critical, girly eyes watching the boys at their pleasures.

This is why Washington is so crazy about stag events.

These strange rites are standard even among the tribunes of the people, the press.

The male White House press corps threw a stag party for NBC's John Palmer upon his marriage. (The ladies of the corps, led by Lesley Stahl of CBS and Associated Press's Maureen Santini, promptly tossed him a hen party.)

But revenge was impossible for the stag birthday party given for columnist Robert Novak, half of the Evans and Novak team, at the Georgetown Club.

"No female faces must be seen," Bob McCandless, the evening's ayatollah, decreed.

Two women reporters covering the event for their newspapers ate lonely dinners closeted in purdah off the dining room. It came time to "roast" Novak, with the primitive warrior wit reserved for such events. ("You scratch that evil surface, and underneath—he's evil.") It was feared that a glimpse of icy female eyes would inhibit the hilarity. Both reporters crouched in a service hallway, ears glued to a crack in the door. The wit flew. Novak sat there stone-faced. As it turned out, he had succeeded in out-machoing the machos. Throughout his roast, he listened blank-eyed to the earplug of a transistor radio as the Maryland basketball team went into triple overtime and won its game.

Men reporters are furious when it works the other way. In his heyday, Henry Kissinger graciously made himself available for interviews with both Barbara Walters and Meg Osmer. He denied Marvin

Kalb. Marvin was so enraged he refused to shake hands with Henry on subsequent meetings.

The Gridiron Club, a journalists' organization for the *crème de la crème,* only recently admitted two or three women members.

Old-timers swear it has crashed downhill ever since.

This built-in bigotry is particularly rich in the light of the media's ever-quivering sensors to ethnic insult.

When Emperor Hirohito of Japan visited Williamsburg, the only words reporters heard him say at all were "Ah, so."

A New York *Times* scribe dutifully quoted them. He was reproached as they were blue-pencilled out: "Too much a racial cliché."

There is something called the Alfalfa Club whose only purpose is once-a-year male bonding. The membership assembles annually, nominates a distinguished public figure for president, and he responds as funnily as he knows how.

(At a recent one, Georgia's Sen. Sam Nunn was the fortunate nominee. He brought the house down with his line, "I ask every one of you to stand shoulder to shoulder with me on November 2, so that, when the curtains are pulled, and the final returns are counted, this nation will give a clear answer to that question: 'What great president has come from the sovereign State of Georgia?' And, gentlemen of the Alfalfa, that resounding answer will be: 'Nunn!' "

*"Deejay wanted. Prefer long flowing hair. Must look good in a gown."*
        —SEXUALLY NON-DISCRIMINATING AD PLACED
        BY A LOCAL RAMADA INN

*"There are many great national libraries in Europe, but we don't want to be like one of* those, *where there's just a* woman *in charge."*
        —DANIEL BOORSTIN, LIBRARIAN OF CONGRESS,
        AROUND THE SAME TIME

Is it something in the Perrier? Some miasma off the Potomac? Radioactivity seeping from the cement of the J. Edgar Hoover building? Or is it truly the human condition?

No one knows. But the city's best clubs are for men *only*.

This is disquieting when you think how political figures are constantly quitting clubs with racially restrictive membership policies on principle. (West Virginia's governor, Jay Rockefeller, is the most idealistic. He has actually quit the same club twice. He resigned from the whiter-than-the-washing Edgewood Country Club in Kanawha County in one fit of ethics in 1970, and in another fit in 1980.)

Even men who fancy themselves exemplars of well-balanced liberalism trip over their own intentions.

The *New Republic* book-and-author dinner, for example, grandly invited *New Yorker* writer Elizabeth Drew as its guest speaker one year. A woman! The organizers glowed with self-approval. They then proceeded to hold the dinner at the Cosmos Club, a hive of macho. All were astonished and rather hurt when Drew withdrew.

With the Reagan victory, Washington feminists girded their collective loins for the death struggle.

Indeed, things looked grim.

The wooden stands erected for the inauguration itself—allowing, as they did, a mere eighteen inches breadth per bottom to watch the festivities—implied a callous disregard for the adipose distribution of the tender gender.

Congresswomen had received the same advice on costume for the event as congressmen, from the Capitol Hill inaugural committee: a gray morning suit.

Worst of all, immediately after the election, Phyllis Schlafly, foe of the Equal Rights Amendment, opened an office of her lobbying firm, the rather bizarrely named Eagle Forum, two blocks from the Capitol, and began to wail for the old womanly ways.

On the plus side, women had two thin straws to cling to: there was Reagan's vow to appoint the first woman Supreme Court justice. And there was the knowledge that Bonzo, the president's late co-star in *Bedtime for Bonzo,* had, in the closet, been a girl—or woman—chimp.

*"They are not about to get rid of me. Elizabeth Dole
and I are the only women the president has who are
special assistants."*
         —WHITE HOUSE STAFFER KARNA SMALL,
         QUOTED BY ROGER MUDD IN 1981

The Reagan Department of Interior did not get off on the right
foot with its women.

At the swearing-in of Ray Arnett, its newly appointed Fish-Wild-
life-and-Parks man, he quite unaccountably told a packed auditorium: "Secretary Watt just whispered a joke to me, and I'll pass it
on. It was about a woman lawyer who'd dropped her briefs to become a solicitor."

Then came the wildlife: loud hisses and boos.

"It sounded kinda like a snakes' nest in the Sierras, and kinda like
a hoot-owl convention in West Virginia," said one of the environ-
mentally aware in the audience.

The following afternoon, a page-long demand for Ray Arnett's
public apology for "unsolicited remarks" went around the department to be signed by dozens of "insulted and offended" women.

There are always plenty of fine ways to get insulted and offended
in Washington. Some women have lower insult thresholds than others. Some object strongly to the use of "Mrs." or "Miss," while the
men with their "Mr." are left mysteriously free from incriminating
matrimonial stamps.

"Ms.," now the standard form of address to women on government business stationery, is not enough for some, who would like an
entirely sex-blind title that can be used for those whose sex is unknown: Mx. You say it "Mix"; you use it for Mr., Mrs., Miss and
Ms.; you pluralize it "Mxs." To purists, supporters cry that X repre-
sents the unknown, and besides, everyone's got X chromosomes.
This pleasant conceit has never gotten off the ground.

"Unisex nomenclature does not advance the cause," one feminist
rather irritably pointed out.

There was great excitement when the Labor Department Building was baptized the Frances Perkins Building to celebrate Federal Women's Week. The hitherto inadequately celebrated Frances, a woman, had been secretary of Labor in the thirties and forties.

Still, there was an undercurrent of discontent.

"I wish she'd been christened Mary Lou, just to rub it in a bit more," sighed one woman.

While honorifics remain in no-woman's-land in government, things move swiftly on another front. Sexual harrassment memos have become an art form.

Carter's Energy department unleashed the model version: it "will not be tolerated," wrote Deputy Secretary John C. Sawhill. Harassment was defined as "deliberate or repeated unsolicited verbal comments, gestures or physical contacts of a sexual nature *which are unwelcome.*"

With exemplary evenhandedness, it went out to all personnel, male and female.

D.C. Mayor Marion Barry, no *naif* himself, went into much juicier detail on what not to do around the District government: "Verbal harassment or abuse; subtle pressure for sexual activity; constant brushing against another employee's body; demanding sexual favors accompanied by implied or overt threat concerning an individual's employment status," and a long, graphic list of conventional amusements including "unnecessary patting or pinching."

"Unnecessary to *whom?*" several people of both sexes giggled.

There is no point in getting insulted by the fact that a woman's place in Washington is spiritually closer to the Blue Plains sewage plant than it is to the swift and strong Potomac.

Here, after all, the male animal is on the front lines. Here he makes what surely must be his sincerest effort to square with the sisterhood. Here he makes the laws. He also makes the gestures.

*"Title IX of the Education Act Amendments of 1978—
Equal Opportunity in Sports—provides that Bob Carr is*

*as eligible for a bridal shower as his imminent bride,*
*maybe more so, because he's not as pretty . . ."*
    —INVITATION TO A BRIDEGROOMAL SHOWER FOR
    REP. BOB CARR. IT WAS HOSTED BY REPS. JIM
    LLOYD, PETE STARK AND PAT SCHROEDER.
    SPEAKER TIP O'NEILL SENT A SILVER TEASET. HE
    DID NOT ATTEND.


Every now and again, there is a flicker of progress.

For some reason, perhaps something to do with the Bicentennial, 1976 was a nodal year on Capitol Hill.

Senators Dick Clark and Jim Abourezk, and Reps. Bill Cohen, Tom Harkir, Pete Stark, Ron Dellums, and Pete McCloskey all humbly tended bar for a fundraiser for the Women's Campaign Fund.

For the first time, political husbands got a taste of the wife's traditional press perception: announcing Bella Abzug's run for the Senate, the New York *Times* wrote not a syllable about the candidate's costume or hat. But it noted that "Mrs. Abzug's husband, Martin, stood at her left side in a navy blue suit, white shirt, and red and blue striped necktie," and that her campaign manager, Douglas Ireland, "once a mountainously plump man . . . (is) now slimmed down to 213 pounds."

That year, too, Jim Schroeder, husband of Congresswoman Pat Schroeder, and Bill Burke, other half to Rep. Yvonne Braithwaite Burke, were both invited to the Congressional Wives' Club lunch. Both accepted.

"Heaven knows what they'll wear. You wouldn't want them to wear the same thing, would you?" asked a Schroeder aide, enjoying the game.

On the surface, things look fine on the Hill.

A congresswoman in her glory is one of the local sights, like the "BOOKBINDERS DO IT IN LEATHER" T-shirts at the Folger Shakespeare Library nearby.

Out of context, however, she's just a woman.

At a New Jersey civic meeting, Sen. Clifford Case turned to the strange, pretty woman sitting next to him.

"Excuse me. Would you mind getting me a cup of coffee?"

"Why, not at all," she said sweetly. "How do you like it?"

She tripped back like Hebe, meekly bearing his cup. Someone later mentioned to him that she was Brooklyn Rep. Elizabeth Holtzman.

*"Equal Opportunity is good. But Special Privilege is better."*
>     —ANNA CHENNAULT, THE REPUBLICAN DRAGON
>     LADY AND WIDOW OF FLYING TIGERS CHIEF
>     CLAIRE CHENNAULT

*"Give ten percent of your salary to the Revolution! How do you think the churches got so rich?"*
>     —GLORIA STEINEM, IN 1981

The physical city of Washington was not designed with women in mind.

A quick reconnaissance will show, for example, that almost no Washington public building has adequate women's toilets.

Until late 1979, even the District Building, home of the local government, offered one small commode and one handbasin for its eighty women; fewer than forty of the unfair sex shared five large commodes, four thingies-on-the-wall, and three handbasins.

All Washington theaters were designed with fly-fronts in mind. At every intermission, lines of fidgeting women snake down stairwells and through chattering clusters of the fortunate sex.

At the relatively new Capital Center, women ignore the signs and stalk into the men's without warning.

Some Washington women habitually tackle strange men to request escort service to the almost-empty gents'. Women at the end of interminable lines at the National Theater began to simply gang up and invade the gents' en masse. The result was miraculous: more johns, or janes, were built.

The only exception to this odd imbalance is the National Gallery of Art. Presumably, its architects had seen enough painted nudes to understand *la différence.*

(Even the staffs' facilities are elegant, by the way: the gents' marked with a reproduction of David's *Napoleon in His Study.* The ladies' has Ingres' *Madame Montessier.* )

The inhumane lack elsewhere is strange in this city of all cities. Where else in the world are foreign dignitaries greeted with the words, "I'm sure you'd all like to wash your hands?" (Lee Annenberg, Reagan's former protocolian, always started the ball rolling that way.)

*"As part of the department's observance of International Women's Year, the Maritime Administration is presenting a program on alcoholism on Wednesday, August 27, at 10 A.M., in the auditorium."*
      —MEMO SENT OUT TO STAFF AT THE UNITED
      STATES MARITIME COMMISSION

Washington restaurants are in the forefront of the revolution. Many now dribble the wine for tasting into both the man's and the woman's glass, and set the check smack in the middle of the table to imply equal opportunity to pay.

"A great leap forward," one woman observed rather bitterly.

Unless everyone knows she is a mistress, it is assumed that the woman luncher with a man is a business acquaintance. Men never eat lunch with their wives downtown. If they do, everyone presumes they have been to see their lawyer about a divorce.

*"Experience?"*
*"Yes, and very good references."*

*"Married?"*
*"Yes."*
*"Happily?"*
*"Oh, yes."*
*"Do you drink?"*
*"No."*
*"Gamble?"*
*"No, not at all."*
*"Well, I don't think you'd be very happy here. You
should find a job someplace else."*
       —A DOWNTOWN RESTAURATEUR INTERVIEWING
       AN APPLICANT FOR A WAITER'S JOB


Washington handles its other stereotypes quite efficiently. In religion, of course, everyone thinks that everybody else believes ridiculous things, and it's best not to talk about them. Racial gaffes, which deserve a book of their own, are often handled with swift élan.

The little plaster figure of a black jockey standing in an Uncle-Tom-helpful pose outside the Red Fox Inn in Middleburg—Liz Taylor's old territory—drew a few irate complaints. Simple to fix! Overnight, the jockey's skin was painted white. No more grumbles.

Women have tried to adapt similarly.

At one government department, to the horror of all, a top woman manager suddenly announced that she was undergoing a sex-change operation. It was not until she reached that awkward in-between stage—pin-striped suits and ladies' undies—that the impact of the decision dawned on her co-toilers: "She's been one of our showcase women. Now, our Equal Employment Opportunity Commission quota won't be met." Meanwhile, at the Capitol, guards refuse to permit women, even those with floor passes, on the floor in pants—even skirtlike gaucho pants.

In several government offices, including the Reagan White House, women are proscribed from wearing trousers at all. In some, they are merely "discouraged" from wearing them, even in deepest winter. In one government department, the release of the new Reagan Era policy was greeted by women lawyers with whoops of joy. Even those who had not worn pants for twenty years turned up sporting them next day.

Some women mourn that it's difficult to remain "feminine" and be successful at the same time.

Barbara Walters revealed her secret at a dinner she had for columnist Bill Safire. While she and Bill were both working for publicist Tex McCrary, she said, Bill had bought her a black lace nightie.

"I've still got it," she lisped, "to remind me about femininity."

Most Washington women don't need reminders. There are plenty.

On Capitol Hill, reporters Cassie Mackin of ABC and Roberta Hornig, then of the *Star,* conferred in whispers about procedures in the Appropriations Conference Room. Representative John Myers of Indiana spun around: "Will you ladies stop yakking? Mr. Magnuson! There are two ladies behind me yakking!"

Justice Sandra O'Connor found herself celebrating her appointment at a luncheon—not with twenty-four senators, but with twenty-four senators' wives.

And in the White House's West Wing, the business side, gym privileges are, practically speaking, denied women. Elizabeth Hanford Dole, complaining that she no longer had time to stay in shape or to groom herself the way she wished, was offered a solution by Arlene Dahl at lunch one day: "Lie upside down on a slant board, darling. And turn off the ceiling lights in your office. They just show circles under your eyes. Substitute *lamps,* darling, which *don't.*"

"Does Ed Meese lie upside down on a slant board? Does he, in fact, worry about his circles?" asked one of Dole's staff.

Even Gloria Steinem has been reminded of her femininity in Washington. Startled patrons of Maxine's restaurant listened to her beau, Stan Pottinger, ordering her dinner ("I know what she likes!").

"What am I to believe in?" enquired an electrified feminist at a nearby table.

"Anatomy is destiny" cackled her date.

Is it? In an effort to give everyone an equal start, Georgetown University Hospital boldly abolished its pink-blanket-for-girl-babies, blue-blanket-for-boy-babies ethic in the nursery. White blankets were ordered for all. During the transitional period, before the white blankets arrived, strict orders were given that newborn girls must be shown to their papas for the first time in blue blankets, and newborn boys in pink. Of course all the new fathers thought they were being shown the wrong baby.

The Battle of the Sexes rages on. There are frequent outbreaks of guerrilla fire. Some of these are aimed at the name issue.

Washington women who have made careers in their maiden names are reluctant to give them up when they are gripped by the life force and marry. They lose if they do, they lose if they don't.

Embattled in-laws fear that their friends will think them illegitimate grandmothers. Husbands fear remarks from their piggish friends. Everybody dreads the boredom of introductions and explanations.

A charming solution was found by Philip Johnson, the chairman of the Commodity Futures Trading Commission. He wed a law grad named Laurie McBride. The pair juggled their names so that he became Philip McBride Johnson, and she Laurie Johnson McBride. This may catch on.

More typically, a local lobbyist sent out an announcement saying simply that he'd married "a Big Apple actress after a chance meeting at the Tavern on the Green." Invitations to a celebration were mailed; *nowhere* on announcement or invitation was the bride's name mentioned.

"Good practice for being a Washington wife," grunted a woman who had just quit that job.

The same week, the egalitarian Women and Health Round Table group auctioned off a vasectomy at its fundraiser. It was bought by a single lady in the catering business.

And so a new minefield is entered in the ancient war.

We must all tread warily.

# ON PARADE

# The Finer Feedbag:
# How They Tie It on
# in the Capital

EARLY-MORNING commuters surveying the scene from their cars spotted the corpse of an unlucky deer. It had been hit by a car during the night. It lay near the house of Jimmy Carter's National Security adviser, Zbigniew Brzezinski, on Old Dominion Drive in McLean, Virginia.

By the time the commuters drove home, the body had vanished. In its place lay a small heap of guts and other unattractive parts.

Between rush hours, Muska, Zbigniew's charming and artistic wife, had raced from the house, tools in hand, and efficiently butchered the beast. The Brzezinski freezer was then firmly packed with venison for the dinner-party season.

*Bon appetit!* Man must eat.

Particularly in Washington, life revolves around food.

Loving descriptions of every morsel served at a White House dinner are read almost as hungrily as the guest list. Newspaper food pages are written with seething sensuality. Food, in fact, is Washington's answer to sex.

*"Instead of sandwiches at tomorrow's press conference, salmon and crab legs will be served. Senator Stevens will*

*discuss national issues and answer questions on Alaska.*"
—ANNOUNCEMENT THAT LURED RELUCTANT
REPORTERS TO A SENATOR'S LAIR

As free-cheese lines straggled along unfashionable streets in early 1982, a distorted mirror-image reflected the scene in the smarter parts of town. On Embassy Row, in official residences, Georgetown lobbyists' mansions, Senate Office Building reception rooms and art galleries and museums in the throes of fundraising, smooth-faced, scented figures, also in line, patiently awaited their stab at tables groaning under *pâté de foie gras,* filet of beef, butter-drenched lobster claws, crabmeat quiches, creamy Brie, poached salmon, caviar, and so on.

Perhaps because of the richness of the on-the-circuit Washington diet, longtime residents develop uncontrollable hankerings for simple foods.

This is called Washington Pica. It is a local version of the malaise that gives people in other cities an urge to eat clay or suck stones.

Jerry Ford, for example, favored two gigantic slices of Bermuda onion with horseradish slathered in the middle after church each Sunday. Soviet Ambassador Dobrynin and Madame have been sighted at a suburban shopping center, gorging shamelessly on kosher hot dogs. Elizabeth Taylor nursed a passion for fried chicken wings, and arranged frequent home delivery from the local Hamburger Hamlet. Charlton Heston, who spends a lot of time in Washington, is mad for peanut butter.

Nancy Kissinger fights a constant private war against a yearning for potato chips. King Hussein, when he comes to town, sends the Blair House limo bowling down to McDonald's to retrieve burgers, fries and a shake. The list goes on.

En route to this condition, the Washington stomach has become an exquisitely tuned instrument.

Is a first-rate *pâté de foie gras* reposing in the middle of a lobbyist's buffet at the Rayburn House Office Building? Its scent twangs a siren chord to the growling cavern within the hungry congressman. He will hunt it down ere dusk.

Is there a plate of caviar within a two-block radius? A delicate sensor inside the Washington tripe quivers toward it like a compass needle to north.

Caviar has mystical overtones here. It is the greatest compliment any Washingtonian can think of. It is served at parties greeting very, very important people.

So tenderly is it cherished by Washingtonians that, although strictly non-kosher, it was once the major attraction at a reception thrown for Israel's Knesset by the Senate. It's the thought that counts.

*"Hey, where's all this caviar I keep reading about?"*
*"Don't be silly. This isn't a hello party. It's a goodbye party."*
        —OVERHEARD AT A PARTY FOR A DEPARTING
        AMBASSADOR

Caviar is never wasted on farewell parties. Who cares what flavor lingers in the mouth of the dear departing? It is reserved for the arriving, for the profitably impressionable, for the influential, the worshipful, the right honorable, the receptive.

The only exception: after the shah of Iran was deposed from the Peacock Throne, journalists visiting the about-to-depart Iranian Ambassador Ardeshir Zahedi were sent out from the embassy heavily laden with splendid beluga caviar and champagne. It then appeared everywhere; it was traded on the circuit like gold dust in a mining rush.

Later, there was to be the great ceremonial Moslem dumping of all the embassy's Dom Perignon down the drains. (The first act of disciples of Ayatollah Khomeini was to obey the priggish prophet on the alcohol question.)

Washington's partygoers almost fainted. Would the fanatics flush the *caviar* down the toilets, too?

Luckily, the prophet didn't give a damn about caviar. After the revolution, regular A-list freeloaders had that familiar *frisson* of delight. Something dark, glossy, grainy and saltily familiar began to appear on the party scene all over again. The Iranian Embassy's unmistakable pearls of the Caspian had been peddled around town at bargain prices by thoughtful Persians, either incoming or outgoing. You could eat the precious little fish eggs well into the Iranian hostage crisis, flavored with a patriotic pinch of guilt.

*"Dear Ted: Did you ever think of eating an apple at noontime? I used to send apples to the boys at school. They are very good in New England at this time of year and much more thinning than other types of desserts."*
—ROSE KENNEDY, IN A LETTER TO SEN. EDWARD KENNEDY

The four-year grits hiatus fell over official Washington's gustatory life like a pall of chitterlings.

The Carters' first dinner in the White House was fried chicken and corn soufflé. (The couple was joined, history might like to know, by son Chip and his then-wife Caron; singer Cher and her then-husband Gregg Allman; and the president's mother, Miss Lillian, escorted by a man who ran a night spot called "Pips" in Los Angeles.)

Washington was enthralled. It leaped to learn the joys of grits soufflé, peanut pâté, catfish fritters, spoonbread and a homespun concoction called the Plains Cheese Ring, apparently containing several pounds of cream cheese and a lot of Jello.

Washington restaurants did their best to salute the New Simplicity. The old Sans Souci, in its time the most fashionable luncheon spot in town and very close to the White House, introduced *amusant* dishes made with peanut butter. (*"A la Française* means with parsley," it kindly explained for the benefit of incoming Georgians. They didn't come in, anyway.)

The Press Club served stuffed tomatoes with black-eyed peas cooked in fatback, with McIlhenny's Tabasco sauce. Chinese restaurants eliminated "Peking Duck Henry Kissinger" in favor of "Carter Chinese Chicken with Georgia Peanuts."

Pisces, the Georgetown club, offered its members Carter Coffee, made by whirling hot coffee in a blender with sugar and peanut butter. Local greasy spoons introduced a "Jimmy and Billy Special: Pabst Blue Ribbon beer and peanut butter sandwich, $1.25."

Washington newspaper food pages rhapsodized over Rooster Pepper Sausage, a favorite delicacy of Carter's Attorney General Griffin Bell.

Mr. Democrat, Bob Strauss, during that peanut-and-pork-chop era, would haunt the best restaurants as usual. He would also defiantly mount the shuttle back from New York, toting large shopping bags laden with the best pastrami, Jewish rye bread, bagels and kosher dill pickles. He even took Rosalynn Carter to the now-defunct Duke Ziebert's to try his beloved matzoh-ball soup one lunchtime, in an effort to broaden her gustatory horizons. The effort was wasted.

The nation's governors, piling into the White House for a luncheon in July 1977, joked about the comical possibility of fried chicken and beer on the way in.

They were confronted instead with Italian hero sandwiches and chocolate chip cookies, washed down with Coca-Cola.

*"Something low on the food chain, please. The governor's concerned about energy."*
—JERRY BROWN'S AIDE ORDERING HIS
SALAD-AND-SANDWICH AT THE MAN IN THE
GREEN HAT RESTAURANT

*"Oh, the president never eats tomatoes."*
—NANCY REAGAN

Traditional Washington on-the-circuit food is the costliest the purse can buy. But the juiciest major item on the menu at chic restaurants is Who Else Is Here.

Corner tables for two are the most deeply desired in all top Washington restaurants, so that you can see the major item. Local maîtres d', responsive to the habits of expense-account lunchers, have refined seating as well as eating.

French restaurants have mastered the subtleties best. Lion d'Or, the most expensive, changes reference numbers on its tables frequently, so customers cannot craftily reserve by number the four coveted corner tables for two.

Le Bagatelle, another swarming spot for the mighty, deliberately created nineteen corner tables in its design, to make everyone a star.

Dominique's—notorious among tourists for rattlesnake steaks—is a splendid French restaurant with many corners, yet the only one of its ilk where table does not matter. Locals go there go for a good time. (It was Liz Taylor and John Warner's favorite anniversary celebration spot.) The highest spirits the city shows in public is at Dominique's annual Bastille Day Luncheon and Waiter's Race. This includes a revolting escargot-eating contest. It was once won by a man named Muskrat, holder of the Guinness world record for oyster-eating.

A point, now: *every* Washingtonian is a Muskrat to the now-resident Californians. The Westerners are sickened by the sheer quantities of food Washingtonians ingest. Successful lobbyist-lawyer-media Washington-macho eateries—like the Palm and Mel Krupin's—serve vegetable side-dishes big enough to sustain an active samurai for several weeks of combat.

Because of this, Washington diet plans spring eternal. Some have elaborate names and systems. The Reagan White House's 1982 Easter Renewal Project, in which sixteen staffers dropped more than 230 pounds among them in five weeks, was called by Ed Meese more complicated than most government budgets.

In the 1970s, Liz Carpenter (formerly Lady Bird Johnson's press secretary) formally founded the House and Senate Committees on Corpulent Responsibility. Liz, Tip O'Neill and twenty others weighed in every Monday morning in the Senate Appropriations hearing room.

Naturally, the news from the scale was always bad.

Washingtonians *need* solid fuel for their arduous daily climb. They are not pleased with *nouvelle cuisine*. To Frenchmen, *nouvelle* might accentuate presentation at table and presentation of food. To Washingtonians, it accentuates presentation of bill. *They want their money's worth.* First-time Washington lunchers at Le Pavillon, an exceeding chic *nouvelle* restaurant for the thin and rich, were often seen slinking across the street to McDonald's for a bag of fries afterward. It was sold and transformed into a Chinese Restaurant.

The elegant 209½, *nouvelle* but generous and close to the Capitol, is most popular with lobbyists wooing palate-smart senators. Its tables are close together. Many of the Hill's finest rumors are spread there accidentally. Nearby lunchers have eavesdropped on classic quartets (conservative columnist George Will, Gov. Jerry Brown, Washington *Post* publisher Donnie Graham and political consultant Mark Shields jump to mind) and fine scenes, like the congressman's wife slurping from the creamer before locking herself in the unisex toilet.

Perhaps because of the eavesdropping factor, some restaurants develop Republican and Democratic seating wings. A fixture in the Ponte Vecchio's Republican wing, for example, is John Mitchell, Mr. Nixon's former attorney general; Walter Mondale, Mr. Carter's vice-president, heads the Democratic wing. Trader Vic's used to subscribe to similar discreet segregation. Diners in the middle have witnessed, in one corner, Julie Eisenhower breast-feeding her infant Jennie at table and sipping a Mai Tai; in the other, a group of Zombie-guzzling Democratic mayors debated marijuana laws.

On the whole, Washingtonians flock with their own kind at feeding time.

Hotshot media, for example, will swarm to places like Germaine's, which serves elegant Franco-Oriental food and is famed for its exquisite flowers. (Queen Noor of Jordan, on a visit, sighed happily over the shrimp and lobster in rice paper and, democratically, fed her bodyguards the same.) Mo and Joe's, downtown, is heavy on media

and lawyers, and its food is therefore substantial Washington macho.
The dining room at the Jefferson Hotel, vaguely *nouvelle,* is popular
with media executives. The hard-working daily press masses at the
Class Reunion, a pub with plushy red walls and middling food; the
company is what's important. Hill lobbyists take senators weary of
the Senate dining room to the 209½, the very pricey Hugo's at the
Hyatt or Basil's, an uncomplicated but elegant spot.

Workaday Capitol Hillites and younger congressmen congregate
at pubby places like Jenkins Hill, Pendleton's, Bullfeathers, or The
Man in the Green Hat. (The last is named after a bootlegger who
hung out around there during Prohibition, providing alcoholic suste-
nance for the Senate.)

Good old Irish heritage boys on the Hill go to the Dubliner and
the Irish Times. The latter was once Hawaiian and still bears traces
of its heritage, so oldtimers grinningly call it the Toora Loora Luau.

(It's worth noting, by the way, that the entire city rises gallantly
to St. Patrick's Day. Green bagels are passed around Capitol Hill by
the Irish caucus, which is headed by an Italian. Italian restaurants
serve green noodles; Hawaiian, green Mai Tais; French, green onion
soup and green whipped cream; Chinese, green eggrolls; German,
green dumplings; McDonald's, Shamrock Shakes, and Thai, green
shrimp crisps.)

Back to the round: downtown lawyers and power brokers pack
Mel Krupin's, which is also where the Reagan White House (and
other people who wish to give the impression that they are so vital
to the nation that they must work on Saturday) goes for Saturday lunch. This is deeply Washington macho, with the best kosher
pickles in town and, as well as mammoth steaks and just-like-
momma-made chicken-and-matzoh-balls-in-a-pot. The Palm—
where the waiters sing happy birthday to you, if you're someone like
Bob Strauss—has even huger servings of everything. The Prime
Rib, Dominique's, Tiberio and Il Giardino are other choices of the
movers-and-shakers.

Sophisticated lovers slink off to Vincenzo's—on the lower level of
an old brownstone near Dupont Circle. (Its best dish: *pasta put-
tanesca.* This is a favorite of ladies of the night in Rome, because,

depending upon business, it can be served hot or cold. The maitre d'hotel, Piero, is from Florence. He likes to serve a light red wine, slightly cooled, with seafood.) Csikos is another lovers' lair. It is a Hungarian restaurant below an apartment building where the cimbalom, a dulcimerlike Hungarian instrument, is played to great romantic effect. Here, passion swells with thick bull's-blood Hungarian wines and substantial protein-packed meat dishes. Practical lovers tiptoe off to the Tabard Inn, a small, old-fashioned hotel in the middle of genteel Old Washington, with a very hip restaurant menu. Extraordinary romantic liaisons bloom there, particularly among journalists. (David Stockman, Reagan's budget architect, likes the bill of fare, although his more frequent haunt is a pubby Northwest spot called Quigley's.)

Upper-income city singles on the prowl—and a few people like Don Nixon, Richard Nixon's brother—go to a place called the Sign of the Whale in search of amusement.

Young Georgetown movers-and-shakers go to Clyde's for brunch. At night, they pack its very long bar, or go to F. Scott's, an art-deco spot with dancing. Rich Old Georgetown haunts the Rive Gauche, a pricey old Washington restaurant which suddenly moved everything but its toilets up the street into a hotel; or to the 1789, a charming and rickety place done up in the Revolutionary manner, with substantial Anglo-French-Colonial food.

Everybody rich goes to Le Lion d'Or for classical and very expensive French food with a few surprises, and to see and be seen. Their fresh fruit soufflés are superb. *Time* columnist Hugh Sidey eats lunch there almost every day.

People like Teddy Kennedy's daughter Kara slip into Annie Oakley's, a sort of Western rock bar.

Casual publishing moguls fancy Chez Camille (which they spell Shake-a-Meal, just for fun.) Administration big-timers favor the close-by-the-White House Maison Blanche during the day, or Jean-Louis at the Watergate in the evening. (The Reagans' fresh fruit sherbets come from Jean-Louis' kitchens, where their manufacture is carefully overseen by security-cleared White House stewards.) They also like La Marée, a small but swank seafood restaurant.

Out-of-power presidents are drawn magnetically to the Hay-Adams dining room, the Madison's Montpelier Room, and Trader Vic's. Ask not why, there they are.

The CIA boys kick up their heels at at an unmarked eatery known informally as Chez O'Toole in McLean. Whenever the owner plans a trip to Ireland, he ups the price of beer by a dime. Loyal spooks wouldn't dream of going anywhere else.

*"White House Leeks; Panama Quenelles; Human Rice with Peas in our Thyme; Lustful Hearts of Palm Salad; Juanita Crepes; Sheik 'n' Begin Chicken . . ."*
—PART OF A CARTER ERA MENU AT THE FARM PICNIC OF HAROLD FLEMING, PRESIDENT OF THE POTOMAC INSTITUTE

Like everything else in Washington, food is profoundly symbolic. Ethnic mixes delight the town.

California's Sen. Sam Hayakawa, for example, invented a dish called Sukiyaki Cacciatore the very week that Supreme Court Justice Lewis Powell ate his first bagel. The media took note of both events.

Political sundaes are another symbol-fraught Washington food form. Jellybeans turn up in a dozen Reagan sundaes around the city. Earlier, Carter-Mondale sundaes were made from peanut butter-and-peach ice cream with jimmies. The campaign before, the Ford-Dole sundae was vanilla ice cream, pineapple syrup, "and a banana peel served in your lap."

The Janet Cooke affair, in which the young reporter returned a Pulitzer Prize after revealing that her famous Jimmy, a nine-year-old heroin addict, was not completely extant—led to a rash of edibles around town named for her. In hard-hearted Georgetown, Bob's Famous Ice-Cream Shoppe advertised its jimmie-sprinkled Janet Cooke Sundae: "You Trust Us Completely and We Make the Whole Thing Up."

Status can be measured not just by what foods are named after one, but by what one is fed. A well-tuned, fighting-fit Washington guest can case a buffet with a single flicker of the eye, register meatball-and-fish-puff or caviar-and-crab-claw, and instantly gauge his perch in the social pecking order, as an invitee.

There was the case of the Democratic National Committee's grand executive dinner. It was held at an old status-conscious U-shaped table in 1977. Those at the head of the U got steak; those sitting along the legs got broiled chicken. Several legmen left the DNC shortly thereafter.

Fresh, uncategorized foods are best for confusing this unpleasant issue. The quest is constant and the competition fierce among caterers to find something original enough to disguise its cost to spring on the buffet circuit. Meats glazed in killer bee honey or etiolated cave-lettuce salads tossed with fresh violet blossoms can and sometimes do make a single-shot sensation. Caterers know that the grazers are constantly combatting finger-food fatigue and need waking up.

On the consuming end, politicans usually take care not to be photographed around lavish buffets. Some photographers are restrained by their employers from snapping candid shots of dignitaries at the trough.

"It looks bad, bad, *bad* to see a senator shoveling food in his mouth," a political aide once told me. He added that the taboo is lifted only at barbecues.

"Voters like to see their man gnawing bones," he explained. He hinted that voters might feel a wave of counterproductive envy at the sight of a man ladling rare Beef Wellington down his golden gullet.

The most consistent and photogenic food symbol in Washington is the Official Cake. Every occasion has one.

For Teddy Kennedy's forty-ninth birthday, his staffers caused to be created (and served at Pendleton's, mentioned above) a cake shaped like Massachusetts. For his fiftieth, there appeared a structure somewhat like the Jefferson Memorial, cunningly illuminated from within.

The city's finest cake ever blushed almost unseen. It was the one created for a Reagan inaugural ball. It was seven feet high, boasted five tiers, and measured twenty-four feet around its base.

Its bakers, all from Massachusetts, trucked in its parts to the Army-Navy Club in Washington for assembly, proudly lists its contents: 500 pounds of buttercream frosting, 720 pounds of flour; 480 pounds of eggwhite; 880 pounds of sugar; 480 pounds of shortening and butter; and 85 gallons of milk; and, of course, cream of tartar, baking powder, and a pinch of salt. The bakers assembled it in the club, then applied the trimmings. There were golden eagles soaring up around one tier, icing flags flying bravely around another. Profiles of Ronald Reagan and George Bush and seals of state added a sense of occasion. The whole was crowned by a scale model of the Capitol Dome. Red sugar roses were stuck on the corners.

Beaming Republicans from Massachusetts gathered to bid adieu to the great *gâteau* before its odyssey to the Kennedy Center for the ball.

Alas. It now weighed 3,742 pounds. It could not be budged.

The day after the ball, more than a hundred cooks, cleaners and waiters at the Army-Navy Club crept out under cover of darkness, carrying large and authorized plastic bags stuffed with huge slabs of cake. More cubic footage was stuffed into the club's freezer, to emerge later as part of various desserts.

For months, all over the city, locals of every creed, color, class, and national origin discovered icing stars and pieces of George Bush's edible nose floating in their flans, sundaes, charlottes, cobblers, pandowdies and trifles.

Honestly, now. Would that happen anywhere else?

# The Image Game:
# How They Play It
# in the Capital

*"I was too tall, too beautiful, too rich."*
    —BESS MYERSON, ON WHY SHE DIDN'T WIN THE
    DEMOCRATIC NOMINATION FOR SENATOR FROM
    NEW YORK

IN WASHINGTON, your most important possession is not your Mercedes. Toss away your diamonds; abandon hope of love. Here, you cultivate your image.

Everything, you see, is not exactly what it seems.

Take the handsomely bound editions of the Harvard Classics, neatly arranged behind the glass doors of a fine mahogany secretary in the White House's Red Room. Does anyone pluck down and peruse Adam Smith's *Inquiry Into the Nature and Causes of Wealth of Nations?* Who sings along with Bobbie Burns's *Poems and Songs?* Nobody. They are not books. They are gilded leather spines, glued onto plywood.

A poem of praise for Rep. Claude Pepper is printed in the daily *Congressional Record.* ("Men improve with age . . . / No one person has done more./ The State of Florida is lucky!")

Does it matter that it was inserted in the official publication by the congressman himself?

Not a bit! Why be modest? There are plenty of people delighted to be modest on your behalf. Self-promotion that would make a rock star blush is the norm, not the exception, on Capitol Hill.

"People aren't looking for truth in Washington," points out Barry Jagoda, who was Jimmy Carter's image man in Washington until the Georgia Mafia elbowed him aside for the Atlantan, Jerry Rafshoon. "They're drawn to success."

There's a sunny side to this. Struggling to catch up with one's own successful image probably pushes more Washingtonians toward success than anything else.

Are you director of the Mint? Washington will be astonished and, frankly, disappointed, if you don't have a medal struck of yourself. Besides, it gives you something to aspire to. Stella Hackel, as director, had a bronze coin struck showing her face in serene profile; the very next year, an excellent plastic surgeon tackled a few minor imperfections on the real thing. The happy result: nature imitates art; friends are satisfied; foes are deceived; everybody wins.

Are you chairman of the Republican Congressional Committee? By all means put your picture on the cover of your magazine, *Congress Today,* with as much purple praise as possible and some very flattering pictures. Rep. Guy Vander Jagt, who made the keynote speech at the Republican convention, did. The congratulations poured in.


*"Oh, no. I don't like the Musk. I'll take the
Sandalwood. [Senator] John Stennis will love that."*
    —SENATOR JOHN WARNER, SNIFFING COLOGNE IN
    A WASHINGTON SHOP, BEFORE HIS SEPARATION
    FROM LIZ TAYLOR


To Ronald Reagan, image comes as naturally as breath.

As Baltimore's Democratic Rep. Barbara Mikulski said, "Any time you've got a President—after they've tried to knock him off—who walks in like John Wayne, sounds like Bob Hope, and got his program out of the *Wall Street Journal*—of course they're gonna love him."

Democrats despair at his easy manner. They threw up their hands when, in his very first televised budget speech, Reagan demonstrated the current worth of the dollar with a little small change.

"That took an actor," grumbled one Democrat. "Carter would have emphasized all the wrong words. Ford would have fumbled and dropped the cash. Nixon would have pocketed it."

Reagan's own idea for his inaugural parade from the Capitol to the White House was a masterpiece of image-awareness. He wanted to lead the parade astride El-Alamein, the superb snow-white horse that had been given him by Mexican President Lopez Portillo just after his election. What a show! The Secret Service blanched. There was frantic talk of bulletproof union suits, armored hats, a steel-lined wig. A quick-change stop was planned in Sen. Mark Hatfield's Appropriations Committee gents' room.

Finally, the President's physician, Daniel Ruge, talked him out of the notion. He has the white-horse image anyway.

Nobody was particularly surprised at Reagan's response to the rumored death threats from Libyan leader Qaddafi, when it was carefully leaked from a meeting with George Bush. It was: "Hey, by the way, George! I don't know how you feel about it. But I'm ready to call Qaddafi and tell him I'll meet him over on the Mall and we'll settle this thing." It didn't hurt a bit.

Nancy Reagan, on the other hand, has had image trouble. (See chapter, "Nancy Through the Looking Glass.") She wears borrowed clothes to balls, and borrowed jewels to a royal wedding. She is trying to project the image of a rich world leader's wife. She succeeds. Ergo, she is perceived as absurdly extravagant. Conforming to image creates image. Her image created, the press gathers, ululating like Zulus, and begins to lob its spears.

She withdraws. The solution: hire the right mercenary for this war. Image man Landon Parvin was brought in to write wisecracks for her to fling among the enemy and plot strategies. Criticism for the White House china gift? Let her refer to "The Nancy Reagan Home for Wayward China." The press, distracted by the bauble called "good copy," lays aside its spears and bustles back to the kraal. All is calm until news of the latest image atrocity filters back, and it's time for the tribe to hoist its weapons again.

Even the perception that you have an image at all becomes part of your Washington image. The late Hubert Humphrey noted that "people just flocked in droves to follow me" when he had a cameraman dogging his steps. Strolling the streets of Washington alone, he was ignored. You want to be noticed? Hire a man with a camera. You want to be noticed favorably? Toil on your image first.

*"If the Soviet Union invades Poland . . . President Reagan is going to come down on them with all four feet."*
—JOHN R. BLOCK, THE SECRETARY OF AGRICULTURE

But be warned. Fashions in image change in Washington. At this writing, a hard-line, grit-stiffened image beats a soft-line, wishy-washy image hands down. (*Esquire* defined Sen. Ed Muskie as soft-line after he cried in New Hampshire; Eldridge Cleaver, the former Black Panther, after he came back from Algiers to design trousers with tubular satin codpieces.) Hard-line convicted Watergate burglar G. Gordon Liddy now makes a very comfortable living speaking around the country on virtues like loyalty and grit and guts. Hard-line fiery-faced Alex Haig triumphed over pale soft-liner Richard Allen in a war of will and image at the White House.

Quite a few old-time hard-liners had suspected that National Security Adviser Allen's stint was to be short-lived early in the game. The clue was his performance for the White House Press Corps one day —an excellent imitation of Richard Nixon's double-V salute, with jowl a-flutter.

Not a good image. Soft-line humor against one's own party member makes Washington clutch up with fear. The murmur goes around: who's the next target?

All National Security advisers after Kissinger are bound to have image trouble. Zbigniew Brzezinski, his immediate successor, had to fight the war on three fronts. As a hard-liner in a soft-line administration; as a Kissinger epigone; and as a man of fairly refined tastes who aimed to please white-sock Georgians. He trod the tightrope delicately. His small—very small—luncheons catered in his office, with damask, flowers and candles, were screened from tightwad Georgian eyes; though often photographed with beautiful young women, he pointedly told *W* that he wished only to be photographed with elderly matrons. (Of course, he was never seen with one.) He never achieved the image he wanted. The point was made when he played host to Andy Warhol in the presidential box at the Kennedy Center for a Liza Minnelli show. Later, Andy took him backstage.

"Liza, darling, come and meet Mr. Brezhnev."

"Oh, the Russian? What's he doing here?"

"No, no, no. This is the president's security man."

Liza chatted benignly for some time, under the impression that Zbig was Carter's bodyguard.

Henry's own image had begun at an advantage. Few remembered his predecessor with any affection. Henry is memorable. He has the greatest image tool of all: quotability.

He plays on his image like a harp. After he had given a five-page eulogy at Nelson Rockefeller's funeral, he sent out copies to the entire Congress, his business card coyly stapled to one corner. He is master of the press. Right after the Reagan election, but before the inauguration, Henry took off on an international swing in an private jet. The media watched in awe. Every stop-off was noted, every meeting quoted around the world. Columns appeared in influential papers heralding his "growing clout—he's quietly building a position of power and influence as advisor to the Reagan Administration."

As it turned out, he was not. The trip was in CBS chairman Bill Paley's corporate jet. Paley had taken along socialite Brooke Astor and Henry for fun.

Yet who could blame Henry for giving his image an airing at that crucial time? The Reagan Administration did not nibble and hire him. (Even worse, he was rudely not elected by his peers to the

Council on Foreign Relations, one of whose members jokes that
Henry signs his mail, "My Excellency, Henry Kissinger.")

But, as Truman Capote once remarked, a boy must sell his book.
Henry's image still glows enough to net him more than ten thousand
dollars a pop for speeches, which he makes before groups like the
Potato Chip/Snack Food Association and the National Tire Dealers
and Retreaders Association.

*"Before I met Ella, I thought she'd be a great big fat
woman, kind of a sweaty thing, you know. But she's just
the opposite! Charming! Not fat! Not sweaty!"*
—MISS LILLIAN, PRESIDENT CARTER'S MOTHER,
CAMPAIGNING FOR THE LATE ELLA GRASSO IN
CONNECTICUT

Fat is always out of fashion; wit always in. In age, on the other
hand, there are fluctuations in chic.

It was considered extremely poor taste to be old in Washington
during the Carter Administration. Rosalynn Carter denies it, but
before going into the White House, she had a ten-day face wrap and
chemical peel at the International Skin Clinic in Miami Beach, according to the owner of that spa. (She is Sylvester Stallone's mother,
Jacqueline Stallone. Jacqueline re-married since having Sly, but understands the image value of her son's name.)

Jimmy Carter looked quite youthful before his election. Shirley
MacLaine even called him "Howdy Doody."

Getting the candidate to look "presidential" was his image man's
first chore. Later, the challenge was to give him a vigorous young
man's image, presumably in striking contrast to Ronald Reagan.
This notion, projected via Carter's inexplicable running sprees, led
to a two-fold image disaster: his much-photographed near-collapse
in a race—who can forget the picture of the exhausted president
half-fainting in his sweatband?—and the loss of so much weight that,
by the summer of 1980, his image man begged him to pile on ten

pounds so he wouldn't look so old and drawn on television.

Even sensible Clare Boothe Luce turned down dozens of chances to be a panelist on the National Town Meeting during the Carter Era; she did not care to sit on a platform among the young, looking old. Finally, when she consented to appear, she looked positively girlish. Her co-guest was the delightfully elderly historian Henry Steele Commager, who also neglects to mention his date of birth in *Who's Who*.

Clare discovered the most important image tool of all: the Relativity Gambit. After the dawn of the Reagan Era, she began happily pulling in six thousand dollars or so on the speaking circuit, the ultimate arbiter of image.

Now, self-consciousness on the score of age is very unfashionable indeed. There are no Hams and Jodys; men well past middle age locked in power struggles at the White House seem in the very flower of their strength. The President's nickname among his staff, "O 'n' W," ("Oldest and Wisest"), sets the tone. Under-thirties suddenly seem out-of-place in Washington, or they must be somebody's children.

The Reagans' elderly-vigor image is a masterpiece.

And no wonder. In one of Amy Carter's old rooms, a temple of exercise equipment awaits its daily worshippers. The First Bodies stay trim with brisk strolls to nowhere aboard a treadmill, and long rides astride an exercycle; they pump iron on a pressing bench and wield dumbbells; they jump into a machine that pulls them in several different directions at once; they bounce on a trampoline.

The finished product is then groomed to the teeth. Immediately after the election, Nancy's California manicurist flew to town to teach the staff at Lord and Taylor how to do the First Nails. Battles between Monsieur Marc and the divine Julius for the privilege of crimping and coloring Nancy's hair make headlines. Reagan himself avers that "All I do for my hair is bake it in the sun, boil it under the shower, comb with water and use a little dab of Brylcreem to hold it down." (And a reporter who stole a sample of his hair from a barbershop and had it analyzed during the campaign was disappointed to discover that there was, in fact, no trace of dye.)

Regardless of what it takes to make it so, the shady side of sixty is now a chic age-range.

Height is not so fickle an image gauge. The wise newcomer to Washington is tall. Even West German leader Helmut Schmidt, having noticed that he was two inches shorter than Jimmy Carter when the leaders met in London, arrived in town a perfect twin in height. His use of the Relativity Gambit gave him the odd gait of one not accustomed to lifts in his shoes, but the meeting was eyeball-to-eyeball. His image was safe.

A rule of thumb, here: try to be the same height as your peers; remember that it always is tactless to tower over your leader.

One whispered reason that Ed Muskie was dismissed as an unsuitable vice-presidential choice for candidate Jimmy Carter was that he loomed above the Georgian; all photographs of the two together, stoop as Muskie might, had a comical Mutt-and-Jeff air; what president wants to be visually sawn down to peanut proportions?

A man can afford to be short in Washington only if he is a very active millionaire—like the late Joe Hirschorn, who created the art museum of the same name, or Joe Allbritton, the tiny Texan who owns WJLA-TV and much of Washington's Riggs Bank, and heaven knows what else by now.

Joe Canzeri, the last powerful short person, was perhaps the best gofer the Reagan White House had.

Canzeri had done wondrous things for Nelson Rockefeller: he had acquired a Water Pik from a closed drug store for the boss's dental work; he had found a home in Georgia to offer the shah of Iran when it counted. When he came to Reagan, he made himself so useful that nobody thought he needed an image at all. But foes accused him of double-submitting his expenses, and he was out. A tall man like Reagan's communications chief, David Gergen, definitely makes fewer foes.

Fat is the image foe of the Washington wife. She must often stand next to a buffet table and ladle things into her mouth to keep the truth from popping out.

Ursula Meese, wife of top White House aide Ed Meese, and Marilyn Lewis, wife of the secretary of Transportation, both jump off their hors d'oeuvres on trampolines, the great distaff image aid of the Reagan Administration. (Introduced, I believe, by Nancy Reynolds, Mrs. Reagan's long-time best friend and a vice-president of Bendix.)

An acceptable accent for optimum image impact, of course, changes with the administration. A non-accent is popular at the moment. A gray veil slides over the eyes of Washington listeners at the first twang of a Georgia diphthong. Texan has regained respectability, after disenchantment brought on by Lyndon Johnson's mealy mouthings on the Vietnam war. Like height, accent is relative. Henry Kissinger always says that he likes to go to Texas because down there they think he has a Harvard accent.

But there are certain image muddles the newcomer must thread his way through that are non-relative, sui generis, and inextricably entwined with his role.

You cannot, for example, head a Committee on Environmental Quality and buy a house with an Astroturf lawn. A New Yorker tried it. The town twittered. Hastily, our hero pulled up the offending plastique and traded it for a Chippendale mirror and two Redskins tickets. Excellent choices. Both articles play leading roles on the stage of image here, yet do not reflect a priggishly environmentist outlook on their owner's part—like, say, a table hewn out of a large boulder.

A secretary of Education does not send his children to private schools; he lives where public schools are decent, probably in the suburbs. A secretary of Defense is not a practicing Quaker. Joe Califano, as secretary of Health, Education and Welfare went so far as to give up smoking. He even railed occasionally about the evils of alcohol, but did not go overboard and give it up.

*"We'll be able to get servants real cheap [in Haiti] . . . We pay them a buck twenty-five a day and they're raking in the money."*
—TEDDY MONDALE, SON OF THE DEMOCRAT (THEN VICE-PRESIDENT), IN INTERVIEW MAGAZINE

Luckily, image gaps in not-applicable-to-you categories do not count. For instance: it would not be seemly for James Watt, the embattled secretary of the Interior, to maintain large plastic blue spruce trees outside his department, lightly hung about with gilt signs saying "Made in Hong Kong." But it's perfectly okay for the Department of Transportation to do so. In fact, it does. One of the city's most charming sights each fall is the gardeners industriously mulching the roots of the *faux* trees in their concrete planters. What's Transportation to do with trees? Nothing. Likewise, nobody minds when Henry Kissinger lets Nancy take out the garbage. His image doesn't depend on his garbage skills.

The joy of all appointive office is that you only have to tend one image at a time. This is how your image problems vary from the man who was elected by a fickle public to his niche in history.

*"You know, Bob, Ah'm gonna walk off the Senate floor*
*for the last time, and Ah'll bump into one of mah*
*constituents. An' he's gonna run up an' say, 'Humman!*
*You know who Ah am?' An' Ah'm gonna say, 'No, Ah*
*don't. And Ah don't give a damn.'"*
—DEFEATED SEN. HERMAN TALMADGE, TO
DEFEATED SEN. BOB MORGAN, 1980

If you are a politician, you may find yourself in perpetual conflict with your own image. This could be because your image started out fitting you like a good suit, but parts of you have grown out of it. Or, it could be that it was never tailor-made, and didn't have a large enough seam allowance for alterations.

Teddy Kennedy is constantly on guard against his unwelcome image as a womanizer. (Around Capitol Hill, he is known as "Wynkin." Blynkin and Nod, the other stars of the nursery poem, are Sen. Jeremiah Denton—who as a prisoner of war blinked out the word "Torture" in Morse code to a television camera—and Sen. Sam Hayakawa, known for dozing fitfully on the Senate floor.)

At his forty-ninth birthday party at Kennedy's house, a very young woman from the Madeira School danced innocently with Teddy. She asked a friend to snap a photo of the memorable moment. As the flash popped, Kennedy's mind leaped ahead.

An image *crise* was brewing here.

"Get that film out of that camera!" he bawled to press aide Bob Shrum. Then, abandoning his partner, he raced over and ripped it out himself.

The picture could end up, somehow, he knew, on the cover of a tabloid on every grocery checkout counter in the country, under three-inch red type announcing "TED'S TEEN TRUE LOVE."

Yes, image is still made by the press. Its two branches, the sleazy and the respectable, are poised pincerlike to grip the elected official and pinch him until he squeaks.

Over the long haul, it is the respectable press that can do the most damage—the major Washington and New York papers and the news magazines. This is because the respectable press writes, mostly, for its own members. They speak the same language, a semi-insider's shorthand, predicated on similar prejudices. A sort of mythic truth is formed from a collection of facts, perceptions and rumors that never really surfaces in print. These become the self-perpetuating underlying wisdom of the big time. Pretty soon, they are the assumptions of most of the people who read, too.

This seems elementary. It is odd that most people who worry about image in Washington don't notice it until it's too late.

Jerry Rafshoon, sadder and wiser after his image blitz failed and Jimmy Carter lost the 1980 election, ruefully told a political newsletter what he would advise Ronald Reagan, were he working for him:

"Court the [columnist] Hugh Sideys of the world. Let them see the president at least every two weeks. It will buy you a good column, but you have to renew your good will constantly. Don't talk about what you're going to do. Do it. Then talk about what you've done. Over and over and over. Keep in mind that Washington is the kind of town where the leading citizens will line up and be character witnesses for a John Connally. That tells it all."

Not quite all. He did not touch upon the exquisite sensibilities of the Washington press, the Establishment and Capitol Hill. If insulted or downgraded, their vengeance is inevitable. When Jimmy Carter invited members of Congress to the White House for egg-and-bacon breakfasts and then billed them $4.75 apiece, they were outraged. Carefully, they kept track of his expenses. The first year, they noted, he spent only $1,372 of his $50,000 entertainment allowance, and was able to pocket the rest. The second year, he spent $13,000. By 1979, Congress quietly ruled that all unspent presidential entertainment monies were to be returned to the Treasury.

Small insults—not returning phone calls, ignoring courtesies—fill little backwaters of dislike and hurt in this vain town. You can detect the first thin trickles over the dam in a particularly Washingtonian form of *Schadenfreude*—a whooping delight in small errors made by the arrogant ones.

When Ham Jordan handed out White House report cards for staffers, with questions like "Rate this person's political skills," there were hoots of laughter all over town when the possible answers ran from "Naive" to "Savy" [sic]. And when Frank Moore, Jimmy Carter's congressional liaison man, sent out memos to members of Congress about the SALT treaties on White House letterhead, upside down, the entire Hill cackled and rubbed its hands over the "distress signal."

The ultimate revenge lies downriver, when the tide turns. Almost all high administration officials can expect high-paying job offers when they leave office. This did not happen at the close of the Carter White House.

*"Vulnerability attracts the sharks."*
　—JODY POWELL

You cannot, under any circumstances, come on swinging an ax and declare your own image to be leaning one way, if it is listing severely to the other side. Environmentalists, for example, say that to Interior Secretary James Watt a wilderness is a parking lot without any lines.

It did no good for Watt's well-intentioned friend in the Senate, Steve Syms, to pass out buttons saying "Another Friend of James Watt." Brave allies sported them to environmentalists' meetings and parties.

"Who's the first one?" the hosts sniggered. The buttons vanished.

Watt ended up in this predicament simply because he had neglected his image-tending from the start.

"Can you tell us how your p-r department is set up?" enquired a puzzled group of public-relations people he addressed in mid-1981.

"I doubt it," he said vaguely. They gazed at each other slackjawed with shock. Washington's first rule had been broken: no one was minding the image.

Within three weeks, the Reagan Administration had launched a massive image war. All major undertakings by each department were to be written up for the White House, along with summaries, press releases, and proposed editorials for newspaper use. All speeches, statements and news releases were to be filtered through the public-relations office of each agency; and, most crucial, all meetings with reporters by staffers were to be reported and fed into the White House computer. This way, when unfavorable leaks occurred, their sources could be pinpointed instantly. This, they hoped, would stop stories like the one concerning James Watt's legendary flow-chart: "God–Watt–Interior Department."

Image repair swung underway. For most Washington people and institutions, though, it is an intuitive art, like flattery. And, like good flattery, a single well-placed line can do the trick. One was used to meet the roars of outrage that greeted AFL-CIO leader Lane Kirkland's trip to the swank Homestead in Virginia.

"A non-union hotel in a right-to-work state," snarled his henchmen, as he left for a closed-door meeting with heads of Exxon, General Motors, et al.

"I hope to do a little missionary work," explained Kirkland modestly. His image leapt to par.

*"This shows what happens to a politician who tries to be a good sport with the press! From now on I'm going to be a stuffy S.O.B!"*
—TEXAN SEN. JOHN TOWER, A SHORT MAN, PHOTOGRAPHED AT A PARTY IN A SUPERMAN SUIT

Image aids that might be priceless in other cities are worthless in Washington. Want to flaunt your diamonds? Forget it. Most of the rich here have them stashed in vaults, and wear phonies. Proud of your education? Pipe down. Here, Georgetown bars advertise for busboys with two years of college, and Ph.Ds run liquor stores. Think you're tasteful with the engraved invites? When Cable Network News announced the opening of its Washington bureau, it did so with engraved cards, with little tissues inside the envelope; Washington would know that Ted Turner meant business. But so do all the lobbying firms and discos and bars that do the same thing.

Excesses of all sorts are warmly greeted in Washington, as long as they're not paid for with tax money. To put it baldly, everyone's dying for a bit of excitement.

Socks, for some reason, are highly cathected image objects. The Carter Georgian crowd was divided into two groups: the white-sock crowd—the Ham-and-Jody set—and the dark-sock, white-wine crowd, like Griffin Bell's aide Terry Adamson.

After the Reagan victory, the winds of change blew first over socks. Georgia Congressman Ed Jenkins gloomily bought one hundred pairs of calf-length black socks, and sent them to his colleagues in time for the inauguration.

"I certainly believe it is important that we get off to a good start with the new administration, and the country can ill afford a 'white socks' scandal at this time," he wrote. "Moreover, black socks don't really look as bad as you may first believe. Many people wear them regularly."

Many others had worn them irregularly.

Fellow travellers on a plane from New Orleans to Washington

have watched fascinated as Sen. Russell Long girds up his feet for their capital high-stepping with a ceremonial sock-change.

First, he carefully removes his shoes. Then he lovingly, and perhaps reluctantly, plucks off a pair of pale, baggy socks. Then, reaching into an important-looking briefcase, he produces with a flourish a dark, silky, longer pair—definitely Washington socks. After a brief wiggle of the senatorial toes in the aisle, these are carefully donned and smoothed. He is ready to take on the slickers on the Hill.

The truth is, Washington image doesn't travel well. You are bound to encounter people who do not understand it. Ignore them. Think of Barbara Thomas, a good-looking New Yorker who is the youngest Securities and Exchange commissioner ever appointed in Washington. Her own image, a smash on Wall Street and in her handsome office in Washington, leans toward immaculately tailored pin-striped suits and discreet diamonds. To most people, an impressive and distinguished combination. To Elizabeth Taylor, who happened to be aboard the same Eastern shuttle flight en route back to her then-beloved Sen. John Warner, the image was that of a stewardess. "Hey, hon. Would you get me a glass of water, please?" she asked. The commissioner thoughtfully went about her business.


*"IMPEACH LANGHORNE BOND"*
    —BUMPER STICKER ON THE CAR OF LANGHORNE
    BOND, WHEN HE WAS FEDERAL AVIATION
    ADMINISTRATOR


A soupçon of pretension is expected of anyone in the public eye. Over a certain level, you can forget it. Two who have crossed the line into the upper ether are Abby Rockefeller, daughter of David, and Robert Redford. Abby has made her life's mission the Clivus Multrum, a toilet that brews up garbage with human waste to manufacture compost—not a good image for a politician to carry around— and Redford has long been happy as a clam with his much-publicized appointment to the post of sewer commissioner of Provo, Utah.

But something happened to Redford. When he was in Washington this year laying the groundwork for a movie about the right wing, the plumbing went awry at the headquarters of Richard Viguerie, the conservative direct-mail king. Redford, perhaps unthinkingly, rolled up his sleeves and tried to fix it. A Viguerie vice-president strolling into the executive john mistook him for a plumber working on the toilet. Everybody had a good laugh. The minute the press got wind of it, his publicity people leaped on the horn to say it wasn't true. Naturally, everyone who heard the story immediately assumed that Redford was planning to run for the Senate.

That, you see, is when the image going really gets rough. If you run for elective office, quite apart from the ordinary insults and imputations you may expect from your opponent, you face degradations undreamed of by your happy brethren in the real world.

Your portrait and words may be emblazoned on toilet paper dubbed "The People's Primary." If you allow reporters into your house, they will sneer at your taste in sofas and grumble about the quality of your booze. If you're rich, they'll think you're on the take. If you are not on the take, they'll wonder why your house is so shabby. If you don't let them in, as the Phil Cranes wouldn't during the last Republican primary, they will suspect you're hiding something. Everything you do is read like a rooster's entrails by your audience.

Does Jimmy Carter move his hair part from right to left? Shouts of "Political metaphor!" fill the air. Does Teddy Kennedy plant geraniums around his house in McLean? The neighbors all nudge that he's getting ready to run for the presidency. (They were right, too, last time. But everybody knew he *really* meant it when he cut out cream, french fries and gravy, dropped twenty pounds and jogged a mile around the geraniums every day.) Nobody has seen a president with a fat image since William Howard Taft. Just before the Democratic primaries during the Carter Administration, in fact, the Waist Watcher suddenly appeared on the White House mess menu, too.

*I'm not running. I'm enraged, but not enough to*
*..... ,,r office."*
—CLIFF ROBERTSON, IN 1978


*"A campaign is a sensual community of the spirit. The*
*smell of it, the taste of it . . . the feel of it . . . it's just*
*like a good shot of cocaine right in the nose."*
—JACK VALENTI, IN 1976


So you win. You're in. But your image battle is not over.

Instead, you now have something to lose. Like Sen. John Melcher. He was accidentally described as a vegetarian instead of a veterinarian in a local social magazine named *Dossier.* Furious mail poured into his office from the home districts in cow country, Montana.

Emergency image-repair was launched immediately. Photographs were taken of the senator-vet engulfing large, bloody steaks. Eight-by-ten glossies were mailed by the score to papers and people back home, proving unquestionably his carnivorous integrity.

Even among the most sincere meateaters, small deceptions must be practiced, built around the basic image premise: a photographer may be watching. Picture the horror of brand-new Sen. Warren Rudman, fresh from Manchester, New Hampshire, at the Reagan inaugural ceremonies. He was perfectly content to sit between two Democrats until pious Sen. Mark Hatfield, who ran the show, boomed to the assemblage that all should join hands to sing "God Bless America." Flashbulbs popped and cameras rolled to capture the stirring scene.

Later, Rudman sidled up to Hatfield: "Why didn't you tell me we were going to hold hands? I would have sat next to Jesse Helms."

On Capitol Hill now, image has soared as a full-time concern since videotapes came to whir perpetually on the House side. There is no more droopy double-knit attire. Nobody has seen what is called a Full Cleveland for years. (White shoes, belt and tie.) Flattering dark suits and quiet figured ties are favored; hair is neatly combed at all times, and the House beauty shop is well stocked with Nice 'n' Easy hair dye.

On the Senate side, where the cameras have not yet arrived, the pressure is from peers. Occasionally, the urge to break away from the quietly distinguished pack image drives men wild. Senate Majority Leader Robert Byrd is a splendid fiddler and man-of-the-people. He worships daily at the altar of beauty in the Senate salon and sports a dramatic pompadour. He favors bright red vests. But he has curbed his inborn sartorial taste to the point where he sports simple figured blue-on-blue ties.

One day, his eyes fell on a loud, balloon-patterned piece of flash on the neck of a reporter; they misted with longing.

"Trade you even up," he said softly. The deed was done. Image forgotten, Byrd beamed and donned the scribe's dazzling jabot. Next day, the fever fled, he was back in dreary blue-on-blue silk.

Rebellion boils beneath the surface. A sincere push to break away from the upper-crust WASP-Brooks Brothers image was launched by former Rep. Ed Beard, the Rhode Island housepainter who came to the Hill and proudly founded the Blue Collar Caucus. Insted of the usual Wagner-on-the-hi-fi, Robert Motherwell-on-the-wall image so beloved by the hip congressmen of his generation, Beard merrily played Elvis on his eight-track stereo and glued up posters of Marilyn Monroe. He didn't last long. The Blue Collar Caucus is now dead.

Some people might jump to the conclusion that being elected to office means you must be pretentious.

Not at all. The proper place for pretension is in appointive office. There, you can't be voted out from below.

As an elected congressman, for example, Marylander Gil Gude would never have dreamed of dropping windy words, let alone peppering his speech with Latin. But the minute he was appointed Director of Congressional Research at the Library of Congress—*mirabile dictu*—a great carved cinnamon-hued sign appeared over his office door: "MINISTERIUM CONGRESSIONALE DE STUDIIS."

Immediately, in the basement, a jealous janitor began stencilling the sign for his broom closet: "CUBICULUM JANITORIS." This would nowadays be called trickle-down image.

Making unpleasant inevitabilities seem pleasant is the objective of every image-aware administration. At least once every four years a movement is launched to rename "Public Housing." Invariably, "People's Housing" is dismissed as sounding too much like Communist China; "Personal Housing" sounds too fancy; the whole thing shudders to a halt. Public Housing remains sounding just like what it is.

The most enjoyable effort along these lines by the Carter people came during the gas crisis. The oil companies were seeing just how high they could shove the prices before America began to howl for their hides. There were gas lines; government office buildings turned off their hot water; thermostats across the land were clicked down to the bottom overnight. The administration hired the J. Walter Thompson advertising agency to manufacture rose-colored glasses for the citizens. The delightful theme of their campaign: "Keep It Up, America!"

At the White House, Hamilton Jordan cannily perceived a hint of a double entendre. Luckily, Ann Wexler, who had the say-so, did not. America got the campaign, and many a good giggle to see it through the chilly nights.

For the socially active denizens of Embassy Row, the Washington image game takes on a comical warp.

The delicate balance that must be struck between wooing the Yankee devils and appeasing the stinkers back home gives the ambassador and his underlings many a sleepless night.

The roaring social rush that the late shah of Iran's Ambassador Ardeshir Zahedi gave Washington's upper crust—jetting them to Teheran for parties, plying them with carpets and caviar, flirting with Elizabeth Taylor—called for a rapid switch in his tactics as the shah's regime tottered to its collapse.

Suddenly, the horrified lounge lizards of the media, accustomed to receiving pretty little illuminated books and silver letter openers from their most attentive embassy suitor, found in their morning mail stout booklets crammed with indigestible statistics on Iran's textile and steel mill industries. Too late. They had already been caviared into goofiness. After the fall, many of the media had to tend their own image. The embassy leaked out the three Zahedi "gift lists" —lists of what presents he had given to whom in the media, the Congress, and social Washington. Reporters who owned Persian carpets for any reason hastily banished them for a long holiday at the dry cleaner's.

Any diplomat's life is a constant fumble for the pulse of image, American-style. Just before they retained Billy Carter, the Libyans threw a huge party at a hotel. There, they gave out copies of the *Sayings of Qaddafi.* They were handsomely bound in green suedelike material. They looked, probably on purpose, like small imitations of the *Washington Social List,* which comes similarly bound. Guests were delighted. No one understood the *Sayings* at all; but everyone knew the Libyans' hearts were in the right place.

The French fancy themselves very cunning on this account. Months before a visit by President Giscard d'Estaing, advance men piled into Washington, and toiled earnestly to work up a hundred possible questions for American newsmen. The president, for his part, polished the required hundred snappy answers in English. It worked quite nicely, as he simply pretended not to understand any of the other questions asked by newsmen.

The British do not sweat the small stuff. They just ship in a royal every now and again to dazzle the natives. One British ambassador, Lord Cromer, sometimes greeted guests at the embassy sporting a splendidly cut but bulging old blazer with silver buttons, endearingly dotted about with large spots of hearty English breakfasts of long ago. Most British ambassadors are far more concerned with the image of the embassy lawn. Under a cloak of high secrecy—these being troubled times at home—Sir Nicolas Henderson imported $20,000 worth of high-class English lawn seed and great buckets of nitrogen-rich elephant poop to transfuse Washington's anemic city soil. About the same time, Buffy, the lawn-digging British Embassy cat, mysteriously died. The grass at the embassy is splendid now. The English beam with satisfaction: they've got this Washington image nonsense beaten, they nod.

*"You ain't in Paris."*
        —D.C. MAYOR MARION BARRY, TO HIS FORMER
        PRESS SECRETARY FLORENCE TATE, THE DAY SHE
        WORE THE GOLD KID BOOTS

On the whole, on the Embassy Row party circuit as elsewhere in the capital, the sort of thing *W* defined as Quiet Quality is considered the standard Washington image: the single strand of pearls, gin and tonic, Bill Moyers, impeccable napery—they're still talking about the day the French had paper napkins with lunch, and it was before the Socialists won their election, too—"The MacNeil-Lehrer Report," and George Bush.

Strange image warps result when the old, genteel Washington upper crust that sets these standards lets down its hair. The day it rained for the Smithsonian's Fourth of July Picnic, for example, ambassadors and socialites all turned out in sportive jeans and plaid in the museum's American pottery section. The waiters, of course, all wore black tie, lest there be some terrible social mixup. They served hot dogs, fried chicken, hamburgers, baked beans, and corn on the cob on checkered gingham tablecloths, carefully laid over the white damask. Most of the older *Social Register* males wore sock garters under their jeans.

By now, it should be clear that Washington's image standards are nothing like, say, New York's. There, constant image pressures keep springing new surprises. Just when New Yorkers think they've got it down, along comes somebody like Diana Vreeland, former editor of *Vogue,* confessing to a magazine that she has her shoe soles restained by a French wardrobe mistress after each wearing.

"You lift your shoes and the soles are not impeccable! I mean, what could be more ordinary?"

In the capital, no one will notice your shoe sole. Neither will they notice your immortal soul. You will be defined, alas, by What You Do. Your image is simply how you seem to be doing it and how everybody seems to feel about that.

There's no anonymity or fleeting escape from your role in Washington, such as even Mick Jagger can find striking up conversation with a little old lady in a New York restaurant.

"Such a nice quiet young man," she said afterward. "Not loud and crazy like most of today's generation."

When it gets depressing, I like to think of the times the images are dropped: Supreme Court Justice Sandra Day O'Connor and her husband moving household oddments into their $300,000 condominium with a Ryder rent-a-truck; CIA head Bill Casey and Bill Simon, the former Treasury secretary, happily lapping ice-cream cones together on the beach in East Hampton; Henry Kissinger stripped to the waist in the men's at the International Club, shaving and humming Mozart.

Meanwhile, there are some questions even the image men can't answer. Republican polls showed President Ronald Reagan least-beloved by women over forty, and they were scratching their heads all over the city.

"It goes against everything we know about his image. It doesn't make sense," said one.

Rep. Guy Vander Jagt proposed the simple answer: "Maybe they remember his movies."

# The Best Bestiary:
# God's Other Creatures
# Are Washingtonians, Too

No Washingtonian is an island. The need for human warmth springs eternal. Often, this being a fickle city, the need is met with *non*-human warmth.

Washington is a great city for pets.

As president, Jerry Ford used to get up in the middle of the night to let his dog Liberty out from his White House bedroom to do his business.

As Jimmy Carter's press aide, Jody Powell took into his house a crippled crow with a broken wing. Every day during its convalescence, Powell would tiptoe down to his basement to hand-feed the darkling pure corn and country ham. ("Just like he feeds us," cackled hard-hearted newshounds around the press room.)

Ed Day, who was once the postmaster general of the United States, keeps a yak at his Potomac weekend farm. She is named Yakima. He is so attached to the shaggy beast that it was feared one year that he would ride her in the staid Potomac Hunt.

A dog is, of course, the ideal companion for the politician.

In the early nineteenth century, as a congressman, Virginia's John Randolph would bring a pack of hound dogs to lie at his feet in the House. "I prefer them to people," he would say in his odd piping voice. This is quite understandable for a man in that position.

Old Blue will not give a congressman a lot of lip about unkept promises. He will sleep with the master when he hasn't had a bath. He will loyally trot at the heels of the lawmaker who has just voted against his interests. He will pay keen attention to a bore, and give a man a nightly ticker-tape reception even if he's just suffered a crashing defeat on the House floor. The cold nose of Blue, thrust into the well-manicured congressional hand, has saved many a jump from slightly too-low Washington apartment balconies.

Men of frozen logic and glacial calculation turn into warm slop around their dogs.

Tyler, who owns Henry and Nancy Kissinger, is a lolloping Labrador retriever. The couple beamed indulgently as Tyler taught Nelson Rockefeller his favorite game—having a milk carton tossed for him to retrieve. The carton turned out to be half-full; Rocky's eight hundred-dollar suit ended up sopping in Grade A Homogenized; the pair still beamed.

In his youth, Tyler had to be taken daily by Nancy and a Secret Serviceman to frolic around the vice-presidential manse's grounds for his exercise. Later, in the Georgetown park where he let off steam, he developed a reputation as the most indulged pet in Georgetown.

"He had a troubled childhood," a moist-eyed Kissinger equerry excused him as he bowled over the Georgetowners' Yorkshire terriers, poodles and Scotties in his mad race around the park. "He had to move from place to place all the time, you know."

Doubtless his peripatetic youth caused his medical problems. Paw injuries, bronchitis, tummy trouble—the poor hound for awhile suffered a diet of cottage cheese, almost identical to Nancy's.

The Golden retriever, a photogenic breed, is the pet of preference for all Republican presidents, presidential hopefuls, and other generally tall people near the throne. (Of course, there are exceptions. Richard Nixon picked an Irish setter by mistake, and look what happened to him. Small politicians choose small dogs, for photographic reasons.)

Golden retrievers live up, visually, to imposing Republican names: Freedom, Conquest, Cannon and Glory frolic the parklands of

Georgetown with dignity and vigor.

The Jerry Fords still play with their Golden retriever, Liberty, in Rancho Mirage. The current First Dog—and the Reagans' favorite among many, even though on one occasion he bowled the First Lady completely off her feet in front of prying cameras—is Victory. Victory, of course, is of the Golden retrieving persuasion.

Although a rather small man, Nancy Reagan's former chief of staff, Joe Canzeri, was allowed to have a Golden retriever puppy. (Mrs. Efrem Zimbalist, Jr. gave it to him when he flew with the Reagans to Palm Springs for the Walter Annenbergs' New Year's party.) Buffington, as the dog was called, being a Palm Springs native, got only one sniff of Washington power. He flew back to town in the cockpit of the press jet. Perhaps luckily for the dog, before he had a chance to get attached to a way of life without a proper name like Integrity, Canzeri was out.

Although grand names are important, a good Washington dog can develop its talents without them. Kovan, ("Novak" spelled backwards) a large black part-Labrador, is the dog of columnist Robert Novak and his wife Geraldine.

It was Geraldine who discovered his rare skill. She had set a pair of diamond earrings on her bedside table one night. Late next day, she discovered that one was missing. A frantic search ensued. Shoes were emptied, rugs beaten, crevices in the wainscotting fingered. Kovan watched the hunt with avid interest that slowly turned to hangdog guilt. Suspicion struck the human side of the household. A rapid trip to the nearby animal hospital's X-ray machine revealed that it was justified. There, deep within the dog, twinkled the little gem. Kovan, more precious than he knew, was transported back to *chez* Novak. In the fullness of time, he deposited the diamond, along with less valuable offerings, in the back yard. Geraldine went through the unenviable retrieval process. *Voila!* The diamond had evidently profited by its adventure. It was now far brighter than its twin.

Democratic dogs have ordinary names. Ethel Kennedy's rowdy pack includes two huge Newfoundlands, Buckwheat and Kulba; Loco, Spanky and Blarney, who are soft-eyed cocker spaniels; and two rather grand King Charles spaniels, Pumpkin and Soufflé, who, reportedly, occasionally enter into sexual liaisons with Thomas Babington Macauley. (Mr. Macauley is the King Charles spaniel of Jack Valenti. Jack, being a former LBJ aide who is now president of the Motion Picture Association, probably calls his dog "Tom" when no one is listening.)

All the Kennedy pack is only halfheartedly housebroken. Yet, when one wanders away, Ethel offers the grandest reward she can think of for their return: a large, glossy, autographed photo of Teddy Kennedy.

The busier a man, on the whole, the smaller his pet. William Baroody, head of the American Enterprise Institute, keeps a rather insignificant snake. Top Reagan aide Michael Deaver began the administration leaden-eyed every morning: "Roberta!" he would explain. Roberta turned out to be not the Other Woman, but a gerbil belonging to his daughter Amanda. The little creature's nocturnal scuffling, trotting, munching, bustling and chattering kept him awake all night.

Sleep is extremely important to the Washingtonian.

A certain well-known Washington media figure who needs a great deal of sleep to keep up his hectic pace was not enamoured of his neighbor's cat. When the moon was high, the beast would howl and croon at the sky for hours on end.

One night the media figure leapt from his bed, grabbed a shotgun, leaned from his window and put an end to the feline aria forever.

Next morning, bright-eyed and well rested, he gave the corpse a simple private funeral at the local dump.

The night after that, the shooter and his wife smilingly tripped out to dine with the owners of the late lamented moonlight serenader.

It was a charming evening. The chat was of everything but cats. The shooter wended his way home afterward, still smiling to himself, and slept soundly.

"And I have slept soundly ever since," he told co-workers, nodding pleasantly.

Of course, he is not running for office. But he would be very well suited to the job.

# Mind Your Manners, Please: Standards on the Circuit in Washington

ROBERT MITCHUM made quite a splash at the embassy of Cyprus during a state visit by the King of Spain. It was a very formal party. Bob had already passed the stage of singing "The Spaniard who blighted my life" a couple of hours earlier. Dinner was over. The Austrian ambassador rose with raised champagne glass to give an eloquent and witty toast. Then, the ambassador from Cyprus, all elegance, stood and offered a lapidary string of remarks. The civilized patter of applause died down. The actor stirred.

"Would you like to say something, Mr. Mitchum?" enquired the Cypriot Ambassador.

"Yes," said Mitchum, lurching to his feet. "I'd like to pee."

You must not imagine that Washington manners are like manners anywhere else in the world.

In other capitals, you can content yourself upon meeting your sparkling new circle of friends with a simple "How do you do?" Then you're on your own. You must gauge your new acquaintance via a series of elaborate computations: humor, accent, clothing, grammar, jewelry, fingernails, shoes, haircut, tie pattern, sock length, allusions, wallet and interests will combine to give you a general picture: would you like to know this person better?

In Washington, it's much easier. The salutation is not "How do you do?" It is "What do you do?"

Foreigners are embarrassed by this. They make up funny answers: "I am an anchovy curler at the British Embassy." "I am the Vice-President's taster." "I stick the little worm in bottles of Mexican booze."

Washington is not amused. It cares deeply what you do. That is how it knows whether or not it wants to know you better. The entire future relationship between the quester and the questioned, over the next three minutes and the next several years, is based on your answer.

Not only that: the type of manners you can expect from a Washingtonian are almost entirely dependent on What He Does, vis-à-vis What You Do.

"Who are you?" guests ask Trudi Musson, social secretary to people like the the John Sherman Coopers. Often, her answer evokes no response, just a broad expanse of back.

"It used to bother me. Now I think it's funny," she says.

The only men expected to have exquisite manners in Washington are ambassadors, spare men—the ones you invite to dinner for the melancholy contingency when the senator forgets to come—decorators, and men of the cloth. Anybody else who is gallant or mannerly is presumed to be Mafia, CIA, a spy, a hustler or all of the above.

Washington manners are totally rank-dependent.

It's considered normal, even rather charming, for a high-ranking White House staffer to leap to his feet with no explanation halfway through a dinner party and bolt. Everything a White House staffer does is charming, you see.

Senators no longer RSVP to invitations. ("Hardly anybody does," mournfully interjects a social secretary.) Maybe they'll come, maybe they won't. They almost certainly won't be on time, unless you are a generous contributor to their campaigns, or plan to invite several who are.

One Washington hostess made the tragic mistake of inviting a half-dozen senators to a dinner party. Two did not arrive. One came on time. One was two hours late. And South Dakota's Jim Abourezk arrived announcing that his wife had decided to paint the basement instead.

If you really, really want someone to come to a party, you nag daily, for about a week in advance. Even Cabinet members can feel social guilt. Some couples—the James Schlesingers some years back spring to mind—have found themselves blackballed for weeks from sit-down dinners, having left gaping voids at table once too often. They are then doomed to eat at buffets and talk to the least useful person in the room until they mend their ways.

You can always get hold of a couple of congressmen. They make happy and grateful dinner guests, for reasons I'll go into below. Some are witty.

*"How do you manage to keep your eyes open?"*
*"Amphetamines."*
     —REPARTEE BETWEEN CORETTA KING, WIDOW
     OF DR. MARTIN LUTHER KING, AND PRINCE
     CHARLES OF ENGLAND

You may expect to be introduced to your fellow guests at a Washington dinner party, but not at a cocktail party.

There may be an announcement of your arrival above the babble. One quite beautiful Washingtonian tells how she is frequently greeted: "Oh, here's Sandra McElwaine." All conversation clicks to a halt; all heads swivel. The assemblage believes it is hearing the words "Senator McElwaine." The error is registered; the chatter swells again. She's on her own.

The choices of an arrival who is not a senator are limited. You may sail in looking vague and circle the periphery, hunting for a familiar face; you may belly up to the buffet and discuss food with strangers; you may scowl elegantly in a corner and wait for someone to find you fascinating; or you may barge in where you're not wanted. All types of behavior are perfectly acceptable.

Perhaps you are barging in on a coversation where, plainly, business is being attended to? The signs are unmistakable. The Powerful One is examining the ice in his glass, head tilted, and listening closely to the supplicant, gesticulating passionately beside him. At one point, the Powerful One drains his glass.

This is when the expert barger-in gently lifts the glass from his hand. "Let me fill that for you, senator." *Voila!* When he returns, he steps into the shoes of the original supplicant, who gives him a look that would shrivel a squid.

*"I whipped two little devils about sassy talk. One was Jimmy Carter. His ma came to see Miss Julia about it. Well, I hope to hell I get asked about it."*
—WALTER LAING, JIMMY CARTER'S HIGH SCHOOL TEACHER, IN HIS JOURNAL, DECEMBER 18, 1940.

A few procedural notes. At fancy Washington winter parties, a maid will gently lay your coat on a bed upstairs. If you are a woman, your coat is dark mink. This means that it is quite likely to get confused with everyone else's. Trying on other people's coats at the end of the evening often livens things up. If you are ill-mannered enough to own a cloth coat, it is polite to kick it under the bed, so as not to bring down the tone of the place.

It is very poor form in Washington to use your host's bed for any purpose other than storing outer clothing. Even a rather hip D.C. crowd was enraged on going to the bedroom of one chic political journalist to retrieve their coats. They found them buried beneath an amorous New York journalist and his then current belle.

But in Washington, it must be clear, manners are not on the bottom line. A drunk at a grade-A party is simply assigned a butler or waiter as a guardian angel; powerful men have knocked back the contents of their fingerbowl and have been asked if they'd like a refill.

Almost every social gaffe has been witnessed and forgiven. There have been black-tie fisticuffs in the middle of *Lohengrin* at the

Kennedy Center Opera House. There have been great thundering dinner-party scenes where Joe Alsop shouted and Clayton Fritchie strode scarlet-faced from the room; there have been betrayals, swindles, scandals, suicides, tears and all the sins of Sodom.

But there is only one breach of manners the city finds completely unforgiveable: neglecting the Code of the Call.

Along with eternal helpful hints like the one engraved near the roofline of the National Archives—"THE PAST IS PROLOGUE" —some practical philosopher should engrave the words whittled on the heart of every successful Washington official: "RETURN THY PHONE CALLS."

Nobody really gave a damn when Hamilton Jordan was reported to have spat Amaretto-and-cream down the bosom of a young woman in a bar. In fact, hostesses began serving after-dinner drinks called Jordan's Lotions—Hamilton maddeningly pronounced his name Jerden, remember—and guests joked happily about "going from Great Expectations to Great Expectorations."

That was not the reason he was not swamped with job offers after the great defeat: it was because he was bathed in the sallow afterglow of thousands of unanswered calls.

The Carter White House disobeyed the Code of the Call almost constantly. Rarely, after some public-relations catastrophe, a short-lived wave of calling back would sweep through the West Wing. Instantly, word spread around the city as though by tom-tom.

Places like the local Jiffy John company would be flooded with calls from White Housers, returning calls from "Mr. John" or "Mr. Yurin." Vengeance in Washington is swift, sure and touchingly childlike.

This was all quite unnecessary. The Code does not even decree that near-greats return their own calls. A polite trusted near-near-great aide with a lavish apology, vows of discretion and can-do promises of help, works almost as well.

While the Code of the Call is immutable, acceptable table manners vary sharply from administration to administration.

Washington is swift to jump into line. It had to learn fingerbowl-doily juggling under the Kennedys, and how to gnaw barbecued ribs under Lyndon Johnson. It had to jump back to *cuisine ordinaire* under Nixon and Ford, gobble grits with a grin during the Carter Era, and nibble veal and raspberries under the Reagans.

The city is breathlessly anxious to eat à la mode.

All Yankee eyes were glued to Jimmy Carter the night of the Georgia state dinner, as the catfish was served. How should one ingest the bony delicacy? They learned that it is properly chewed with the mouth open, to allow for sudden rejection of parts. Then, at the end, you pick little bits out from between your teeth with your thumbnail.

Teddy Kennedy's staffers hide food from his sight constantly during campaigns, to prevent his eating in public. The very words "Pat Lawford's chicken sandwiches" or "sandwich eaten in back of limo" are enough to produce gales of laughter among cognoscenti.

Through thick and thin, certain eccentricities in personal manners of the distinguished are accepted without comment by the circuit. Bobby Kennedy, Jr., when in town, chews and spits tobacco. Joan Braden, a woman of much personal charm and perennial hostess to the great, habitually combs her hair at table, as stray hairs waft into the mousse. Her friend, the late Nelson Rockefeller, always stirred his coffee with the tortoiseshell earpiece of his glasses. He would then shake the glasses briskly. He did not wipe the stem before replacing it behind his ear.

*"Please! Call me Keke! Or Mrs. Anderson! But 'ma'am' makes me feel fifty years old!"*
—KEKE ANDERSON, WIFE OF PRESIDENTIAL CANDIDATE JOHN ANDERSON (SHE WAS 49 AT THE TIME.)

Just as the undone waistcoat button of King Edward set off a fad that lasts to this day, so little oddities among the great become Washington habits.

That famous front-page photograph of Rockefeller giving the

finger to a heckler gave Washington a new word (the Rockefinger), a new wave of jokes ("Now we know how they turn down a loan at Chase Manhattan,") and an epidemic of Rockefingering in fashionable Georgetown.

People began flashing the uncouth signal from taxis and limos. Pedestrians strolling by the window of Clyde's Restaurant began playfully dipping the digit to patrons seated within. The gesture was used as a greeting for a while among people of like political views. One young political aide who adopted it as an all-purpose salute was finally beaten up by a Marine on Dupont Circle.

After Rockefeller died, an affectionate ten-minute film of his life was shown at a $1,000-a-plate GOP fundraiser. Cut from the film was the Rockefinger photo.

"The family would have found it in poor taste," explained a spokesman.

"Rocky would have loved it," grinned one close to him. "Several people at the dinner had pushed to have him dropped from the Ford ticket in '76."

The gesture is now completely out of fashion.

Its last gasp was heard in September 1980, when Rita Jenrette, still devoted to her then husband John, flashed it daily in the halls, during the Abscam investigation, at government informer Mel Weinberg.

Current manners in the White House are decidedly genteel.

After all, Nancy Reagan herself is a woman of exquisite manners. Who else, craving a cookie at night, would instead sit up in bed and silently peel and eat a banana, so as not to disturb the slumbering president?

Everything at the mansion now is exactly as you remember it from *Advise and Consent*. There are furs and formality. There is "Ruffles and Flourishes"—that trumpet fanfare that heralds "Hail to the Chief," which in turn heralds the president—and a smart Marine guard, absent since the Nixon years. Styrofoam cups for secretaries' coffee breaks have been banned; china cups only may be used. Trousers on women are *verboten*. There is a standing rule that Nancy Reagan must be referred to at all times as "the First Lady." (She is privately called "Mommy.") Bosses and secretaries must no longer hail each other by their first names.

At the end of a White House evening, guest are urged homeward not with a bum's-rush flicking of the lights, but with the insinuating strains of Brahms' Lullaby.

Naturally, the high-toned atmosphere encourages visitors to behave themselves.

Sometimes they get carried away. The question of curtseying to other people's royals, which everyone thought was resoundingly answered with the Declaration of Independence, got a stormy re-airing with the visit of Prince Charles of England.

There, smack on the front of the Washington *Post,* was the Reagan's first chief of protocol, Leonore Annenberg, caught by the camera's eye at the airport in mid-crouch in front of himself.

A storm of wrath broke over her head. Before the private White House dinner that Nancy Reagan threw for the prince in May, the "fun group" she invited racked their brains and thumbed their etiquette books. This was the most agonizing manners crisis the city had encountered since wondering what to say about LBJ's gall bladder scar: to bob or not to bob?

"Are you Going Down?" friends called to ask one another.

Evangeline Bruce went down. (Her husband had been ambassador to England.) Pat Buckley, wife of William F. Buckley, Jr., did too. (She's a British subject.) Diana Vreeland, former editor of *Vogue,* did. (She thought it was elegant.)

As the Royal Ballet's fiftieth anniversary affair in New York drew nigh, the British consulate in New York insisted that curtseying to a prince is "good manners, according to *Debrett's Correct Form,* " the Bible of the British upper crust.

But Peter Hall at the British Embassy insisted that "The Palace would never try to establish correct form for Americans, or any other non-British."

The world watched with narrowed eyes: what would Lee Annenberg do, now that the wisdom of the western world had had a chance to bat the topic about? As it turned out, she gave the prince a warm handshake. The Battle of the Bob was over, until the next time. Each woman remains alone with her conscience.

Less rarefied problems tended to bedevil the Carter White House during foreign visits. All they had to do was put a spittoon in Blair House for Mr. Teng, the Chinese vice-premier. He himself handled trickier aspects, like the fact that he couldn't bear American food. For some reason, he was always served rubbery veal and broccoli. He simply wrapped it his napkin and smuggled it out in his pocket to flush down the toilet.

Other foreigners, on other visits, have slipped unfamiliar morsels into their shoes or under the table. This might explain the periodic mouse-and-roach explosions at the White House. Mousetraps lurked in corners of public and private quarters, and the Oval Office through most of the Carter administration.

A party was thrown there to salute the opening of the Department of Education. A thousand schoolteachers rolled in. They were there, palpitating with excitement, to meet the new secretary of Education and to engulf champagne and strawberry shortcake in the East Room. The line was long, the wait was weary. A two-inch cockroach sauntered from his lair, and began to promenade slowly the entire length of the room, parallel to the line. As the roach reached the halfway point between the portraits of George and Martha Washington, schoolteachers dropped to their knees with cameras to snap candids.

"To educators, all things are educational," explained one.

White House visitors these days have tougher tests of their substance. All must submit to thorough searches and electronic friskings. Manners in the eighties dictate that you look rather pleased with all the attention. Do not shed objects on your way in.

In fact, do not shed objects at any time during the evening, if you can help it.

Henry Fonda once popped out his hearing aids at a rather grand White House dinner, just as the music struck up. The small pinkish *objets* were found later, listening hard in a corner all alone, after everyone left.

"Luckily nobody says anything interesting at White House dinners," observed a friend.

This is true. The most consistent rule of manners on the circuit in

Washington is to leave your passions, pro or con, at home, with your shotgun and your sweatsocks.

This has always been the case on Embassy Row.

Barbara Howar, in the long ago, dined at an embassy and, in a fit of political conscience, turned a flattering portrait of Richard Nixon to the wall. Then she passionately proposed a toast to a newsman "who's been in the same job for seven [effing] years!" She was not invited back.

A man who let loose a strange, loud cry at the Swedish Embassy during a visit by the king was pounced upon instantly. The Secret Service pinned his arms to his sides and wrestled him to the floor.

"All I said was 'God Save the King' in Swedish," he sputtered as he was led off.

Enthusiam and conscience are the twin foes of politesse. A glamorous dinner was tossed before one opera ball at the Chilean Embassy. Representative James Scheuer, after several pisco sours, decided to give his opinions an airing. He gave the ashen-faced ambassador an earful about Chile's repressive policies; he cried that his presence, and the fact that he was eating Chilean food and drinking their pisco, must not, under any circumstances, be mistaken for approval of Chile's wicked ways.

Other guests squirmed with horror and glee.

"My God," moaned one regular. "If you had to go around approving everywhere you went, that would be the end of Washington life as we know it."

At the next big ball, the Beaux Arts, there were the Scheuers again. (Mrs. Scheuer is popular decorator Emily Malino.) This time, the scene was the Greek Embassy. The assemblage paled as the congressman rose to speak.

Well, he said, flushed with generosity of spirit, he just wanted to say that whereas he had been morally bound to tell the Chileans what he thought, he wanted to say he was simply *crazy* about the Greeks. Always had been!

Rubbing in one's views or emphasizing differences before it is necessary to do so is bad Washington manners: the differences will surface soon enough in the ordinary press of politics.

*"Ah, yes, this is a Cuban cigar. A Havana. But I always*
*peel off the label before offering one to Ronald*
*Reagan."*
    —KING JUAN CARLOS OF SPAIN, TO HOUSE
    SPEAKER TIP O'NEILL, OCTOBER 1981


If you are talking on the telephone to somebody who is fairly
high-powered, or exceptionally interesting, or works for an embassy,
it is only polite to presume that his phone is bugged.

Some people in Washington, and in Langley, Virginia, headquarters of the CIA, answer all their phone calls with a "Hi, everybody!"

Because of this, it is rude to expect people you are calling at the
White House or at the top of Cabinet departments to be completely
candid on the phone.

Some people go so far, however innocent the call, as to never
mention their own or their friends' names. This seems a little too
delicate for most cases. A good gauge is probably the callee's office
security measures. Do the secretaries there lock up their typewriter
ribbons at night, as they do at the National Security Council? Do
they have scrambling devices on typewriters, so that gadgetry of
people on the Other Side cannot figure out which keys have been
struck in what order? Are all calls coming in or going out logged?
Then simple courtesy dictates discretion.

"After years of trial and error, I've decided to be completely
honest," sighs a journalist bored and irritated with the etiquette of
discretion. "You just have to presume that the people you *think* are
your friends are your friends."

"Friends" is another term fraught with unique meaning in the
world of Washington manners.

You must not be too deeply hurt if, after an election that affects
your pecking position on the Washington social scale, you suddenly
find some friends are not as friendly. The only inviations you get, to
put it bluntly, are those to annual reunions of the Outs.

The sad truth, in Washington, is that "friend" is often a loose term
for a tight but temporary alliance. Paul Feinberg, a photographer

who published a book on friendship all over the United States, concluded that Washington, D.C. and California are the most sparsely populated with true friends.

Meanwhile, it is extremely common, in this wicked city, for almost everybody to refer to powerful people as "My friend, So-and-So."

This is not good manners. For one thing, nobody believes you.

It has long been thought excellent Washington manners, on the other hand, for the powerful to refer to the *less* powerful as "My friend, So-and-So."

Jimmy Carter tried this early and often.

After he had called two men who left his government in disgrace, Bert Lance and Peter Bourne, among his "closest friends in the world," the *National Journal* ran a list of his other "friends."

He called House Speaker Tip O'Neill, who despaired of him, "someone who in such a short time can become one's closest friend." Among "best friends," "good friends," "personal friends" and "very close friends" was a delightful ragbag including Andy Warhol, British Prime Minister James Callahan, Anwar Sadat, King Hussein, Doug Fraser, Hubert Humphrey, Max Cleland, the president of Mexico, the shah of Iran, Johnny Cash, the prime minister of India, and Abe Beame.

The poignant upshot was that Carter probably left office with fewer friends than anyone else, including Richard Nixon.


*"Do you want to use the bathroom or something?"*
    —JIMMY CARTER, MEETING EGYPTIAN PRESIDENT
    ANWAR SADAT AT ANDREWS AIR FORCE BASE ON
    THE OCCASION OF HIS FIRST HISTORIC VISIT


Carter wished to be generous. He had good intentions and terrible luck. Moves intended as *beaux gestes* constantly ended up leaving a peculiar smell in the air.

Once, after a World Series baseball game between the Orioles and

the Pirates, he cornered Earl Weaver, manager of the Orioles. He
was oozing sympathy.

"Ma motha, ma self and Rosalynn would lak to extend our condo-
lences on the loss of your motha."

Actually, Weaver had merely lost the game. His mother was spry
as a sparrow. It was the mother of the Pirates' manager who had just
gone on to that great baseball diamond in the sky.

Michael Blumenthal, his secretary of the Treasury, was fired right
after Carter made his return-from-Camp David speech. In this one,
he quoted an anonymous source as saying "Mr. President, some of
your Cabinet members are disloyal."

To Blumenthal's astonishment, two months after his firing, he
opened his mail to find a handsomely bound copy of that very speech,
warmly inscribed: "To Secretary Blumenthal. From your friend,
Jimmy Carter."

Carter's genuine mannerly instincts were duly observed by the
media in Vienna, as he accompanied Leonid Brezhnev from a meeting at an embassy there. The Soviet leader tripped and stumbled.
Swiftly Carter reached to catch and support him; Brezhnev was
saved from a nasty fall.

"Lyndon Johnson would have picked Brezhnev up by the ears,"
mused a man who'd known all the recent presidents and presidential
aspirants. "Nixon would have pushed him down and then left. Jerry
Ford would have fallen on top of him. And Teddy Kennedy would
have waited twenty-four hours, and then figured something out."

*"He never says thank you."*
    —A WHITE HOUSE BUTLER, ABOUT JIMMY
    CARTER.

Some people were charmed by Amy Carter's attendance at White
House dinners, her nose buried in a book. (Lord and Taylor, creating
a model White House dinner setting, set a place for little Amy and
stuck a book there.) Others were not. At one dinner, Sen. Ed Muskie

sat beside her on one side, repeatedly enjoining her to "Eat your spinach, Amy."

On the other side of Amy seethed a New Yorker. She had laid out $7,000 for her enchanted evening. She had bought a Stravropoulos evening gown, rented a suite at the Madison, given herself a little party to swank to her friends before she left New York, and hired a limousine. There she sat in her glory, plonked next to Amy, hearing Ed Muskie telling her to eat her spinach.

"Did you write a thank-you note?" a friend enquired.

The thank-you note is one of Washington's most beloved skills. It ranks higher on the sincerity scale than flowers, because it is more of a nuisance to send.

One of my favorites is from Effi Barry, wife of Mayor Marion Barry, after her enchanted evening at a Junior Chamber of Commerce benefit for D.C. General Hospital:

"The evening, if planned for disrespect, rudeness and embarrassment, went well for the Jaycees and humilitatingly for the Washington community and myself . . . The MC twice introduced me as Effi Bailey. I was presented with a Peaches and Herb gold record with the inscription Mary Barry. (Barry's previous wife was Mary.) I was detained at the door and told I could not enter the affair without a ticket. I was told not to sit at the table assigned to me and directed to another one. I was rudely swept away by a Secret Service man to meet Mrs. Carter and once she arrived thirty minutes later I was left standing there . . . The First Annual Spring Benefit appeared to be rooted in the deepest layer of insensitive human behavior."

She did not send flowers.

At most Washington social events, it is polite to stay awake. Traditional exceptions are the movie premieres at the American Film Institute—as long as the stars are not sitting directly behind you. It is rude to sleep where people are sweating strenuously to please you —at tennis tournaments, the circus and the ballet, for example. (Hamilton Jordan snoozed soundly throughout the Stuttgart Ballet's "Sleeping Beauty." That was fine because he was in the Presidential Box. Anything is fine in the Presidential Box.)

It is conventional to doze during after-dinner speeches at think-tanks. The Brookings Institution, on the left, and the American Enterprise Institute, on the right, would both be disappointed if a few guests did not nod off into the soufflé. It is an indication of the importance of the speech.

At AEI dinners, you are likely to be logged. An hour-long speech on the economy, by former Chairman of the Federal Reserve Board, Arthur Burns, had them snoring like tired puppies. Carla Hills dozed for twenty minutes; Rep. Phil Ruppe was out cold for fifteen; David Packard racked up about forty-five minutes.

The only complaint came from a neighbor of David Packard: "He is a dreadfully fitful sleeper. He snores for a while, then starts wildly. He really kept me awake with all his fidgeting."

Shortly afterwards, incidentally, Burns received $50,000 for making a similar speech in Japan. He is now ambassador to Bonn. There, he and his wife hand out song sheets to guests at many events, and everyone stays awake.

In Washington, song sheets are not distributed. People have better things to do with their mouths. Those who are not gossiping are ensuring they get their daily nutrients.

Several financially strapped congressmen, the sort who are not asked to fill in for senators, live exclusively on buffet food at House and Senate office building receptions. They prowl the corridors of power at six o'clock like vampires wakened by the moon, sniffing for the aroma of rare roast beef. Some must be satisfied with less. Representative Jamie Whitten, chairman of the House Appropriations Committee, has been seen loading up napkins with half a dozen fish sticks, and jamming them into his pocket. One regular on the grade-A party circuit often stuffs both suit pockets, thoughtfully pre-lined with Baggies, with caviar.

Some ambassadors still follow the lead of the dear departed Ardeshir Zahedi, the late shah of Iran's envoy. Selected guests at the top of the pecking order never approach the buffet. A servant brings a pre-loaded plate from the table to the mighty one as he receives supplicants, to save him from the shabby inference that he is eating from hunger rather than politeness.

This is not so odd as it seems. A half-dozen gallant and shaky old aristocrats in seam-shiny evening clothes owe half their daily bread to food stamps, and the other half to the groaning buffets of Embassy Row. (Other regulars on the circuit know that it is bad manners to interrupt while they are grazing.) Some practical, usually female, reporters habitually carry capacious totes to the city's finer fiestas. Down their gullets go the meatballs. Into the totes they shovel a stream of high-protein shellfish, steak tartare, rare roast beef, pâté de foie gras, turkey breast, eggrolls, lobster claws, cheeses and two or three handfuls of *crudités. Voila!* Dinner is served, for about a week.

"Doncha *hate* to see waste?" one asked me once, trickling a dozen cherry tomatoes atop her loaded tote as garnish.

Important Washington skills include attending very large funerals, and walking in step with the music during ceremonial events. (Henry Kissinger, despite his lifelong ambition to be a spear carrier in an opera, never mastered this. "Actually, everyone else is out of step," friends grinned.) Jerry Brown got several black marks from the manner-mavens when he was spotted busily signing autographs on the steps of the Washington Cathedral at George Meany's funeral.

Unfortunately, with all the formality and pomp, good Washington manners must retain an underpinning of accessible humanity, under all circumstances.

*"I'll never forget the impression I had of him. When he shook my hand and said a few words to me it was almost chilling how hollow it was. I never forgot that, and it had a lot to do with my attitude about politics."*
—ROBERT REDFORD, DESCRIBING HOW, WHEN HE WAS 13, HE RECEIVED A BOY SCOUT TROPHY FROM SEN. RICHARD NIXON.

Humanity, of course, does not extend to getting drunk. It is exceedingly bad manners to acknowledge that anybody of importance in Washington ever ties one on, despite the fact that Washington has the highest per capita liquor consumption of any American city.

It matters not that reporters often spot the mighty tottering and reeling from receptions. No social scribe ever recorded the spectacle of former Speaker Carl Albert and his wife staggering from ballroom to hotel lobby to car; none note the basic law that a senator plastered on the Senate floor is usually escorted to the cloakroom by another senator.

Some senators have actually learned to control the manners of the press. Teddy Kennedy, while campaigning in 1979, fully expected a lot of uncouth questions about womanizing and Chappaquiddick. Reporters were expected to ask them, too. Teddy took with him, to news conferences in places like Los Angeles, his teen-age daughter, Kara. She sat beside him throughout, fresh-faced and demure. A tattered shred of reportorial gallantry still clung to the furious scribes. The questions died on their lips.

Often, the best manners in Washington are shown not by the mighty, but by those who surround them. A well-known Washington widow is a habitual shoplifter. If caught, she simply nods graciously.

"I'm just trying these things out," she says. Shopkeepers send a bill. It is usually paid.

You are now almost ready to go on the circuit. A few final hints: you will probably be greeted, after your maiden expedition, in one of three ways: with a two-cheeker kiss, (if you are a woman); with a Rostropovich bearhug (if you are a man—it was introduced by the maestro); or with the Elephant Hug. (This is Nancy Reagan's favorite greeting. It involves her arms around your neck, and your arms around her waist. Everyone in Georgetown can now do it perfectly.)

After it is over, you must never turn to whisper loudly to a nearby observer, "Who was *that?*"

Write it on a napkin.

Remember that at some Washington dinner parties, women are still expected to leave the table while the men have brandy and cigars. You may be surprised to learn that this is a largely Democratic practice. Both Averell Harriman and Sargent Shriver subscribe to it. You might enjoy making a fuss about it. Sally Quinn did once, at the Harrimans', and had to leave.

At some parties, you are still expected to turn the table—talk to the person on one side during one course, and the one on the other side during the next. This saves stiff necks, and does not leave one person staring vacantly across the table at the only other person not engaged.

Meanwhile, forget the seventies-style instant first-name-only intimacy. (It now smells of California wife-swapping clubs; only waiters address peole they barely know by their first names any more.) Do not tip anybody at embassies. Learn to tie your own black tie. Master the "you call and I'll raise" ploy of Washington gossip, which separates the frosh from the old hands.

One whiz on the social circuit explains: "You keep your mouth shut and hope someone else will bring up the topic. Then, you just add the most interesting details you know. That way, you get the pleasure and the status of gossip, but not the blabbermouth reputation."

The final commandment of Washington manners, especially as an administration enters its fourth year: Thou shalt not, ever, mention a subsequent administration.

This is where the maestri of manners get a chance to show their stuff.

Just before the last election, the Office of Management and Budget prepared the budget. The election was in November; to even the most obtuse, there was a chance that Carter might lose; the presentation of the budget was to be in January. No one could mention the unmentionable.

The solution for OMB was to put together two completely different budgets. One, boldly labeled "A La Carter," was bruited about merrily. The other, tentatively tailored to fit the Reagan philosophy, was never mentioned by name.

*And it was only discussed in the men's room.*

It was the best-kept secret in Washington.

With the exception of Robert Mitchum, at the beginning of this chapter, who talks about what goes on in men's rooms?

That brings us, finally, back to Ham Jordan.

His remark toward the end of Barbara Walters' big Egypt-Israel reconciliation dinner, in December of 1977, was a more formal echo of the Mitchum ploy. It was widely reported as "Well, this administration's got to go take a piss."

("Is that the royal wee?" enquired one wag.)

Even more widely reported was the young man's remark to the wife of Ashraf Ghorbal, the Egyptian ambassador, as he peered down her modest decolletage: "Well! Now I've seen the pyramids of Egypt."

Dr. Ghorbal, a man of elegant manners, hushed the uproar as best he could.

"In Egypt we have a saying: 'He who repeats an insult is the one insulting you.' " And privately, he pointed out, "Actually, we have three pyramids."

Meanwhile, playing on Jordan's pronunciation of his name as "Jerdon," a brief flurry of bumper stickers emerged with the message, "HAMILTON JORDAN IS A JORK."

Washington manners allow you to say anything at all on your bumper sticker.

# TROOP
# MORALE

# Access: Getting to Know Them, or Moving in on the Shakers

*"The best way to stay normal is to stay away from the White House."*
—DAVID EISENHOWER

ARE YOU coming to Washington for the scenery? Enjoy! Most people are mad about the azaleas, of course. But they are here for the access.

Access means that you can talk to somebody who can do something for you. The only person in the capital not worried about access is the president. He can talk to himself as often as he likes, and to anyone else whenever he wants. Around the sun of himself, lesser planets frolic, thumping into one another's orbits, knocking each other off their axes.

If you simply wish to tug a respectful forelock or say hi, access is easy. The mighty lead ordinary lives in Washington.

You can catch White House Chief of Staff James Baker jogging 'round the track at American University, in a baby blue T-shirt labelled Fat Cat. You can expect to watch the attorney general, William French Smith, darting about in tennis whites at the Arlington Y.

You'll bump into House Speaker Tip O'Neill at big Democratic dinners and ball games. Vice-President Bush Christmas-shops at

Bloomies, picks up his preppie togs at Brooks Brothers, and jogs by the canal, with his spaniel Fred and Secret Service puffing in his wake.

You'll encounter Chief Justice Warren Burger riffling through pages at Discount Books. (Somewhat less frequently since he was tackled by a young black woman who, taking advantage of the access, chewed over the Bakke decision with him for forty minutes before he could escape to his waiting limo.)

You can spot Defense Secretary Caspar Weinberger if you linger at the frozen food section at the Georgetown Safeway. Sooner or later, he'll trundle through, pushing a cart laden with proletarian frozen pies. You'll probably see President Reagan at worship at the National Presbyterian Church. (You must expect to address the Secret Service and the FBI before you have access to either your president or your Maker there, these days.)

But chances are you want want more than a howdy.

If you're a lobbyist—and some days it seems everyone is—you want lingering and repeated contact with senators and congressmen who can push your or your clients' causes; you want a word over the Christmas eggnog with appropriate Cabinet members; you want people at the White House to return your phone calls.

That is access. Generally, access is not cheap.

"I like having senators to dinner at my house," says a lobbyist in a frank moment. "But be realistic. If you have a senator as a friend, he's going to say to you, 'For God's sake, help me raise some money for my campaign.' That's how you endear yourself to them. You give 'em a thousand dollars yourself, too. Then, you've got to keep your nose clean. If he's at dinner at my house, he doesn't want to pick up the paper a couple of days later and see I've just been indicted."

If you're a Cabinet member, you are in a good position for presidential access. But not the *best* position. Drew Lewis, the secretary of Transportation, nodded that yes, he had the president's ear at Cabinet meetings. "But Holmes Tuttle [Reagan's car-dealer friend] was at the president's birthday party—and that's where the real decisions are made."

Please, don't expect access like Holmes Tuttle. But different kinds
of access serve different purposes.

*"The President doesn't want any yes-men and*
*yes-women around him. When he says no, we all say*
*no."*
     —ELIZABETH HANFORD DOLE, THE REAGAN
     WHITE HOUSE'S TOP RANKING WOMAN

Journalists, for example, have a sort of anxious access. Their ace
in the hole is that somebody wants to tell them his side of the story.
They may get leaks from people who trust them; all are carefully
designed to serve a purpose. When there's an exception—a shot of
off-the-record truth, such as Budget Director David Stockman gave
to his friend Bill Greider, who promptly splattered it all over the
*Atlantic*—it is often short-lived. No journalist has had easy access to
David Stockman since the doubts he expressed to his friend sprang
into print.

For continuing access sought by people who are trying to accomplish something—for their firms, for their countries, for their for-
tunes—there is a golden rule:

"Don't waste your time fiddling around at the middle level."
Counsels one lobbyist who has made access an art form: "Go *straight*
to the Power People."

It's not easy. The closer to the throne, the tighter-packed the
throng around the Power People, and the sharper the elbows waiting
to dig you in the ribs. Your access, you see, inevitably means the
diminishing of somebody else's.

This is what gives the game its thrill; it's also why people must be
so fast on their feet to play at all.

Luckily for the players, Power People, like everyone else, have an
Achilles heel. This is their social life. Perle Mesta, the hostess with
the mostes', said all you have to do is hang a pork chop in the window
and they'll beat a path to your door. Not quite. You hang a pork

chop in the window—*along with the delightful and useful prospect of meeting other Power People.* You dream up a logical reason to get them all together. "To meet the new secretary . . ." "To salute . . ." "To hear . . ." You give them a convenient time and setting. And, confident that they're going to the right place at the right time with the right contact, in they pile. (See chapter, "Some Enchanted Evenings.")

The best time to build access is at the very beginning of a new administration. The old Power People are afraid of being left behind. The new Power People fear they are missing something they probably should know. This is when the access hound, nose quivering, ears pricked and adrenalin rushing, trots most gloriously on the trail of his helpless quarry.

Lawyer Steve Martindale, when he first came to town, launched his career of amazing access with a party for John Lennon and Yoko Ono. The two, who knew nobody in Washington, wished to live in the United States without a lot of nonsense over their alien green cards. At Steve's urging, they came to meet Power People who could help them—Henry Kissinger and various senators and journalists. The Power People came, atwitter with excitement, to meet John and Yoko. A perfect match. Steve had had nothing to do with either side before.

The assemblage made a media splash. After it was over, his name dropped without shame from several formerly pursed Washington lips. Then it became a simple matter, with sensitive planning, to arrange for the ultimate access evenings: the Little Dinners.

The Little Dinner is second nature to access-aware Washingtonians. You choose two Power People you know would sell their socks for access to each other, and use each as bait for the other. You build the dinner around them, inviting others you wish to impress. It is a seated dinner, of course. Currently fashionable is a dinner for twenty-four, with three tables of eight, but twelve or fourteen is acceptable if almost all of the guests are equally high-powered.

"Are you free to come to a little dinner I'm having? Ming the Magnificent will be there," you say in your first conversation to Bobby Bigtime. Then the call goes out to Mr. Magnificent: "I'm hoping you can come to dinner on the thirtieth. Bobby Bigtime's bringing his wife, they'll be back from Ruritania. He knew your mother there. Harry Scrivener, one of my *dearest* friends, is flying in. Have you met his wife, Tessa Tube Star? She's a riot." (Of course, you invite at least two media people. Word must get around somehow.) The ball is rolling.

A certain level of boyish personal charm is an enormous help; and money matters insofar as it means you can supply respectable surroundings.

*"Oh, God, I'm not going to have time to do my wash*
*next week. Queen Sirikit's coming over again."*
  —STEVE MARTINDALE

You do not wish to be a flash-in-the-pan accessmeister. The wise man or woman, in it for the long haul, takes other steps to ensconce himself in common perception as part of the scene.

Some people in Washington actually crash the classier funerals and weddings, specifically for this purpose.

If you meet someone you wish to have access to at someone else's party, you pounce to cement the relationship immediately. You invite them to lunch: "Let's go tomorrow, to the Bagatelle/Mel's/Lion d'Or," depending on where you best know the maitre d'. (See chapter, "The Finer Feedbag.")

Sunny Adler, editor of *Dossier* magazine, suggests that it's important for newcomers to stay in a hotel—the right hotel—when they first come to Washington to sniff the air. She recommends the Jefferson, Fairfax and Madison hotels—personal hotels where the manager is willing to shepherd the social lives of her or his guests.

If you decide to entertain your new friends, you don't want to plunk them down at another Little Dinner immediately. You want them to see the other people you have access to. Perhaps you have them over for a drink at, say, six o'clock on a weeknight. Nothing formal. For God's sake, don't expect them to wear black tie at that hour. This is a drop-by, at a location convenient to Capitol Hill or their houses, or perhaps one of the above hotels.

This is a good time to develop and set up sports access. Tennis is still a desirable sport for this purpose. You can expect to see everyone you ever wanted to meet on the court at St. Alban's, or at the Arlington Y, the Mount Vernon courts, and others. If you are a good player, you are in demand. The high-powered club courts are always looking for fourths.

At the moment, squash is a desirable access sport; paddleball is popular with many members of Congress.

Competitive sports have one disadvantage: you might win. ABC newsman John Scali has been seen playing tennis doubles against Secretary of State Alex Haig, and muttering to his partner, Brit Hume, "Throw the match!"

Even the non-competitive camaraderie of the swimming pool is not free of danger. A major who had daily access to then Defense Secretary Harold Brown in the Pentagon pool on one occasion accidentally kicked the secretary in the face, hard, bloodying his nose and scratching his eye. These are possibilities to be weighed in the lists of access *sportif.*

Some people think that an important part of access in Washington is your listing in the *Green Book,* the local social list.

You can get in by being Old Social Washington, by being a millionaire active on the charity scene, or by being a presidential appointee.

You can also worm your way into the hearts of some of its nouveau entrants, and bald-facedly ask them to lobby for you with the book's publisher. (There is always much talk of a committee, possibly apocryphal.)

Steve Martindale tiptoed into the *Green Book* via a circuitous route: he rented a house in the Hamptons one summer, spending $30,000 on his "season." He was promptly listed in the *Blue Book* of the Hamptons. Friends brandishing copies of this pushed for the ultimate honor here.

Having been listed in the *Green Book* as a father's daughter, a wife and, along with the florists and engravers, a journalist, I assure you that it gets you nothing but sale announcements from the better shops. But it means that most likely you have not yet been caught in a murder, a scandal-ridden divorce or the seduction of somebody's small son. That counts for something in Washington.

Essentially, it has symbolic value. It is also a popular item among burglars. They steal the new one each year to figure out who is likely to be away at their summer homes during peak burgling months.

For more specific access to more specific figures, on a regular basis, the handiest tool is a common faith.

Naturally, it doesn't have to be *yours*.

John White, when chairman of the Democratic National Committee, had trouble reaching Jimmy Carter's ear, an organ usually reserved for Hamilton and Jody. White promptly joined the First Baptist Church. That was where the Carters worshipped, so confident of their own access to the Almighty that Rosalynn shucked her shoes while singing hymns.

White became a pillar. He was even asked by the church elders to address the congregation at its 176th anniversary dinner. A mistake. To the straitlaced Baptist family men, their blushing wives and wide-eyed children, the born-again political access man cried, "Speechwriters are like artificial insemination! Effective, but somehow it takes all the emotion out of it!"

He was not asked to speak again; but then his mission had been accomplished.

Robert McNamara, hard to reach as head of the World Bank, occasionally took over his late wife's Bible class. When a major job at the bank opened up, several upper-level staffers who had shown a limited interest in the Gospels until then—including two Jews— suddenly began turning up for McNamara's class with shining morning faces on the appropriate Sundays.

Washington political access is not universally powerful. Although Mrs. Howard Baker, wife of the Senate majority leader, could probably ask any favor from the president, she could not get Luciano Pavarotti to sing at a Ford's Theater benefit through her husband's influence. In fact, she was turned down flat. But politicians' wives learn there are many routes to access. She took the route circuitous. Her manicurist, Elena, hailed from Luciano's home town of Modena. With heads together, Joy Baker and Elena wrote the tenor in Modenese dialect. They explained how precisely Ford's Theater resembled the opera house at home. Pavarotti, charmed, consented instantly.

Within the city, fleeting, one-time, short-term access is almost laughably available to all. Waiters at certain Georgetown fundraising events sidle up to guests and murmur, "Can you help me with Immigration?" An ambitious young artist got to mingle with his desired artistic contacts by going to a reception for them at the vice-president's house. He drove the truck for the band.

"Well," said a friend, pleased with his chutzpah, "if everyone in Washington had to say how they got where they got to, nobody would go anywhere."

How true.

*"Look, there's Mrs. Sadat, Nancy Kissinger and Happy Rockefeller. Should we applaud?"*
*"Good heavens, no. This is a private club, you know."*
—OVERHEARD AT THE F STREET CLUB

In Washington, the most constant fount of access is the club. Belonging is a sign that you are Here To Stay.

Perhaps, if you are among the blessed, your club is the Metropolitan Club.

The Metropolitan is very picky about who steps beneath its blue-and-yellow flag and through its handsome double portal at Seventeenth and H streets Northwest.

The late Guy Burgess, the homosexual British spy of yore, tried to join the Metropolitan when he was in Washington in the forties. As he was a spy working for the KGB at the British Embassy here, the access would have been most useful. The club's elaborate research into his background made him uneasy. He withdrew his application, and flounced off to join the National Press Club instead. The ironic note is that he was, finally, approved at the Metropolitan, but it was too late; he had left the country.

"Might have been a different sort of fellow if he'd joined," mused one member, told of the near-miss.

But the Metropolitan does not seek exotic members of any sort. Its racial exclusiveness sticks in the craw of high-minded administrations. Carter appointees who were members of the Metropolitan Club, like his Secretary of State Cy Vance—"Spider" to club members—and his HEW Secretary Joe Califano, were ordered to resign before they could ascend to the Cabinet.

The banned club gallantly rallied from the blow, and tried to fling itself into the spirit of what was plainly a temporary era. Its Carter Inauguration Day special invitation urged its blue-blooded members: "Y'all come! Bring your Ladies and Youngst'rs for Peanut Soup 'n' Clams, $5 . . ."

Late in the Carter Administration, when the president hired sophisticated Washington lawyer and club member Lloyd Cutler to try to repair the hopeless mess at the White House, Cutler was willing to take almost every privation. He did not mind the $250,000 salary cut. He laughed at the $300 annual expense allowance for his entire staff. He was willing to toss in the towel on his business connections; without a whimper he abandoned a plush suite on K Street for a squalid office in the bowels of the West Wing. But he stoutly refused to drop out of the Metropolitan Club.

It has all the best prejudices. Club members do not wish to hear, except on very rare social occasions, the tinkling laughter of women. When the tender gender is reluctantly admitted, en masse, for events like the Winter Dinner Dance, the club makes a great fuss: it decks out the gents with a saucy little sign saying "Ladies." Then, to complete the hospitable illusion, it packs the porcelain pissoirs with fragrant mauve-and-white hyacinths. Even at such an event, risk of inadvertent access by the wrong sort is cut to the bone: not only are tickets issued for dinner placement; they are also issued for the drawing room in which one should sit for cocktails beforehand.

"Never know who'll tag along with some people and pin you in a corner." explained one member.

The Chevy Chase Country Club is another WASP's nest of pride, prejudice and Old Washington access. One out-of-town member, a distant relation of mine who had not visited her club for twenty years, arrived one morning without fanfare. The doorman greeted her simply: "Mornin', Miz Brown."

That is what Chevy Chase Club members expect.

What they do not expect are people of the wrong sort intruding on their serene retreat.

Aspiring members, even those like Hugh Sidey of *Time,* must be sponsored by entrenched upper-crusters like Clark Clifford and Stu Symington, and still run a cruel gauntlet. Brigadier General Godfrey McHugh, who was President Kennedy's air force aide, was reportedly blackballed by a member whose dog had been bitten by McHugh's dog.

Jews are not warmly welcomed. Henry Kissinger's membership, though pushed by both Symington and Henry's old foe from the Senate, William Fulbright, took more than six months to push through.

Of course there are other clubs. The F Street Club, where the Reagans chose to entertain the city's high-flyers before their inauguration in order to emphazise the difference between theirs and the Carters' style, is the club of choice for moneyed Old Washington. Senators and congressmen often crash parties at the F Street Club. It was founded by a woman, so has no sex discrimination. You must not expect to read much about it. Its members felt shamefully overexposed after the Reagans came in, and reestablished its iron rule: no press, ever; and no photographers, except at members' weddings.

The Federal City Club was founded in the Kennedy Era to make room for those who disapprove of the prejudices of the other clubs, including many newspapermen of principle. Of course, many others react like Groucho Marx: who wants to join a club that wants me as a member?

The only club that wants you as a member no matter what is the one through which you give money to your political party. Republicans buy access to their leaders via the $10,000-a-year membership in the Eagles, a group that supports Republican candidates for the Senate. The Democrats have something similar: the Senate Democratic Leadership Circle, chaired by Sen. Alan Cranston. For $15,000 a year, 164 members get to rub notions with the Democratic mighty at four big sessions a year. These currently dwell gloomily on Reaganomics and the Republican defense posture, but also offer lively parties with at least 35 Senators in attendance. They are mostly for out-of-towners who pay to talk to Teddy Kennedy and hear George Mitchell of Maine talk about his first filibuster. Snoozing on an army cot next to John Warner, he said, "I knew it wasn't too bad if John Warner'd give up a night with Liz Taylor to be with me."

Lots of laughs.

But the sincere access-hunter paddles warily in political waters.

Washington old-timers hastily detach themselves from any political commitment the minute their side loses an election. These days, if you call Robert Strauss, the most powerful Democrat long before Carter and probably the most powerful Democrat of the future, he will sigh heavily and say, "Ah'm not a politician, now. Ah'm a lawyer."

This tactful evasion is most important in your club life.

The Woman's National Democratic Club, for example, is extremely popular at the beginning of Democratic administrations and in the waning years of Republican ones.

It is disaster to join at any other time.

Nancy Reagan's social secretary, Muffie Brandon, had the misfortune to apply for membership in the summer of 1980, just before Reagan's election. She was sponsored by Pamela Harriman, wife of the Democrats' grand old man Averell Harriman; also by Maddy Kalb, mate of newsman Marvin Kalb, and Karen Mayer, married to a lawyer in Lloyd Cutler's law firm. Of course she was accepted. It happened just before Reagan won the election. Imagine her horror when she was offered this excellent job with the Reagans. What could she do? The only sensible solution: withdraw. She approached the club with her withdrawal request, which had a hilarious proviso attached: nobody must gossip about her having joined. Of course, nobody could talk of anything else for months.

An excellent hunting ground for access during the reign of either party is the golf course of the Congressional Country Club. There, Republicans are always in season; yet Tip O'Neill swings his way around the course like a woolly mammoth, and caddies regularly flee the approach of former Maine Senator Ed Muskie, who almost never tips.

Tipping members at Congressional are tended lovingly: a doctor who beat a goose to death on the golf course with his club was suspended for two months, and considered severely punished. Another member, who attacked the locker attendant with his eight-iron, was penalized with a two-drink limit at the club bar.

Nowadays, most of Washington's WASPiest clubs seem to have Latin help. All are occasionally raided by Immigration. At a raid at one of the very best, to the surprise of members who were not there that day, only three illegal immigrants were nabbed. Members who happened to be present knew that, meanwhile, the ladies' john was jammed solid with hairy-legged birds roosting in the stalls. The club's sauna was packed tight as a sardine can with swarthy young men, sweating in their birthday suits. And the cook's station wagon, laden with a happy gang singing "La Cucaracha," was taking a long, scenic tour of the surrounding countryside. Members are passionately loyal to their own, even if they're not *exactly* their own.

Down a notch or two, Pisces, a club in Georgetown, gives access to the night-owl, new-money, good-time set. It was opened in 1976 on the site of the Sundown, a kinky disco, by a man named Peter Malatesta. (His claim to fame: Bob Hope's nephew, Spiro Agnew's gofer, and, for a while, a deputy assistant secretary for tourism at the Commerce Department.) Wyatt Dickerson, husband of Lyndon Johnson's favorite newswoman, was a principal, too. Sister Parrish of New York designed it with a two-story cinderblock waterfall, of which socialite Anne Vanderpool said, "It looks like my basement after a heavy rain." Wheelers and dealers go there to enjoy themselves. The doorman has spurned the likes of William Randolph Hearst, and daughter Patty Hearst, and told big Hollywood stars "I don't care who you are."

"Dreadful for them," sighed one Piscean. "But nice for us." Several clubs of this sort have been born and died, but Pisces soldiers on. The property it is on has been owned by Tongsun Park, the central figure in Korean scandals; he also has had a lot to do with the George Town Club, a pleasant, panelled, old-fashioned club very popular with members of the Reagan Administration.

Those seeking access to the stuffier troglodytes of Washington join the Sulgrave Club. Scholars, explorers, scientists et al, the Cosmos Club. ("Let's whoop it up!" cries an invitation to members for its big hoopla, which turns out to be a 5 to 7 P.M. eggnog party on New Year's Eve.) The National Press Club is populated by journalists, flacks, and, probably, spies. Much of the working press belongs to the rival Washington Press Club.

The University Club is not political in character, but during the Carter Administration the plumbing was stopped up with peanut shells on several occasions. Its ethical challenge these days seems to be whether or not to admit women as members. (Members' wives may stay as guests, provided they race straight through the door and immediately retire to the fourth-floor guest quarters.) Perhaps microwaves are to blame. The club is nestled close to the bosom of the Soviet Embassy, the top of which bristles with unpleasant-looking aerials, and the Washington *Post,* at which about half of the aerials seem too be aimed. The problems appear to be the club's pool, where the great minds of the western world frisk and splash as bare as babes, and a nude slumber room. There seems to be much nudity. A writer named Art met members of both the Federal City Club and the University Club by becoming a masseur. After that, he went on to write campaign material for a vice-presidential candidate.

"Art has access to everyone who's anyone, at least til they put their clothes on," it was said.

Prepare for a shock. Some people are involved in charity benefits in Washington for conscience' sake; but an awful lot are there for something completely different: access.

Charity balls, fairs, parties, auctions and marathons crowd the calendar in Washington. The president's, vice-president's and Cabinet members' wives lend their names to various causes to raise funds; their husbands attend the events with them.

Because of this, the most avid supporters of many charities are lobbyists. Washington charity balls, sometimes costing as much as $500 a ticket, are swarms of the accessers and the accessees. The big three are the Symphony Ball, the Meridian House Ball, and the Opera Ball.

There is a standard technique for getting on the circuit: you check *Dossier* magazine, the glossy local social magazine, to see who is chair of the upcoming ball your first year; you telephone that person and ask to be invited; you go; you make yourself charming. The second year, your spangled little slippers neatly in the door, you offer to be on the ball's committee. You are now launched.

Some people support literally dozens of causes, for access' sake.

You get the kind of good time you pay for. There are different levels of participation in almost every charity membership. If you decide to support the Smithsonian Institution, for example, you can pay a small amount and get announcements of events and the magazine; a larger amount will get you invited to smaller receptions; a generous amount will get you invited to private dinners and rather glittery parties. The same applies to the Kennedy Center, where Friends and the Golden Circle are the high-powered access spots.

Smaller endeavors—Washington Project for the Arts, New Playwright's Theater, Arena Stage—offer a good time and a lively crowd.

Of course your charitable contributions are mostly tax-deductible, even if you are having a good time.

Preferably, you'll choose a cause compatible with your nature.

If you are swathed in furs, for example, you will not hang out with animal lovers.

One Christmas there was almost bloodshed at the very social Junior League. Honorary chair of a two-day benefit event at the Mayflower Hotel was Mrs. Roger Stevens, wife of the head of the Kennedy Center for the Performing Arts. Cristine Stevens is a passionate animal lover. Her most memorable party had been one to which guests came as endangered species. Philip Geyelin of the

Washington *Post* wore a dog-fur hat to the event, and was unpopular for weeks.

Local furriers had promised to show their finest wares in the League's charity event at a fashion display. A New York firm had contributed an exquisite white fox boa for the silent auction.

The battle began. Opposite Mrs. Stevens' portrait in the League's catalog she placed a full-page Animal Welfare ad. It showed a wretched fox, one pathetic gnawed-off paw gripped mercilessly in a black steel trap. Copies of her book, *Facts About Furs,* larded with even grislier illustrations, were brought in as door prizes.

The fur people threatened to back out. The fight raged for days. Ladylike compromise was reached: Mrs. Stevens withdrew her book from the door-prize list; the fur people did not show furs with the fashion shows. But the tension left some socialites deeply traumatized: they now go to New York to buy furs.

If you are anti-gun, you will not wish to support the National Rifle Association. Are you viscerally committed to the other side? You might want to hurl your weight behind the National End Handgun Violence Week. But suppose you do not wish to alienate some excellent contacts whose access you have cultivated carefully, who are on the NRA's side of the fence?

One local woman in this dilemma did not join the Week. But every day throughout it, she walked her small white poodle to do his business on the manicured lawn of the National Rifle Association headquarters.

*"An old desk of Speaker Sam Rayburn's; a 1905 tennis racquet found at the White House with the initials T.R. whittled in; Bella Abzug's hat; Mo Udall's speeches; an uncontested divorce; a pornographic cake delivered in a plain brown-paper wrapper; and Ronald Reagan's gubernatorial jelly-bean jar, emblazoned with the Great Seal of California."*

   —ITEMS BID ON BY A LOBBYIST AT VARIOUS
   AUCTIONS IN WASHINGTON

Almost every charity in Washington, sooner or later, holds auctions. Among the items auctioned off, and blissfully tax-deductible is, of course, access.

Washingtonians bid on luncheons with White House officials in the White House mess; luncheons in the Senate dining room with senators like Larry Pressler; at the National Gallery of Art with its director J. Carter Brown, and with humorous, serious, social and political columnists. High prices have been paid for a wine-tasting at Sen. Tom Eagleton's, a moose roast at a Rockefeller's; a cocktail soirée for thirty aboard a million-dollar yacht; a day at the track with racing writer Andy Beyer; opportunities to editorialize in *The Washingtonian* magazine; and all the beans you can pick on Mrs. Drew Pearson's farm.

Extremely well-heeled Washingtonians offer their houses and grounds for charity benefits, too. It is unwise for access-seekers to rely on these events. A loud wail went up at one $500-a-head fund-raiser thrown by the wife of a grand old powerhouse on her grounds. Guests knew it was outdoors, and that her inaccessible husband would stay within. Several planned a foray to the john, during which they could "accidentally" beard the old man. Horrors. She had locked the mansion's doors and rented port-a-potties for the lawn.

"Wouldn't have come if I thought I couldn't snoop in the house and talk to the old man," complained one critic, emerging irritably from the port-a-potty.

The prey was seen grinning broadly through the french doors as the last guest left.

Some people successfully gain access by pretending to be something else.

In the short term, this works quite well.

Respected author Joseph Goulden *(The Super-Lawyers* and *Korea: The Untold Story)* found it impossible to get embassy personnel to talk to him unless he told them who he was "with." He learned to say, "The New Delhi *Times*" or "The Freeport, Louisiana *Journal,*" depending on the embassy. They talked.

Visiting firemen lending themselves last names like Rockefeller or

Mellon often make reservations in the better restaurants, and enjoy the service thoroughly.

Long-term deceptions, perpetrated in the name of access, are pathetically common. Newcomers sometimes invent elaborate backgrounds to ease access. Often, these work for a while. Perhaps out of habit, Washington takes its newcomers at their face value, unless glaring inconsistencies surface, for four-year stretches.

One unfortunate lobbyist declared himself rich, of impeccable breeding, and from a northern state. He invited the cream of Washington freeloaders to elegant and expensive dinner-dances at a club; he proposed marriage to the daughter of an Old Washingtonian. A few night later, he pushed his male lover through a window. He telephoned his new friends in the press. There had been an accident to an intruder at his house, he said; please don't report it. He was roundly mocked when he tried to pick up another lover at a gay bar. He went home and shot himself. His whole life had been fabricated.

"Barons" sporadically surface—dating rich girls, saying things like "Didn't we meet in St. Moritz in '69?" pulling the wool over the eyes of men who are on the hustle themselves, and being invited to balls by society ladies. They have a merry time, and then slink away with no harm done when unveiled.

Another type of push involves no deception. It is sweet old-fashioned chutzpah. It often comes after success. In this strange, lonely town where all attention is focused on the present power, something is missing in the lives of those who live here as they would in other towns. They must make their own fame.

It's not considered odd in Washington to create a memorial to a loved one while still alive—even if the loved one is yourself.

A Washington lawyer, who works for the Kennedy Center, is determined to immortalize himself with a plaque there. He urged a bill creating the plaque through the House of Representatives, thanks to access to congressmen. Then he cornered Sen. Charles Percy at a prayer breakfast to suggest that he support the plaque in the Senate, and phoned social acquaintance Sen. John Warner to ask him to do likewise.

If the plaque is not there yet, it will be.

Perseverance is a Washington virtue. Al Eisele, who was Vice-President Mondale's press secretary, lists it as the ultimate key to the city of Washington.

"At heart, it's a very small town. There's no Darwinian principle. The fittest don't survive: you get what you want simply and almost exclusively by perseverance," he says.

To maintain access through thick and thin, you must develop several small-town virtues.

Victor Kamber, a highly successful labor lobbyist, no matter which party is in power, lists three: "Credibility: your word is your bond. Humor: you must be able to laugh at yourself. And generosity: don't step on other people on your way up. Here, they don't forget. They'll get you later."

Washington women can gain access in several ways. One of them is sex. It is done here exactly as it has been done throughout human history in every capital of the world. (See chapter "Sex and Sensibility.") What, you may say, about professional, egalitarian access, much as a man of equal rank might hope for? Well. Ha-ha. (See chapter, "Shall we Join the Ladies?") Finally, there is the special and admirable Washington Order of the Grand Pushy Dame.

Frankie Welch, a local dress and fabric designer, is a Grand Pushy Dame. She has designed scarves for practically every candidate, president and cause in Washington, from Lady Bird Johnson's Discover America scarf to Pat Nixon's inaugural scarf. When Jerry Ford was president, he once boomed loudly at a governors' luncheon: "All the ladies' scarves courtesy of Frankie Welch." She designed Betty Ford's ballgown, Jimmy Carter's peanut scarf, wallpaper for the office of the head of the Veterans Administration, and scarves, tote bags and umbrellas for the Reagan inaugural. "Only winners," she says smiling brightly, "and Hubert Humphrey."

Maria Fisher, a pretty octogenarian one-man-band of a lady who used to sing light opera in the Eisenhower White House, is a mistress of the art. She puts on an Ear Ball every year, to benefit the deaf and give scholarships to young musicians via her Beethoven Society. She moves swiftly and with certainty. Popular news anchorman David Schoumacher careened his car into the back of hers on the road one day and bowled her into the bushes. She emerged from the foliage without a glance at the dents in her car. Wagging her finger, she tackled the shaken newsman: "David Schoumacher! I want you on my ball committee." She got him.

It is common to overhear Henry Kissinger discussing his diet's fiber content or Teddy Kennedy confiding his vitamin intake to another Grand Pushy Dame, health writer Trudi Engel. Sporting dazzlingly matched sequined clothes, hats and shoes, she hits every major event in the city. She simply sidles up to the mighty and inquires about their digestion. This has gone on for years. By now, people rather enjoy discussing their intestinal workings and batting about the advantages of papaya, laetrile and never sitting with your legs crossed. (That way lies heart trouble, you see.)

A Pushy Dame named Evelyn Y. Davis has access to government officials and the chairmen of the board of every major company in the country. She buys stock, thus gaining entree to stockholders' meetings. There, she harangues the corporations' officers. Later, she telephones chairmen of the board and presidents at home. She writes a newsletter in which she attacks those who are rude to her—and charges them $94 per copy, with a minimum of two copies—refuses to deal with "flunkies," and holds men with million-dollar salaries in terror. Several companies now plan their annual meetings in far-flung spots around the country on the same day, calling it Evelyn Roulette. The loser gets her. She is acutely aware of the revolving door that spins between government and big business. For years, she has had access, if not popularity, at most White House and Cabinet news conferences.

One New Jersey denizen manages to push herself into the bosom of every administration. Helen Boehm's late husband founded the factory which manufactures decorative porcelain birds. Mrs. Boehm has frequent access simply by presenting to the White House or State Department—or making available to them very cheaply—such birds. They are given to heads of state. When Richard Nixon parted the bamboo curtain, the first gift received by the astonished mainland Chinese was a pair of gigantic china swans, courtesy of Mrs. B. The lady urged her Prince Charles Rose and Lady Diana Rose porcelain floral centerpiece as the official United States wedding present for that royal couple. No such luck. (Mrs. Reagan had chosen a Steuben glass bowl.)

Undeterred, Mrs. Boehm promptly gave the bride and groom the centerpiece herself: transatlantic access in action.

Most ambassadors and their wives have learned access through giving.

Charity ball chairmen now commonly ask embassies to hold dinners before elaborate balls. This, they feel, gives ballgoers their money's worth in glitter. Embassies oblige, to cement their relations with the social upper crust.

Socialist countries jump aboard the glittery wagon along with oligarchies, dictatorships, kingdoms, republics and empires. The Soviets finally succumbed in 1980, and became one of the twenty-one embassies tossing a very non-proletarian dinner party before the Meridian House Ball. Washington's diamond-studded plutocrats battled for the privilege of supping with the Soviets.

"Anywhere else is Siberia," explained one.

The high point probably came when the Communist Chinese were charmingly prevailed upon to host a tea for debutantes. Mary-Stuart Montague Price, who rounds up groups of debs each year and shows their parents a good time, Washington-style, pulled off this little coup. His Excellency, who perhaps had presumed that debutantes played some sport like ping-pong, wised up by teatime. Tea à la Chinoise was served to the rosy-cheeked darlings and their sable-drenched mamas, but, said a spokesperson, "His Excellency cannot be present."

On the whole, embassies are willing to oblige almost any polite request. Anyone presentable can angle an invitation to a none-too-exclusive affair by calling the social secretary. People who crave fancier fare make friends with the social secretary at their choice of embassy, and take her to lunch. Men who wish to be invited back often to embassy dinners must flirt with the ambassador's wife, if possible. That is what makes a charming dinner partner.

*"Ah hurt mah back playin' paddleball with George
Bush."*
     —REP. SONNY MONTGOMERY, EXPLAINING WHY
     HE WAS OUT OF COMMISSION


There is a type of access called Saturday access, which is available
to those who do not mind surrendering their weekends to the hunt.
This can be through restaurants or neighborhoods. Restaurant Saturday Access began when Ronald Reagan told his first Saturday
Cabinet meeting that he *really* planned to stick to a five-day week.
"So if there is a Saturday Cabinet session," he wound up, "it will go
on without me."

A lot of White House and Cabinet business does in fact get done
on Saturdays, and those who do it nowadays lunch at Mel Krupin's
restaurant. That is where sincere access-seekers go for lunch on
Saturday.

Neighborhood Saturday Access is the reason people live in
Georgetown. The Right Kind of people live there, no matter what
the administration.

Specific Access to Reaganists is, of course, at the Watergate. You
will ramble the Watergate Safeway with Reagan pals like the Charles
Wicks; you will slide up and down in elevators and wink at senators
like John Warner or Bob Dole.

The most hungrily sought apartments there, you should know,
have river views. They are on the tips of Watergate South and West.
People paid, in 1982, between $160,000 and $300,000 for a one-
bedroom apartment. (The best addresses, in the South building, are
apartment numbers that end with 04, 05 and 06. John Warner
bought an 06.) An apartment of 1,700 square feet in Watergate has
sold for $535,000.

Naturally, at those prices, a certain standard of behavior is expected of residents.

Shortly after the California contingent moved in, all residents
found little flyers in their mailboxes, requesting joggers not to use the
passenger elevators:

*Many of our Residents have complained about Offensive*
*Body Odors on the part of joggers. It would not be*
*unreasonable to ask these Athletes (whom all of us*
*sedentary people so much admire) to use the service*
*elevator. Also, our rules and regulations call for*
*Appropriate Attire in the lobby and passenger elevators.*
*We recognize that contemporary mores permit and*
*sanction casual attire in our modern-day society.*
*However, it is preferred, at least in* our *building, that*
*people in shorts, etc. should use the service elevators and*
*service entrance to our building . . .*

Two final points to keep in mind: one is that some people to whom
you seek access may be trying to dodge you. Others are simply in
passionate pursuit of privacy. You will not catch New York Rep. Jim
Scheuer on the paddleball courts. He is busily lapping up and down
his pool in the buff every day, giving the neighbors' housemaids a
treat. Rep. Pat Schroeder finds her solitary recreation roller-skating
down the streets of Alexandria. Former DNC Chairman John White
was notable for turning to his wife at parties while surrounded by
suitors and murmuring, "Honey, it's almost ten o'clock. We better
get on home, or we're gonna miss 'Love Boat.' "

Media heavies deliberately jog at dawn or predawn, to avoid recognition, mostly along Rock Creek Parkway by the Kennedy Center.
The last time I looked, there was Bill Plante of CBS.

The other point to remember is that charity events are not designed to give you too good a time. They are to raise funds, cut taxes,
and swell your access. The last group who confused the issue decided
to hold a black-tie benefit showing of *Behind the Green Door,* the
popular porno movie, for Washington's upper crust.

Invitations were mailed. Several enthusiastic acceptances came in.
(One, from a certain George, said "Don't mention this to Lily."
Another, from Lily, said "I'm not telling George.") It all fell apart.
No charity could be persuaded to accept their ill-gotten gains, about
three thousand dollars.

The affair was cancelled. Some people who got the invitations never again spoke to those who mailed them out—or, at least, almost never. Not until they needed access again.

That is how it works.

# Hey, That's Mine:
# A Peep at Crime
# in the Capital

*"One way to make sure crime doesn't pay would be to let the government run it."*
—RONALD REAGAN, DALLAS, 1967

THERE IS a story of a French diplomat jogging through Rock Creek Park, the bosky stretch that slices through Northwest Washington, shielding the unlovely from the lovely parts of town.

As he panted lightly along the path beside the stream, Pierre saw a sinister-looking man running toward him on the same path.

The man jostled him as they passed. Trotting on, the Frenchman felt a wave of apprehension. He fumbled in his jogging-suit pocket. His wallet was missing.

Spinning around on his Adidases, he raced after the jostler, and pinned him against a tree.

"Give me ze wallet!" he cried.

The man, looking appropriately humiliated, reached into his rear pocket and handed it over.

With a proud snort, the diplomat spun again on his sneakers and retraced his route, jogging righteously back to his fashionable apartment near the Shoreham.

Once there, he headed straight for the shower. Sitting on the elegant marble vanity nearby was his wallet.

"As far as I know from first-hand experience," Pierre is quoted as saying, "I am ze only criminal in zis town."

If it's true, Pierre is lucky. Crime in Washington is absurd.

Washingtonians live like a people under siege. They dare not walk their streets at night. They fear to board an almost empty bus. They click down the locks of doors in taxicabs as they drive through neighborhoods where youths loiter on corners. They scuttle from their cars to their houses like frightened mice.

No one is immune. Livingston Biddle, as chairman of the National Arts Endowment, was mugged in the middle of fashionable Georgetown, slammed up against a car by two men holding a knife and gun respectively. As the wife of the chief of police stopped in K-Mart, somebody stole the battery from her car. Ambassador Robert White got back from strife-torn El Salvador without a scratch, even though terrorists had aimed a bazooka into his office there. In the shadow of the State Department, in fashionable Foggy Bottom, he was mugged at gunpoint.

Of course, Washington is not unique. Representative Bob Michel, now the House minority leader, was mugged in Washington in 1978. Outrage over the crime rate of the capital city crammed his home-town Peoria papers for weeks. The following year, Mrs. Michel was mugged in Peoria.

And while the FBI director was addressing the rent-a-cops of the National Association of Industrial Security Agents at the Plaza Hotel in Detroit, somebody was smashing open a locked case and stealing all *their* door prizes.

But crime's persistence occupies a niche in the thoughts of all Washingtonians at all times, under all circumstances, in all neighborhoods.

President Reagan's first choice for assistant secretary for Mine Safety and Health, Bill DuBois, drove to Washington from Nevada in a trailer with his wife. The pair parked their trailer outside town and set about hunting for a house.

They found a pleasant nest in an attractive neighborhood. Being sociable Nevadans, they went calling. Neighbors were pleasant. They remarked that the previous tenants of the house had left after being mugged and robbed.

Taken aback, the Du Boises bustled to their trailer, parked in the suburbs near the University of Maryland. It had been broken into.

The pair had a date to meet Mr. Du Bois' new boss, Reagan Labor Secretary Ray Donovan, a couple of days later; they had also scheduled an appointment with Vice-President Bush.

They did not make the dates. Instead, they slammed shut the door of their trailer and headed for the hills.

A polite letter turning down Safety and Health arrived a few days later.

The fact is, Washington is neither safe nor healthy.

If it is bad for the upper-income Washingtonians, it is even worse for the lower-. The day-to-day terror of casual street crime in some parts of Washington, a city of just over half a million households, cannot even be imagined by the locals who are cloistered in security-conscious Northwest enclaves, delivered door-to-door in limousines, or those who scurry home to quiet suburban retreats at day's end.

But you must not imagine that the criminal heart beats only in the breasts of the poor.

At Washington's Social Safeway—the Georgetown branch where the rich shop—the manager is often forced to move the saffron, truffles and caviar into his office to avoid the sticky fingers of some of his clientele.

At Clyde's, the hip Georgetown bar and restaurant where Nice People go and the staff comes from respectable families, each staffer must submit to lie detector tests. These are to ensure he has not made off with kitchen equipment, dining room furnishings, uniforms, knickknacks, T-shirts, ashtrays, gift certificates or money from the tip bucket.

"How can a waiter make an honest living?" inquired one of their number.

There are the usual burglaries.

There are also the unusual ones. When the house of columnist Rowland Evans was broken into, his wife's jewels were left completely untouched. Rifled and stolen: the jewels of her maid. Friends scratched their heads trying to figure out whose taste was off-key—Kay's, the burglar's or her maid's.

Hunt-country gentleman Randy Reed was robbed not only of his coin collection but of his silk top hunting hat.

Difficulty is no object for the sincere burglar. An airline executive's $30,000, 600-pound Waterford crystal chandelier, held to the ceiling by tow-truck chains, was sawn down from its moorings without dropping a single prism.

The District of Columbia, obviously concerned about its reputation as the crime capital of the free world, periodically launches ambitious let's-cut-the-crime-rate movements. A handsome anticrime flag was designed for one of these. At one precinct, Old Glory and the new anticrime banner flew proudly together to announce the new era. Both were stolen.

Appropriating objects made of cloth is an act apparently without the usual social stigma; it is done in respectable territory by respectable people without a second thought. When friends helped Joan Mondale unpack her pottery purchases from China after her 1979 trip, they could not help noticing that they were rolled in chic red-and-white towels emblazoned "Kwangtung Guest House."

Sixteen pairs of undershorts belonging to Victor Lasky, the author of *It Didn't Start With Watergate,* vanished from the laundry at the Watergate, where he then lived.

Griffin Bell, Carter's attorney general, had his socks snatched as he languished in a sauna at the Federal City Club.

The FTD man who brought flowers to a glamorous Capitol Hill reception wearing a bright yellow Mercury outfit removed his yellow tights, size 40, in the changing room. They were still warm when a base tights-fancier made off with them.

Faced with more formal thievery, Washington's honest citizen is depressingly passive. Only a few—often those who work with the law and see its failings—take enough of a personal interest to try to stem the tide.

As burglars raced down P Street in Georgetown one day clutching typewriters, a man in a three-piece suit sprang from his car to chase them down; he turned out to be Don Santarelli, who rose from Nixon's assistant attorney general to become Johnny Carson's lawyer.

While working on a series about crime and punishment, Tim O'Brien, ABC's Supreme Court reporter, picked up his car at a parking lot one day and noticed that a hubcap was missing.

"So sue me," said the attendant.

Tim did. He picked up $35 in small claims court.

While prevention is tricky, the District of Columbia police department runs splendid undercover "sting" operations to entrap Washington's busy burglar population.

After these, for several days, hundreds of Washingtonians file companionably through police headquarters, identifying valuables fenced to undercover cops, admiring each others' stolen possessions, and sometimes discovering that an object stolen from one had been stolen—long before its penultimate purchase by the fake fence—from another.

These festive and satisfactory occasions are usually followed by a drop in the city's burglary rate.

Although books are seldom among "sting" items recovered, some works of limited literary interest are occasionally stolen, too.

The *Green Book,* Washington's social list, is most often pocketed or bagged as a guide to the better sort of burglees and their summer-vacation migratory habits.

Kennedy memorabilia, too, are popular. Kennedy in-law Sargent Shriver's leather-bound, 300-page *History of the Shriver Family* vanished from his house.

A *National Enquirer* reporter who spent many weary hours trailing the Kennedys was robbed too: his television, stereo, Nikon camera and radar-detecting device were left strictly alone. What vanished were his copious notes, along with eighty or so tape recordings of limited interest.

It is street crime, however, that pads its sneakered path into the nightmares of most Washingtonians.

Almost everyone has a story to tell.

Washington artist Richard Copeland, wearing his painting togs, was checking out the light in the L'Enfant Plaza parking garage when two nasty-looking dudes cornered him and demanded, "Give us your wallet."

"That won't do you any good," said Dick, opening his fist to reveal forty-seven cents in change. "I'm panhandling."

The meaner of the thugs grabbed the money.

"Hey man," whined the artist. "I could really use a quarter."

The dude gave it back to him.

Copeland, however, has now gone off to paint in Oklahoma.

# Money Matters:
# Poor Little Rich Folks
# in Washington

*"The Hon. David A. Stockman requests the pleasure of your company in paying tribute to Dale McOmber for his role in overseeing $4,236,531,000,000 in federal expenditures during his tenure at the Office of Management and Budget."*

> —INVITATION RECEIVED IN MID-1981 BY FRIENDS
> OF MCOMBER, OMB'S LONGEST-LASTING
> BUREAUCRAT

*"Can you give me $1.50?"*
*"My dear good man, I saw my son giving you fifty cents just a moment ago."*
*"Yeah, but I never accept less than $2."*

> —DIALOGUE BETWEEN PANHANDLER AND
> MATRON OUTSIDE A WASHINGTON GROCERY

ALL AROUND the country, people glared at their newspapers and gaped over the breakfast table.

"It says here that White House feller Michael Deaver can't get by on $60,662 a year. What's wrong with those guys in Washington?"

Here's what's wrong. Everyone in Washington must bounce between three totally different concepts of money: the Big Picture, the Small Picture and the Knock-'em-Dead Show.

Every day the newspapers bulge with budget figures. Hundreds of billions of theoretical dollars are being juggled and squeezed and hurled around. This is the Big Picture.

Everyone who has anything at all to do with government—typists, admirals, congressmen, toilers in the poultry division of the Department of Agriculture, lobbyists, secretaries, journalists—talks and writes in Big Picture sums.

The Small Picture is the actual salaries these people get.

It is $60,662.50 for a congressman. An average of $13,500 a government secretary. It's $28,964 (union scale) for a Washington *Post* reporter, and $52,000 for the head of the poultry division, and so on.

These seem like perfectly adequate salaries for ordinary living. Most places, they'd be considered generous.

But Washington is not most places.

You see, Washington salaries are not only compared to the bizarre apogees of the budget. They are compared to the Knock-'em-Dead Show—the huge salaries and expenses of lobbyists who swarm the city.

The lobbyists, in Washington to woo and influence the mighty, spend huge tax-deductible treasuries given to them specifically for that purpose.

Representatives of industries and nations throw money at parties, expense-account luncheons, extravagant offices, hunting lodges to take officials to for more efficient wooing, cars and limousines, charity balls and auctions, call girls or boys, club memberships, bribes, tax accountants, "desirable residences," liquor and gifts.

On top of that, their salaries must be big enough to maintain clothing suitable for the wives of such influential men, and pay expensive school fees. Their children attend St. Alban's or Cathedral or Madeira or Sidwell Friends or Gerogetown Day, because Washington public schools are so appalling and besides, the Right Kind of children don't go to them. Not to mention orthodontists, psychiatrists, landscape gardeners, cooks, caterers, maids, tennis instructors, exercise teachers, florists and pool cleaners.

*". . . and Henry's net worth is only $900,000!"*
—NANCY KISSINGER, MOURNFULLY, IN THE
MIDDLE OF A HUSH THAT SUDDENLY FELL AT
THE OLD SANS SOUCI RESTAURANT, SEPTEMBER
1979

*"Twenty-five grand? Hell, Ah give twenty-five grand for a good table!"*
—ROBERT STRAUSS, OVERHEARD AT A PARTY

Sixty grand? Hell, Michael Deaver sees people giving sixty grand for a good table every day.

He sees the Eagles, a group of men who give $10,000 a year each to the Republican cause. He sees the members of the President's Committee of the Citizens for the Republic, who give $5,000 a year to help push Republican congressional candidates. (This is one of former Reagan aide Lyn Nofziger's major projects, since he left the White House.) He sees that the last Reagan-Bush campaign cost more than thirty million dollars. (Including $2,500 to Michael Reagan for a consulting fee, $12 for a Toledo Mud Hens baseball cap and $250 for the oompah band of Chester, Pennsylvania.) He sees people pouring in to $1,000-a-plate dinners, $2,000-a-plate dinners, $10,000-a-toss inaugural weeks.

No wonder he feels that Old Washington Squeeze. All the un-rich do.

To meet it, some congressmen and women practice law on the side. Three-fourths of the senators, who make $60,662.50 a year just like congressmen, pull themselves up to par with speaking fees.

They average about two thousand dollars a pop. A rather indignant article in the Washington *Post* pointed out that Sen. Richard Lugar made $8,500 for five speeches in a 30-hour period. Newspaper reporters earning $28,964 a year quite possibly don't know that some of their paper's own columnists, editors and executives pull in $8,500 for a single speech.

If you think that's a lot, consider that former President Gerald Ford, addressing the Cosmetologists and Hairdressers of America for thirteen minutes in 1980, got $13,000, and all he talked about was how terrible Jimmy Carter was. "He could have brought Betty so we could look at her hair," complained one of his listeners, unaware that for Betty to tag along costs another $5,000.

*"Jeez. For that amount of money, just knock out three jokes up front and cut it down to twenty minutes."*
—ART BUCHWALD, ADVISING A NEOPHYTE
SPEECH-GIVER IN A MEN'S ROOM AT THE
NATIONAL PRESS BUILDING

*"They don't like me, but they'll pay to see me."*
—RICHARD NIXON TO OHIO REPUBLICANS WHO
HAD ASKED HIM TO SPEAK AT A FUNDRAISER IN
1981

A lot of people in Washington are rich anyway; they came rich, and they'll go rich. People who gain high office often come from monied families.

During the 1980 term of the Supreme Court, now-retired Justice Potter Stewart, a multimillionaire, had to withdraw from fifty-one different cases. All would have provided conflicts of interest with his investments. Justice Lewis Powell withdrew from twenty-four.

On the other end of the scale is someone like Jeane Kirkpatrick, the ambassador to the United Nations. Naturally, she was invited to all the Reagan inauguration hoopla. Ticket prices were scaled to the

California millionaires, Eagles, and the Washington lobbying rich. She was a poorly paid Gerogetown University professor sending three kids to college.

"A hundred dollars a ticket! I just won't be able to go," she shrugged to a friend.

Ronald Reagan's California crowd is, to old-line Washingtonians, almost comically generous—with its own money.

Most rich Easterners would never dream of such a thing. They are generous only with other people's.

In fact, some of the finest pennypinchers have always been from the Washington side of the Great Divide.

As the bride of Sen. John Kennedy, young Jackie Kennedy found that she had far too many wedding presents she did not care for in 1953.

Did she give them to charity? Certainly not. We are talking here about a woman who was later to give her maid a uniform for Christmas. She bundled all the presents up in Jack's old winter underwear —all three hundred items, including Steuben ashtrays, bar accessories, silver traveling clocks, picture frames, the silver box with all the autographs of the Cabinet, bookends, linens, a lacquer tray with sterling inlay engraved JFK. Then, she toted them off to the Walter Reed Antique Shop run by the late Jack Traten in Bethesda.

"She got top dollar for them all," Traten's daughter, Caryl Traten Fisher, says. (Caryl kept Jack's labeled underwear for sentimental reasons.)

How do you think millionaires get that way?

A friend passed multi-multimillionaire Walter Annenberg standing patiently in a long line at Union Station shortly after the Reagan inauguration. He hadn't been able to ride Amtrak's club car, he explained. He was waiting for his $13 refund.

Clement Stone, when in town for the same event, tipped headwaiters a dollar.

The late Nelson Rockefeller, while in Washington, always had the worn collars on his blue oxford-cloth shirts removed, turned and sewn on again.

Old Money always practices clever little economies.

One Georgetown hostess has been known to buy masses of huge potted azalea bushes a day or so before a garden party from a local florist. The day after the party, she phones the florist: "Pick them up, please, and credit my account."

Two of Washington's *grandes dames* and luncheon hostesses to Nancy Reagan—Lorraine Cooper, wife of John Sherman Cooper, and Evangeline Bruce, widow of Ambassador David Bruce—pinch pennies by sharing a butler.

Washington always knows summer is here when a certain local millionaire fills his pool free, from the public water hydrant. A busy little bevy of rich Georgetown matrons buys extremely expensive sweaters from Garfinckel's, runs around to the Woolgatherer needle-craft shop, picks up wool and a few lessons in fancy stitchery, takes the sweaters back to the shop for credit, and knits its own.

*"I had this huge stockpile of Rely tampons, and they were suddenly declared unsafe. So I had the most marvelous idea. I made them all into little Christmas angels, with a few sequins and dabs of this and that, and wings from doilies. Really, they're quite adorable. That's what I gave everyone for Christmas last year."*
—ONE OF THE GEORGETOWN MATRONS

Into this strange temple of public extravagance and private stingi-ness wandered the Carters, like lambs to the slaughter. They didn't like to throw money around at all.

A model housewife for an inflationary age, Rosalynn Carter kept a watchful eye on nickels. Her White House domestic staff was embarrassed to shop from her grocery lists, as she always requested the very cheapest brands. She made her own clothes, sometimes with fabrics from the G Street Remnant Shop. She did her Christmas shopping at discount stores like Evans Distributors in Rockville.

An admirable example for the ladies of Georgetown, yes. But it was in their public lives that Carterites were self-destructively cheeseparing.

For their very first trip abroad, in May 1977, the Carter entourage reserved seventy rooms at Claridges, the fashionable and expensive London hotel. After a little thought, and pondering their leader's image as a man who carried his own garment bag, they cancelled the reservations.

Instead, they went to the cheaper Brittanica Hotel. (With the exception of Alex Haig, who was unaccountably along on the ride and who always stays at Claridges.)

The Savoy Group, which owns Claridges, found itself suddenly stuck with seventy empty rooms.

Quietly and tastefully, it threatened to sue the United States for $10,000. It got the money. The taxpayer, who was told none of this, ended up forking over for two hotels instead of one.

In spite of his $50,000-a-year entertainment allowance, Jimmy Carter could not drop his tightwad habits. Not only did he bill congressmen for their breakfasts during his early days; in the final days of his last presidential campaign, a group of Democratic mayors was invited to fly with him from Pittsburgh to Rochester. A simple lunch was served on board. All thought they were doing the president a favor by making a show of support. Each mayor later received a bill: $180 for his fare, and $6.50 for lunch.

Buffalo Mayor James E. Griffin described the reaction of most mayors as "sore."

*Hello there, Mr. Deadbeat;*
*Know why I'm here?*
*It's bill-collectin' tiiiiiime.*
*It's bin a long time comin',*
*Almost a year*
*You haven't paid a diiiiime.*
    —LYRICS TO THE SINGING TELEGRAM SUNG IN
    WASHINGTON BY EASTERN ONION, TO THE TUNE
    OF "WON'T YOU COME HOME, BILL BAILEY"

A drab cheapskate cloud hung over the Carter White House from the beginning. Refreshments for guests were cheap; White House matchbooks were no longer left around for guests. Cleaning crews were invited to the staff Christmas party *if* they didn't mind having the time docked from their pay. Staffers' wives went uninvited. Senators and congressmen, accustomed to the rich, crested cards of lobbyists and earlier White Houses, were astonished to be invited to a White House picnic with cheese-colored mimeographed paper invitations. Once there, they were entertained by Rosalynn's old music teacher.

Neither Jimmy nor Rosalynn Carter, during their four years, once tried Washington's best restaurant, Le Lion d'Or. Finally, just after losing the election, but before the Reagan inauguration, they went.

Rosalynn's hairdresser took them. As they sat engulfing their *fruits de mer mousseline,* who should be ushered to the table directly in their line of vision but Hugh Sidey. The *Time* magazine columnist had just committed the unforgivable sin of writing that with the Reagans in power, class might return to the White House. Jimmy and Rosalynn's eyes glazed as they ignored him.

"I wondered whether to send over a bottle of wine," he said later.

Eivind, Rosalynn's hairdresser, paid the Carters' bill. He tipped generously.

The waiters were relieved. Carter staffers conventionally tipped about five percent in Washington restaurants. Waiters all over town had sighed wearily at the first twang of a Georgia accent for four years. Carter's Georgia friend Smith Bagley, a Reynolds tobacco heir, was known to the hatcheck girl at the Pisces Club as "Tip Badly." Hugh Carter, Jimmy's "Cousin Cheap" who was in charge of cost-cutting at the White House, did not tip at all. When, late in the administration, he married a beautiful stewardess, friends tittered that it was so that he could get the discount flights to Atlanta.

Doubtless, all must have been bitterly disappointed when their self-denial was not richly rewarded.

Traditionally, a high-ranking administration job is merely a prelude to the life hereafter: the job administration officials will get when their side loses.

For years, the high-profile jobs have led to far higher-paying lobbying jobs with industry; one is presumed to know the way Washington works.

Wonderful stories circulate about the worth of the mind that understands the machinations of Washington's Machiavels.

Clark Clifford, advisor to many presidents and once secretary of Defense, is held up as an inspiration to all.

There is a legend of Clifford's being reached by the head of a Midwestern company frantic about some adverse legislation brewing on Capitol Hill.

Clifford's advice supposedly arrived at the executive's office by mail: "Do nothing." Attached was a bill for $25,000.

The Midwesterner wrote back. Gee, he said. For $25,000, shouldn't he get a better and more detailed explanation? *Why* should he do nothing?

By return mail came the answer: "Because I say so." Another bill was attached, for $5,000.

(Clark hoots with laughter at this tale, told oft in print. He says he first heard it told fifty years ago—starring J. P. Morgan and Elihu Root.)

Lobbyists who cannot charge such fees must do what they can. Padding expenses is not unknown.

One successful lobbyist for a trade association turned in his gigantic monthly expense account as usual. Listed among its items was a fifty-dollar lunch with a local official. His boss happened to be looking over the expenses that month.

The name of the official caught his eye. Hadn't he spotted that name in the Washington *Star*'s obituary column a while back? In fact, hadn't the official been dead a week before that fifty-dollar lunch?

Indeed he had. Snipping the obituary from the old newspaper, he clipped it to the expense account and sent it back to the lobbyist. It came right back to him. The word "Lunch" was heavily pencilled out. In its place: "Flowers."

Even Abraham Lincoln padded as a Congressman, according to Rep. Paul Findley of Illinois. Findley riffled through hundreds of dusty files before concluding that Honest Abe had habitually fiddled with his travel vouchers between Springfield and Washington.

Trying to keep up an illusion of success when they are not rich, not on a huge expense account, not on the take, and not on the speaking circuit has driven Washingtonians to drink, suicide and exile.

A few years ago the Internal Revenue Service began to subscribe to *War Cry.* The Salvation Army's magazine lists the names of the dropouts, the lost sheep who end up in the soup kitchens of the Lord.

Every year, several of these turn out to be people who have fled the horrors of poverty, Washington-style. The IRS cares because, along with bills, they owe gigantic tax debts.

And some of those, before the fall, earned a lot more than Michael Deaver's $60,662 a year.

# FURLOUGH

# Getting Away: Escaping the Potomac Plague

*"God forbid that anyone will ever tell me that the city of Washington is my home. It is not. I detest it. I really do. I cannot think of another place to have a nation's capital in the world that is a worse place to live . . . We shorten our life span by coming to this town. As far as I am concerned, I know of no town—no town—that has a worse crime standard, a worse set of schools, a worse circumstance to live in and work in than the city of Washington. I do not care who knows it. I will tell everyone."*
    —SENATOR TED STEVENS OF ALASKA, DEBATING
    A $75-A-DAY HARDSHIP ALLOWANCE FOR
    SENATORS, IN 1982

THE VISITOR from India sat bolt upright in the cab, his eyes riveted in horror at the scene on the Mall.

"My goodness! What are those poor people running to?" he asked the driver.

At high noon, as far as the eye could see, rank upon rank of almost-naked joggers, streaming with sweat and rolling their eyes with fatigue, trotted through the ninety-eight-degree, stinking miasmic effluvium of a Washington midsummer day.

Panting and gasping among the Athenian-style monuments, they looked like a pack of exhausted Greek slaves bearing urgent messages to wrathful masters.

"They're not runnin' nowhere!" snorted the cabbie. "They're runnin' from their goddamn jobs. Makin' forty grand a year in air-conditioned offices bigger'n my house. Secretaries to get them coffee. Nothin' to do all day but screw around with the crossword puzzle and suck up my tax money. That's why they're runnin'."

A pessimistic assessment. But Washingtonians *do* run a lot. Some are pumping the appropriate elements through their cardiovascular systems. Some are seeking a spiritual getaway with Zen-tinted dedication.

Quite a lot are running off Washington stress.

Who can pinpoint the motives of the secretary of Agriculture, John Block? He rises at dawn every day to run like a deer through the silent city streets. On weekends he pelts along beside the Georgetown canal with his dog, Shadow, galloping at his heels and a score of serious runners thundering in his wake. On one catastrophic occasion, in midwinter 1982, the dog tumbled through the ice of the canal. The passionate runners formed a human chain to rescue him —with Block at the business end. Afterward, soaked to the skin in a freezing drizzle, the cortege headed by the secretary pelted onward for another nine miles.

The running getaway seems to have developed on both sides of party lines and right up the middle.

During the last administration, a high-ranking and laid-back staffer at the Senate Commerce Committee, aptly named Dick Dashbach, couldn't wait to get calls from the White House or Treasury asking for information.

"I'll run it right over," he'd cry.

"Don't worry, we'll be happy to send a messenger"

"No, no, I'll be right there."

Fascinated underlings at the receiving end would perch on the windowsill to await the inevitable vision—the track-shod, jogging-togged hotshot, panting and sweating, carrying his important envelope high like the Olympic torch.

Denizens of Capitol Hill on the whole prefer the gym to the jog for stress abatement. One congressman was briefly famous for liking to jog down the Hill, but requested a staffer to pick him up for the tiresome journey *back up* the Hill.

Senator William Proxmire, best-known for his "Golden Fleece" awards to wasters of tax money, is the patron saint of Senate jogging. He did it before it was fashionable.

Senator Alan Cranston, a dignified California Democrat with presidential aspirations, having shed his wheelchair-bound wife for a newer model, took up the sport himself fairly recently.

He can often be seen trotting along his home street of Constitution Avenue in what appears to be his underwear. One day a passerby noticed a thin, sweating, boxer-shorted figure, presumably a vagrant, jogging helter-skelter up the sidewalk, then stopping to crouch over a grass verge at streetside, plucking at weeds.

Believing that he was lying in wait to ask her for money, the passerby averted her gaze hastily and fell into deep conversation with an acquaintance.

"I see the senator's back from his jog and is cleaning up the block," observed the acquaintance.

Indeed he was.

It was before the dawn of the new age of limousines—and long before quite so many middle-aged men had keeled over with heart attacks halfway through their health regimens—that the pleasures of life afoot caught on in Washington.

Perhaps they flowered most profusely in the wake of Jimmy Carter's historic inaugural walk from the Capitol to the White House.

One local lobbyist immediately took on Kinney's shoes as a client.

He proposed to the House leadership that they all walk en masse from Capitol Hill to the White House for their big bimonthly meeting with the president, wearing, of course, Kinney's shoes.

What an inspiring sight it would be! Gigantic Tip O'Neill in loafers, shambling up Pennsylvania Avenue; lesser congressmen in lace-ups, slip-ons, brogues or boots, depending on their constituents' prejudices, waddling in his wake like dignified ducklings.

Unfortunately, the proposal was greeted coldly by the House leadership. If God had intended politicians to walk in Kinney's shoes, He would not have created limousines or Guccis.

The fact is, as the cab driver implied to the Indian gentleman, no Washingtonian wishes to run or walk *to* anything at all. Walking or running for a purpose is, in the Washington mind, a step away from pulling a rickshaw.

That is why the intelligent Mr. Dashbach's purposeful run seemed so odd.

It is, nonetheless, perfectly fine to run away *from* Washington stress, which everyone understands.

The run as the Washington stress getaway is perhaps the simplest, but still the most current, manifestation.

At its next-simple level, Washington stress escape is maneuvered from what is vaguely called "within."

A little while ago, an epidemic of Transcendental Meditation hit the city. A frightening wave of glassy stares on Capitol Hill one season turned out to be the result of TM seminars held in the Cannon Caucus Room. It was a Minnesotan, Rep. Tom Nolan, who started the craze.

A hundred Hillites turned up to learn how to unplug their teeming brains for the refreshing pleasures of the mindless drift. Among the Hill's closet meditators were several senators, including Teddy Kennedy.

The art trickled down to most of the departments of the government. At an executive training session at the Department of Agriculture, an academic virtuoso of mind freedom came in to lecture high-level bureaucrats on the joys of the brief mental getaway.

"I know it sounds silly," he told the old-timers, who had seen presidents come and go and the central core of Washington life remain as immutable as a cinder block. "But I'd like you to think about this. For complete refreshment of mind and spirit, and a total holiday from stress, more and more executives are undertaking the learning of Transcendental Meditation.

"Now, don't laugh. You take a little time each day. You can do it right there at your desk! You just sort of sit there, gazing at the wall. Clear your mind out completely, like sweeping away cobwebs. For a while, think about absolutely nothing."

"I know just what you're talking about," grunted one old veteran. "Most of us do it about eight hours a day. Heh-heh." Nobody else laughed. He was close to retirement.

More recently, Washington stress has been responding to a delightful new wave of water therapy.

At its spring, water therapy is very Washingtonian.

Jerry Ford, from his days as a congressman, could not have survived without his daily splash. Joe Canzeri, Nancy Reagan's former top gofer, liked to soak his feet in a trash bucket full of hot water when the going got tough. The Finnish ambassador cracks the ice on his pool every day in the bitterest midwinter weather and plunges in.

Some of the frazzled media clientele of Charles the First, the trendies' hairdresser, like to slip upstairs to loll in his tranquillity tank—a large bathtub, four by eight feet. In it, about ten inches of water is jammed with 800 pounds of Epsom salts. The tank is maintained at precisely body temperature. The tranquillity seeker simply flops in, sporting earplugs and little dabs of Vaseline over his or her tender zones, and floats there for about an hour.

There are no phone calls, no secretaries, no memos, no boss, no newspaper and no twenty-four-hour newscasts to intrude on his blessed peace. He has escaped Washington stress completely. He cannot sink, because the salts give the stressed the buoyancy of one afloat in the Dead Sea. The result is said to be like getting away from Washington for two weeks, without the nuisance of packing clothes or giving a jealous rival a chance to elbow you out of your place in the pecking order.

More healing powers of moisture trickled down to the grateful city with the opening of Washington's first hot-tub parlor, Making Waves. This was started by the nephew of the former secretary of the Navy and current ambassador to the Organization of American States, William Middendorf.

Young Chris Middendorf's brainchild pulls in bureaucrats, visiting showbiz stars, a few indiscreet undersecretaries and their staffs, lots of lawyers and lobbyists and their clients, and several Washing-

tonians soaking off their sorrows after paying car-impoundment fines
at the nearby District Court.

So popular has it become that a new party room has been added
with large television screens.

Now, let us be frank. Drugs are used to escape stress in Washington.

Alcohol, of course, plays an important role in Washington stress
control. (See chapter, "Some Enchanted Evenings.") Those who fear
they may become embarrassingly frank under its influence choose
other paths to the stress-free mind.

Alexander Cockburn and James Ridgeway of the *Village Voice,*
who apparently spent some time investigating various substances
used around Washington in the late 1970s, dubbed the Carter White
House "The Snow Palace."

They found sherry to be the preferred high at the Supreme Court
and the World Bank. The alleged unofficial high around Teddy
Kennedy's office at that time, they wrote, was amyl nitrite; the
official, vodka and cranberry juice.

The Capitol's most important release they found to be cocaine,
dispensed at the office of a certain Californian congressman on a quid
pro quo basis. The Georgetown dinner party at that time, they wrote,
offered Colombian Gold and Angel Dust, catnip smoked in a pipe
or an infusion of nutmeg.

(The two scribes noted that at Washington parties *they* attended,
they gobbled limp celery and unspeakable cheeses, swilled terrible
jug wines, and jabbered about politics—expecting no sex, no dancing,
no music, and a mugging on the way home. The catnip must have
been a welcome diversion. Let this be a reminder, gentle reader, of
the importance of getting on the right guest lists.)

*Playboy* polled the House and found twenty-six members who
admitted to pot-puffing. It also claimed to have uncovered five senators who smoked the weed.

In spite of the wave of reefer madness during the House Select
Committee on Narcotics hearing on Drug Paraphernalia, many innocent congressmen got their first glimpse of dope-cutting gadgetry
and the pot pipes commonly called bongs.

"You ever smoke one of those bonkers?" Representative Tom Railsback sternly asked one witness, early in the day.

Halfway through the afternoon, one member of the Select Committee stumbled into the hearing room falling-down drunk. He wove through the throng of drug-haters, plopped to his seat, and crouched there gazing dully at the five paraphernalia manufacturers who had been called to account and their gadget display.

Finally, the committee's chairman, Georgia's Billy Lee Evans, asked if the gentleman had any questions.

With a start, the congressman tugged a dope pamphlet from his pocket. He mumbled its contents for about ten minutes, slurred "This whole thing stinks," thrust the papers back in his pocket, and settled back for a snooze.

Representative Railsback began to call the bongs "bombs." The hearing rolled on. Each congressman continued to deal with Washington stress in his own way.

Massage parlors reportedly do an excellent job of stress release for some Capitol Hill regulars. Occasionally, little brightly colored flyers appear under the windshield wipers of congressionally tagged cars, offering a series of services from the establishments, the finest of which is called the Senator's Special. Such establishments can spring unexpected dangers. One official attended one, lit a cigarette while being massaged with alcohol by a lissome maiden, and set himself afire.

Nancy Reagan deals with Washington stress by sitting in the bathtub and carrying on debates with those who have offended her, in which she emerges the indubitable victor. (See chapter, "Nancy through the Looking Glass.") Both Reagans, of course, ride horseback on their Santa Barbara ranch or, in the president's case, at Quantico.

When the stress of the shah's imminent tumble from the Peacock Throne became too much for him, the former Iranian ambassador, Ardeshir Zahedi, liked to stand on his head.

Henry Kissinger was once asked point-blank by a reporter, "How do you deal with the inevitable stress and guard against diplomatic blunders occurring perhaps just through sheer exhaustion?"

Henry replied, "By beating my dog."

Mr. Reagan's secretary of Commerce, Malcolm Baldrige, relaxes by riding in rodeos and, in Washington, practicing his lasso techniques. He is a champion roper-and-tier of calves, and frequent winner of prizes like the Connecticut Rodeo Association's Annual Team Roping Award. He once lassoed his secretary at the end of a weary day in the Commerce Department.

CBS newsman Bob Schieffer paints portraits on the side. (Among his works: dual portraits of Ronald and Nancy Reagan, and Carter's old friends Bert and LaBelle Lance.)

Actual geographic relocation—just temporary, mind you, not long enough to lose your place—is an important Washingtonian release.

One local, who used to run the Board of Elections and Ethics, spotted a golden opportunity and opened a summer camp for adults in the Berkshires.

Camp Carefree operated, and perhaps still does operate, in a delightfully structured, stress-free Washingtonian way. It was designed exactly like the kiddie camps to which wise Washingtonians send their children every summer. Among its offerings: crafts, organized activities, "free play" along the Mohawk trail, canoeing, volleyball, make-your-own-bed discipline, and campfire singalongs.

Washingtonians wishing for their ramble down Memory Lane could be divided into Yellow and Orange teams. A highlight of the design was the Carefree Color War—"Just like at the District Building," said one native at the time of the announcement.

Of course, most of the upper crust in Washington would rather die than escape thus. The status retreat remains Martha's Vineyard, the Massachusetts island where Jackie Onassis has built her rather peculiar-looking getaway, with its heated towel racks and toilets that flush with hot water.

The grand attraction there is privacy.

In fact, the only public sport on Martha's Vineyard is the Privacy War, and Washingtonians like to play that with the right kind of opponents.

Old-timers trace its origins to the day when Roger Baldwin, the founding father of the American Civil Liberties Union, nailed up large signs around the beach adjoining his Windy Gates property. They proclaimed, "Private, No Trespassing."

Immediately, playwright-author Lillian Hellman erected a cabana on what had been a right-of-way through *her* property, engaged a guard and directed passersby to pass by a different route.

More and more people began to get more and more private. Signs flew up everywhere. Robert McNamara, who then directed the World Bank, tried to sweep the nude bathers from the beach next to his; failing that, he sold his property.

Unfortunately, none of the above had a legal leg to stand on. Anybody at all—"even the most frightful people," as one Vineyarder put it—can legally goggle at the stress-escapers from the beach or walk along it, as long as they stay beneath the high-tide mark and don't cross anybody's property to get there.

This explains why, at low tide, Vineyarders including the likes of Art Buchwald, as well as Carly Simon and other non-Washington celebrities, habitually dodge around to the backs of their houses.

The theory is that everyone there, after a great deal of public exposure, is escaping Stress.

One year, the Frank Ikards—he was a Texas congressman, a judge and the top lobbyist of the American Petroleum Institute, and is now a popular Washington lawyer—rented a house to a tenant with an unpronounceable last name and a whispery voice.

She was a very conscientious tenant.

"Oh! You have no idea how hard it was taking that big woollen rug out on the deck to beat it!" she whispered on one occasion when her landlady, Jayne Ikard, dropped by to see if she could lend a hand. "Tomorrow night, I'm taking out all the pots and pans and scrubbing them thoroughly."

Whenever Jayne dropped by, the tenant would be bustling about some difficult and menial chore, fretting about other chores down the road and whispering what had gone wrong.

"Oh! I don't understand how that big hole got burned in the deck. I put plenty of newspaper underneath the fire before I lit it." Or, "Oh! The door just blew off my house. I'm afraid I'm not making a very good impression!"

It was not until after her constantly toiling tenant had vacated the premises that Jayne, chatting to her neighbors, realized that she was Hope Cooke Namgyal, the former queen of Sikkim. She was simply seeking escape like everyone else.

Closer to home, Rehoboth is the favorite resort of Old Washington. It has also become, more recently, the stress release locale for Gay Washington. North Shores, the campiest corner of the beach resort, is renowned for its costume parties. At one, instructions were for everyone to dress as though for a Chinese funeral. At a later White Soirée, hundreds of white men, in white shorts or slacks and white shirts, wore white high-heeled shoes—Lane Bryant's ran out —drank white wine and discoed until rosy-fingered dawn crept up and simply wrecked the color scheme.

Ocean City, along the Maryland shoreline, is more proletarian. Its garbage trucks bear the legend, "Satisfaction guaranteed, or double your garbage back."

Several rich Washingtonians thought they could avoid Washington stress completely by buying houses in Jamaica. The stress promptly followed them: now, about a dozen well-heeled permanent villagers from the capital retreat to the same island—from Rose Marie Bogley, the hunt-country widow considered the probable next bride of Sen. John Warner, to the Mandell Ourismans, the wealthy local Chevrolet dealer and his wife. Both frequently host political Washington on its little stress-escape runs.

Cultural cruises, set up by the Smithsonian Institution, are popular stress escapes for the locals. These are particularly useful during disagreeable or opposing administrations.

One cruise through the Greek islands, for example, included former First Lady Lady Bird Johnson, author Allen Drury, author-humorist Erma Bombeck, Lady Bird's married daughters, Lynda Bird Robb and Luci Baines Nugent, and Liz Carpenter. To keep the conversational ball rolling, each participant, before sailing, read up on an aspect of Grecian culture. Lady Bird studied Grecian wildflowers. Liz Carpenter (who had been her press secretary) hurled herself into Lord Byron's Greece. And so on.

Most of what was talked on on the cruise, however, was Luci

Baines Johnson Nugent. She floated into one shipboard party wearing a see-through nightie and an awful lot of diamonds.

There was even less to discuss on another Smithsonian voyage to the Galapagos Islands, home of the giant tortoises.

Absolutely the most elegant Washingtonians—Evangeline Bruce (widow of Ambassador David Bruce), Taylor Chewning (JFK's closest pal,) Olga Hirshhorn (wife, now widow, of Joseph Hirshhorn of museum fame)—and several literary figures went along on this one.

The odd note was that many left their highly stressed mates behind.

One distinguished stay-at-home mate who had spent several years in top posts with another administration explained why he would rather suffer the Washington summer than go along.

"If my idea of fun was to tramp around a lava field all week waiting for turtles to move their butts," he said, "I would still be working for the government in Washington."

Washington stress, of the classic ilk, may have its roots in something of the sort.

# All in the Family:
# Who Are Those Strange
# People in Your House?
# (And Can You Get
# Them a Job?)

"The U.S. Department of Jobs for Senators' Sons (Bureau of Long Lists)."

> —FROM FORMS THAT WENT OUT AT THE TIME OF THE LAST CENSUS. A WITCH HUNT FAILED TO TURN UP THE TRICKSTERS AT THE GOVERNMENT PRINTING OFFICE WHO HAD CREATED THE EXCELLENTLY FAKED FORMS.

FAMILIES ARE those strangers that Washingtonians go home to visit every night.

A lot of them are stranded in the suburbs.

Safety is the reason they must huddle out there. It is very practical, too. It keeps Washington wives out of mischief. God knows what would happen if they started mooning around city art galleries and outdoor cafés.

Living in the suburbs also keeps the kids in good free schools, and the whole gang out of the hair of the *real* Washingtonian.

Out in their suburban purdah, dwindling numbers of non-working wives try to give Washingtonians' children cultural advantages. Like all suburbanites, they spend hours every day careening them around the waste land—to ballet classes, music lessons, tennis lessons or baton-twirling practice. Some young suburban Washingtonians have never set foot on a street in the capital.

Working Washington wives—who toil to help pay the gigantic mortgages on their suburban forts—must also ferry, worry and hurry. They stay out of mischief because they do not have time for it.

Only Washingtonian families who are important, quite rich or very poor, may actually live in the city.

The poor send their children to perhaps the worst public schools in the country. Enormous sums of money are bootlessly poured into these schools. Many students emerge unable to read.

The idealistic send their children to the best of the poor public schools for a while—in the right neighborhoods.

Children of the rich, and children of political appointees and well-paid bureaucrats, as well as Cabinet officers, senators, vice-presidents, kings' ex-wives and miscellaneous deposed rulers, diplomats, and well-paid lobbyists, go to excellent schools like Maret, Sidwell Friends, Cathedral, Foxcroft and so on, en route to conventional Ivy League colleges.

Most noteworthy among these schools is St. Alban's, an Episcopalian establishment nestled near the Washington Cathedral. This prepares mostly White Anglo-Saxon Protestant boys for life at the top.

Miraculously, it discourages un-WASPish symptoms of raw ambition, yet sets the youths' courses unwaveringly for later inclusion in the best Washington clubs.

Perhaps the first acquisition for any incoming Washingtonian who hopes to get a handle on the city should be a copy of the St. Alban's yearbook for the previous year.

It is called *The Albanian.* Here are listed the accomplishments, hopes and fears of the upcoming generation of the Washington upper crust. Also listed are their "Obsessions" and "Repulsions."

Young John Warner, son of the senator, was a St. Alban's boy, of course. His father was too. John Jr. counted among his "Obsessions" skiing, growling, jumpsuits, fast cars, beach trips, Heineken Keg, New England, painting, Bali, apple juice, and his mother. (He meant his real mother, the former Miss Mellon. He could not stand Liz Taylor. His "Repulsions" were "withheld due to obscene language.")

Prince Faisal, son of King Hussein of Jordan, was a fellow St. Alban's scholar because Princess Muna, his mother and an earlier wife of the king, lives in Washington.

He listed his "Obsessions" with fine abandon: flying, go-carting, boating, sailing, fishing, electronic devices, his girlfriend Ali, photography, soccer trips to North Carolina, cigarette racing boats, simulators, three-dimentional computer images, Jordanian air shows, aviation books, national defense, helicopters, hunting and firepower displays.

Among his "Repulsions": Zionists, boring chapel, antagonists, political elections, vandals, boring classes, jocks, people who disrupt class, girlfriend jokes, American-made cars, liberal extremists, being late, Arab jokes, ignorant fools, bad food, heavy workloads and heavy breathing.

Meanwhile, Tom Liddy, son of Watergate burglar G. Gordon Liddy, who most people do not realize is upper-crust enough to be an Albanian, declared his "Obsessions" as anything done extremely well: Indonesian eyebrows, profound debate, singing, dancing, prep games, double dates, college trips, flirting and politics. His sole "Repulsion" was "apathy," and he boasted more nicknames than any other student. Among them: Lido, Shuffleman, Tombo, Great God Zulu Nitpicker, Capone, Shovelnose, Hobbit, One-Punch, Maniac-at-Large and The Enforcer.

The children of politicians, you see, are remarkably clever.

You can tell this by the jobs they hold upon reaching adulthood.

Shortly after the Reagan election, for example, twenty-six-year-old Michelle Laxalt—daughter of close Reagan friend, Sen. Paul Laxalt—slipped silently into a $50,000-a-year plum job as deputy assistant director for legislative affairs at the Agency for International Development. (An "ethical administrative determination" squeezed her pay down to just over $32,000, however.)

At thirty-five, Caspar Weinberger's son, Caspar Jr., became a G.S. Grade 15 ($45,000 to $50,000 a year) with the about-to-be-renamed United States Information Agency, working out of New York. (His boss is Charles Wick, Reagan's close friend, who is reshaping the agency.)

Barbara Haig, daughter of Secretary of State Alexander Haig, was hired at the same time as young Caspar.

Talent is not limited to the offspring of politicians.

Several congressional wives have appointments within the administration. Elizabeth Hanford Dole is the most conspicuous in her $66,662-a-year job as Reagan's top White House woman appointee. A lawyer and a former member of the Federal Trade Commission, the wife of powerful Sen. Robert Dole of Kansas is considered well qualified for her job.

She also sees the humor in her role.

Shortly after Elizabeth Taylor split from John Warner, Liddy Dole told a group that her husband sometimes grumbled about having another politician in the family, and asked her why she couldn't be like other Senate wives?

"So this weekend I'm flying to London for a rendezvous with Richard Burton," she said.

Lilla Burt Tower, wife of Texas Sen. John Tower, is a busy woman too.

Tower divorced his wife Joza Lou after twenty-three years of marriage, and wed Lilla Burt in 1977.

She is paid $57,500 a year as director of the government's Institute of Museum Services. One cannot help one's relatives, of course, but it's interesting to note that Lilla Burt's brother, Samuel Cummings, runs Interarmco, the big arms dealership based in nearby Alexandria, Virginia. British police linked Cummings with "major international gun-runners" arrested in New York in December of 1979. A stockpile of Sten guns in England supposedly awaiting shipment to "Latin American revolutionaries" was traced to his stock, but no American laws had been broken.

(Senator Tower, now Cummings' brother-in-law, was not only at the time the ranking member of the Senate Armed Services Committee, but also a powerful force on the subcommittees for Arms Control, General Procurement, Military Construction and Stockpiles.)

The wife of Illinois Republican Congressman Henry Hyde, Jeanne Hyde, earns $20,000 a year in the White House correspondence office as a staff assistant.

Heather Gradison, twenty-nine-year-old wife of Rep. Bill Gradison, the Ohio Republican, was named to a seat on the Interstate Commerce Commission—a neat $58,500-a-year appointment.

Charlotte Conable, wife of Rep. Barber Conable, the New York Republican, is a member of the Federal Council on the Aging, and receives $220 a day when it meets.

Dee Jepson, wife of Iowa Senator Roger Jepson, was appointed to the president's Task Force on Private Sector Initiatives.

She receives no payment for this. But she does have some impressive stationery, with an arrow-bearing eagle seal at the top, above her name. Senate, House and Cabinet wives, most of whom are solidly settled into middle age, were flattered to receive, on this stationery, a letter urging them to a meeting on an unlikely topic.

"Because many of you have expressed an interest in learning about the Billings natural birth control method," she wrote, "I have arranged for Congressional and Cabinet wives to meet informally with the man who pioneered this effort, Dr. John Billings."

Attendance at the informative event, held in a Senate hearing room, was, alas, sparse.

Claire Schweicker, wife of the secretary of Health and Human Services, although on the committee with the thoughtful Mrs. Jepson, was off celebrating the birth of a new grandchild. Several others found themselves unexpectedly called out of town. A few explained that this was the very day they had planned to attend the Pentagon's regular weapons briefing for wives.

Ursula Meese, the wife of Ed Meese, the presidential counsellor, was busy too.

She had recently been created interim director of something new called The William Moss Institute for Studies of Life in the World of Tomorrow, an organization attached to American University. This completely new academic institute is grimly determined to pry into the future twenty, forty and sixty years ahead. It has the financial backing of several millionaires whose interest is more than academic, like Joe Allbritton and William Moss himself. (Mr. Moss' capacious purse is behind the television ventures of Nancy Dickerson, once LBJ's favorite television newswoman.)

Realistically, jobs for the families of administration high officials who wish to work are regarded as perfectly proper. They are akin to the rights of conquering troops to a spot of minor pillage.

Normally nobody pays attention. Few would have noticed, for example, that both the son of Sen. Mark Hatfield, Republican of Oregon, and the son of Bill Clark, now the National Security Agency's head, were very gainfully employed, had they not been in a terrible car crash together in 1981: Mark Jr. was working at the White House, a whistle away from top presidential aide Michael Deaver; and young Colin Clark had a comfortable job at the Labor Department.

Some all-in-the-family arrangements simply flow out of the fact that some clans predictably follow the scent of a political philosophy which, in the cyclical way such philosophies rotate, then proceeds to become fashionable.

Should there be a Teddy Kennedy revival, Washington will be bitterly disappointed if some of the better plums do not drop into the handsomely toothed mouths of the younger members of the clan.

At another level, the entire Dolan tribe has hitched its wagon to the Reagan Administration star.

Terry Dolan is its most conspicuous member. He is the young man who runs the National Conservative Political Caucus. This maintains the political hit list for Democrats and non-conservative Republican members of the House and Senate—set up to dispose of those who don't march in step with the Reagan tune. Robert Redford spent some time with Dolan in 1982, to study a "character" reportedly loosely based on him for a movie about the right wing. (Terry, incidentally, astonished some of gay Washington in April, by publicly apologizing to the *Advocate,* a homosexual newspaper. He was embarrassed about some of NCPAC's remarks about gays. He assured the newspaper that they had come to an end.)

Terry's brother, Tony Dolan, writes speeches for the president. His sister, Maiselle Dolan Shortley, toils in the White House Office of Public Liaison.

The mother of them all, Peggy Dolan, invented the Committee to Replace Sen. Lowell Weicker in Connecticut. The king-sized Republican star of the Watergate hearings was not right-wing enough for the taste of the Dolan tribe or the administration.

"Any Republican is better than Weicker," said Mrs. Dolan staunchly when she launched her movement. "Nothing personal, mind you."

Personal feelings do enter into some entanglements, naturally, along with family connections and sentimental ties.

Also, and this is important, old loyalties outlast old defeats.

Young Marty Mitchell, daughter of the Nixon Administration's late Watergate chatterbox Martha Mitchell, spent the summer after the Reagan election at the White House, as an intern. Anne Haldeman, daughter of Nixon White House staffer Bob Haldeman, has a "patronage" job at the Senate as a doorkeeper.

New loyalties aren't bad either. Sandy Sidey, daughter of the *Time* columnist unbeloved by the Carters, Hugh Sidey, became an efficient toiler in the Reagan White House press office.

Very few Washingtonians are acutely sensitive about the family's taking advantage of employment opportunities. One who was: Gerald Ford's chief of staff, Donald Rumsfeld.

Feeling the squeeze, as do the Michael Deavers of the present day (See chapter, "Money Matters,") he put the family out to work. His wife worked at a dress shop three days a week, his daughter Marcy toiled at the Junior Hot Shoppes, and his other daughter pitched in as a checkout girl in the Safeway.

That kind of delicacy of feeling is rare.

Beyond simple gratitude and likemindedness, Permanent Village Washingtonians—those of long standing—cannot help becoming entangled ("like snakes," a New Yorker observes) and having their lives and careers intertwine.

At a Reagan Kennedy Center Honors Gala, who should end up toiling away as the transportation director for the affair—ensuring that all the stars were chauffeured from White House to hotel to Center—but the son of White House Social Secretary Muffie Brandon.

The Reagan White House-Kennedy-Muffie connection is one of the most delightfully entangled of all Washington sagas.

During the Nixon Era, when the FBI bugged the telephone of Muffie's husband, London *Times* reporter Henry Brandon, they got a bigger treat than they had bargained for: intimate conversations between Joan Kennedy and Muffie Brandon on Joan's Teddy problems. (Being gentlemen, of course, the buggers did not pass on the tidbits to their boss, Mr. Nixon.) Had things worked out a little differently all around, it's well known, Muffie was keenly interested in becoming Joan Kennedy's social secretary.

Nobody, of course, is born into a vacuum.

There were chuckles all around after the last election when a young man named Frank Sinatra turned up working in the office of New York Sen. Al D'Amato. But no. He was no relation at all to ol' Visine Eyes. He did turn out, however, to be the grandson of Carlo Gambino, reputed Mafia head.

"It was a shocker when we found out," acknowledged the senator's press secretary, "but he's a great kid. He's in law school, you know. He just answers phones and opens the mail one day a week . . ."

In Washington, relations who are not as useful as Mr. Gambino might be can show their affection in other ways in a crunch.

At a hundred-dollar-a-head fundraiser for conservative Angry Young New York Bachelor Congressman John LeBoutillier, Miss Gloria Vanderbilt traipsed in to give a fashion show. She is a distant cousin.

Christopher Buckley, a talented writer, is a speechwriter for Vice-President George Bush. He is also the son of columnist William F.

Buckley and his wife—with whom the Reagans went on their little April 1982 holiday in Barbados.

Republican offspring usually head straight for the trough.

Historically, Democratic Washington's children feel obliged to put in some time at the bottom before riding on their connections, to get a flavor of life. The Kennedys are particularly keen to inspect the less fortunate at close quarters. Ethel's daughter Kathleen spent some time on an Indian reservation before her marriage. Maria Shriver, the daughter of Sarge and Eunice, put in a stint as an oyster shucker at the Foundry restaurant in Georgetown.

Young Evan Bayh, son of Sen. Birch Bayh, toiled as a busboy and waiter at the Hyatt Regency Hotel. Terry Eagleton, the son of Sen. Tom Eagleton, went to a special Giant Food store school at seventeen, to learn the correct way to weigh bananas.

At about the same time that Teddy Mondale, son of the man who hopes to be Democratic president next go-round, was graduating from the banana-weighing class to the lettuce-weighing—a distinct step up the social ladder in the giant scheme of things—Melinda Muskie was working in an art-and-frame shop in Kennebunkport, Maine; and Mary McGovern, daughter of former Sen. George McGovern, waitressed in Worcester, Massachusetts.

The son of New York Governor Hugh Carey, Michael, after getting his B.A. from Catholic University, kept himself solvent with a job as a barkeep at the Dubliner Irish pub on Capitol Hill, where Kennedy staffers go to sing sad songs and talk of merry wars.

Kennedy kids too recognizable or too tightly trapped in the Hyannis Port compound have historically found things to do with their time for fun and profit. There is always a family candidate to push.

Back in 1975, when they were forbidden by the authorities from door-to-door soliciting for Sargent Shriver's presidential campaign, one young Kennedy and one young Shriver made it their business to get a license. They ended up panhandling people who came to rubberneck the Kennedy compound, and charging $5 each for a photo taken with a genuine Shriver. (Their total take for the summer was $1,500.)

Notoriously, Republican kids are not quite so eager to muck in. A Georgetown matron walking her sheepdog bumped into a new teenager on the block.

"Wouldn't you like to do a little baby sitting?" she inquired of the girl.

"I can't," said she. "My father won't let me. He's Henry Kissinger."

Politicians are slightly irritated when Republican children pitch in among the ordinaries. During the Ford Administration, an enraged aide at the Senate Rules Committee kept stumbling over a pretty blonde "clicking her Nikon in my face," who turned out to be Susan Ford.

Wives, of course, are different, especially in these liberated days. They usually work synergistically with their husbands. Nancy Thurmond, the beautiful, busy, and, it's said, extremely ambitious wife of elderly, powerful Sen. Strom Thurmond, helps out the family exchequer in several ways. She is a frequent public speaker. She is also a "consultant" with Gray and Company. (Robert Gray, the most successful lobbyist of the Reagan Era to date, helped organize the inaugural balls. But he has been completely forgiven.)

Rare is the congressional wife who launches her own career independently of her husband's. Arlene Crane, colorful mother of eight and wife of one-time presidential possible Rep. Phil Crane, is a notable exception. Perhaps angry at unwelcome attention lavished on her and her family by the media during her husband's run for the Republican presidential nomination, she launched a career as a private investigator. Working for International Investigators, Inc., she pokes into corporate shenanigans and thievery.

"It's what I'm cut out to do," she says.

Marty Davis, the wife of Michigan's Rep. Bob Davis, is a radio and television newscaster. She began a business called No Hang-Ups, with custom-created answering-machine tapes. Among the tapes are the dulcet tones of actors who sound exactly like both Reagans, and an excellent David Stockman soundalike.

The tape the Davises favor themselves has a Mid-Eastern flavor.

"Grreetings! Grreetings to you!" purrs a voice rather like that of the Iranian Bani Sadr.

"I am the Ayatollah Muhammed Kamel Kahrahbi, the Davises' new houseboy . . . I think they are out, how you say, boogalooing. Please leave yourr-a name and number after I make the chicken squawk . . ."

Rita Jenrette vainly tried to use her marriage to Rep. John Jenrette as a launching platform for a career as a folksinger, but it was not until after Abscam and her extreme exposure in *Playboy* that she began to get better offers in her theatrical career.

More typical of Washington synergism is Ellen Proxmire, wife of Sen. Bill "Golden Fleece" Proximire.

Mrs. Proxmire founded Washington Whirl-Around in 1967. It is one of several successful organizations that show members of out-of-town professional societies or trade associations—or their wives—a good time, Washington-style. That, of course, means it lends access. It includes luncheons in House or Senate reception rooms, meetings with officials or speeches by their wives or other Washington personalities, special VIP tours of the White House, and so on. Gretchen Poston, who was Rosalynn Carter's social secretary, and Barbara Boggs, daughter-in-law of Rep. Lindy Boggs, run the group too. Occasionally, rival tour operators accuse the ladies of taking "special advantage" of their positions, especially vis-à-vis the use of Senate and House rooms and catering services. The Rules Committees have found no "wrongdoing."

Families can be a help; they can also prove slightly embarrassing. A Kennedy station wagon pulled up at three o'clock one morning on M Street in Georgetown. A parking meter vanished. Later, into the D.C. Juvenile Corporation Counsel's office marched Teddy Kennedy, Sr., looking grim; then seventeen-year-old Teddy Jr., looking repentant; and then a lawyer, carrying a Georgetown parking meter, looking expensive.

Washington understands such things can happen. It understands worse things can happen. It is, actually, profoundly sympathetic. When Billy Carter was being far too friendly with the Libyans, the city rallied. Even the stuffy Manuscript Division at the Library of Congress, with no fanfare, mounted a small but carefully chosen display of presidential letters through the ages, emphasizing troubles with family black sheep.

President McKinley's brother Abner and his telegraph stock manipulations, which provided many a merry moment for his brother's foes, were featured prominently.

Washington loved it.

# The Outer Washingtonian: Attired for the Fray

*"We do not wear pants. We do not wear clogs. We represent our country."*
    —MUFFIE BRANDON, MRS. REAGAN'S SOCIAL
    SECRETARY, TO *INTERVIEW* MAGAZINE

WASHINGTON IS a town of uniforms. The uniform changes, chameleon-style, from administration to administration, but it is always there.

Dame Fashion trails into town behind each new president and his wife, nodding vaguely toward jeans and sweaters or three-piece suits for men, high-fashion glitter or frumpy classics for women.

Transitions are trying periods.

During the Ford–Carter transition, sensible women like Barbara Howar covered all bases by adopting jeans-with-mink. During the Carter–Reagan transition, the women's uniform was black with pearls, or a long, full Oscar de la Renta taffeta skirt, which was once seen on six women at one party. (For the definitive Reagan Administration look, it was worn with dyed-to-match pumps and matching stockings.)

The current prototypical Washington daytime woman's uniform is an Adolfo suit. The model can be inspected at the Smithsonian. Nancy Reagan gave to that institution the oatmeal-beige Adolfo trimmed with chestnut braid that she had worn to the Republican

Convention, perhaps as a warning.

The genteel no-pants-for-women rule at the Reagan White House is explained to the lowliest typist.

"By the way," one applicant was told during her interview for a typing pool job, "something your should know. We all wear Supphose here."

Congressional and senatorial wives, through thick and thin, must wear good, tailored outfits—preferably a dress and jacket. Clothes must be modest and photogenic, preferably in bright colors. Most politicians agree with Lyndon Johnson, who forbade Lady Bird from wearing "old muley colors."

Liz Taylor, of course, dressed like a madam in purple muu muu effect, but everyone rather liked that.

Rosalynn Carter set one standard. She often made her own clothes with fabric picked up at a shop near the White House. About three yards of black silk fabric with linen weave cost $25 a yard; a set of simple shoulder pads cost about $2. There she was, ready to stitch up a genteel little blazer with which she topped the silky little frock she also made.

Nancy Reagan set another standard. She also likes blazers. But she picked up half a dozen at Leon Block, in New York, for $350 each.

Naturally, this different approach signalled other changes. When Mrs. Reagan moved into the White House, she had Amy Carter's two rooms fitted out with panelled doors all around them, as large walk-in closets. The room with a fireplace where Amy once practiced her fiddle is now the home for daytime outfits, plus a closet of shoes —all slickly color-keyed behind the spanking new closet doors. Exercise equipage perches in the middle. The other room has three closets full of evening clothes, a lot of built-in bureaus, and a little antique desk and chair by the window to lend an officey air.

Nearby is Nancy's built-in hair care center.

Many Democrats believe that Republican women's hair naturally springs into a bouffant formation. This is not true. Some local hairdressers, who complained of slow business during the last administration, after a few drinks now moan with fatigue after their day of dealing with "the helmet heads."

The First Lady's elegant coif is constantly flicked and teased and cantilevered into place by New York's Monsieur Marc or California's Julius, or, more often, by Washington hairdresser Robin Weir.

But all over Washington, hairdressers work harder and get richer than ever before.

*"Dina Merrill is the only woman in the world rich enough to wear a cloth coat all the time."*
    —VIRGINIA GRAHAM

Fur is obligatory for Republicans, in spite of Pat Nixon's famed Republican cloth coat.

However, political wives must not wear mink unless they have private money, lest foes develop an unhealthy interest in their husbands' income sources.

Eunice Shriver, Teddy Kennedy's sister, favors a white mink. This was seen all over town with a long rip in the back one year. Eunice is beloved among friends and family for what the poet called a "sweet disorder in the dress."

The Washington uniform mink for about five years has been very dark, in the Blackglama range. Sadly, by the time everyone rich enough to afford the uniform mink had actually acquired it, at enormous expense, along came Nancy Reagan—with a brand-new Maximilian mink of Lunaraine, a disturbingly different mid-chest-nutty brown hue.

Ronald Reagan had bought it for her just before the inauguration, so there is no hope of a return to earlier uniforms. The true impact of this traumatic event will not be felt for a couple of winters.

For the male of the political species, fur is unthinkable. The usual dress-for-success rule takes precedence: dark, heavy coat. Beneath that is the dress-for-success navy blue suit, white shirt, and tie with red in it.

Beware of unwitting symbolism. Senator Robert Dole was seen one day disconsolately fingering his tie in the Gucci shop at the

Watergate. It was an expensive Countess Mara tie, with her little initials embroidered on it.

"I just met someone who thought this meant Carter–Mondale," he said wonderingly.

Midwesterners and likable Republican presidents may wear brown suits. (Both Jerry Ford and Ronald Reagan did.) Other politicans must wear blue, dark gray or navy. Only Ohioans may wear green. They do it less since the House installed video cameras.

Teddy Kennedy's presidential campaign suits, all dark blue and shapely, were expensively stitched by Dimitri of Italy, at Ethel's insistence.

Almost all busy men must be urged to attend to these details by somebody. Only George Bush—seen elsewhere in this book leaping from vice-presidential motorcade into the semi-annual sale at Brooks Brothers—seems able to take care of his own outer man.

An aide to former Texas Rep. Bob Eckhardt sat with the audience in a Houston church hall, listening to the congressman campaign for re-election. The aide was impressed by a small girl sitting beside him, watching the congressman with rapt attention. Finally, the child turned to her mother, damp-eyed.

"Mama, we just *have* to he'p that man. He looks so poor."

The aide took the congressman aside.

"Look, you really must buy a decent-looking suit," he said. "You haven't had a new one in five years."

"Well, okay," shrugged Eckhardt. "But don't think you're gonna talk me into buying one of those fancy $80 or $90 numbers."

Eckhardt won his next election.

In some administrations, it is fashionable to adopt a very proletarian air. If you decide to do so, you must not be surprised if you are then mistaken for a proletarian.

It is always a good idea for a man to wear a suit, but especially when visiting a jail. As a D.C. government official, Washingtonian Douglas Moore went to visit Lorton Reformatory one day sporting dungarees. He was presumed to be a new tenant, and was promptly offered a job on the jail's house organ, *Morning Count.*

*"I found out that you can walk into a store and buy
suits ready-made."*
     —GEORGE BUSH, TELLING REPORTERS WHAT
     HE'D LEARNED ON THE CAMPAIGN TRAIL


At the peak of the Washington establishment, white tie is what
separates the men from the gofers. On the rare upper-crust occasions
it was worn, before the Reagan era dawned, like opening night at the
Washington International Horse Show—the scent of mothballs
made the horses quite sick.

But Reagan had forked over about a thousand dollars for his
white-tie outfit just before his inauguration, and had no intention of
wasting it. Suddenly, everything in Washington was white tie. Locals
had to relearn the ancient art of tail control: do you sit on your tails,
tuck them into the back of your chair, allow them to flap out at the
sides or knot them over your lap?

Even reporters had to meet the challenge.

At the very first all-star Reagan diplomatic reception, white tie—
which leaves plenty of room for medal display—was grandly sported
by the ambassadors, all the way down to the Castroite representing
Cuban interests in Washington. (Actually, the Zimbabwan boasted
a brown suit, and the gentleman from Tonga a sort of frock, but both
were making important sartorial-political statements.)

A reporter from the Los Angeles *Times,* Don Shannon, wished to
cover the event, so that he could interview the Cuban interests man.
He thought he was more than doing his duty when he sailed in
sporting his tuxedo. No, he had to go home and change.

"Reporters must wear white tie. Only photographers may wear
black tie," a young woman aide reproached him. (Luckily, the scribe
had a son who was on the debutante circuit. He raced home, thrust
on his son's deb-ball uniform, stapled together any gaping parts, and
sped back to the White House in time to sidle up to the Cuban and
get his story. Fellow reporters, mistaking him for an ambassador,
interviewed him.)

Quite plainly, the current White House clothing code reflects the

Hollywood caste system: men who write—equivalents in class to
Paddy Chayefsky or Wolf Mankiewicz—are white-tie material,
something like the stars themselves, but funny looking; they happen
to write the script after the show instead of before it. But newspaper
photographers, bedizened with picture-taking paraphernalia, are
down several notches, like grips or cameramen—fine in black tie, but
not Our Crowd.

At a later White House party, the code was even more refined.
Television technicians were asked to dress the part. The idea of a
black jumpsuit was tossed around for a while—something that would
render them almost invisible, like mimes or puppeteers. It was dismissed as going too far. "A dark business suit," was the final decision.

Shoes are not of vital importance on the day-to-day Washington
upper-crust male round, but brown suede should be avoided at all
costs. They remind all Washingtonians of Abscammed John Jenrette, who stuffed $20,000 in ill-gotten gains in *his* brown suedes.

The real status shoes for this administration are Lobb's, made in
London by the royal shoemaker. Several White House staffers ordered them at the time of Prince Charles' wedding. A few years ago
you could buy a pair of Lobb's for $125. Now, they cost $750, and
Lobb's wooden shoe trees cost $150.

Meanwhile, there are very strong forces lobbying against import-
ing any shoes at all.

Senator John Danforth went to the White House to plead passionately against such imports. Of course, he was wearing his Guccis at
the time.

*"Blue denim jeans, no matter how fashionable or
expensive, are not appropriate attire, and should not be
worn to work in future during the business week."*
      —MEMO AT THE DEPARTMENT OF
      TRANSPORTATION RAILROAD PERSONNEL AND
      TRAINING OFFICE, AT THE DAWN OF THE
      REAGAN ERA

# SHINING
# THE BRASS

# The Media and the Man at the Top: Can This Marriage Be Saved?

*"You can't get a nice piece in the paper about anyone any more."*
—WILLIAM SAFIRE

JIMMY CARTER'S troubles with the press began during his first campaign.

A certain Carter staffer had promised "gonzo" journalist Hunter Thompson—who was staying in Miami at the time—an interview with the candidate for *Rolling Stone.*

"Just fly up from Miami to Chicago," he told Hunter. "When you get there, you can fly with Carter from Chicago to New York. I'll get you sitting right next to him on the plane. You'll get a real good interview."

Obediently, Hunter hopped a plane.

In Chicago he hopped another. Sure enough, he got the seat next to Carter. The candidate turned to the journalist with half-closed eyes.

"I've been up for two days," he moaned. He promptly fell asleep.

Hunter seethed all the way to New York. He seethed en route to the hotel. Late at night, still seething and with a few beers on board, he went around and hammered on the door of the room where the Carter staffer who had set it up was resting with a young woman.

"Go away!" shouted the staffer. "Sleep it off!"

Instead, Hunter went down to the hotel shop and bought a can of lighter fluid. He squirted it under the door of the room. Then he set fire to it. A sheet of flame shot under the door. The young woman and the Carterite ran screaming from their nest.

Gonzo vengeance had been wreaked.

*"Things are going beautifully now, but, you know, your media 'friends' and those beautiful people from the Washington Establishment who are fawning over our man because he is a winner will turn on him viciously as soon as the going gets rough. In their hearts they just don't share his views and they're just waiting for the day when they can safely attack him again . . ."*
—RICHARD NIXON WRITING TO LYN NOFZIGER, THEN A TOP REAGAN AIDE, IN THE SPRING OF 1981

The marriage between the media and any given administration is an uneasy affair.

The administration is the rich old bridegroom. His every waking and sleeping moment is monitored for signs of impending demise.

The media, his restless young bride, is his captive. She is also his captor, and his interpreter to the world. She is fond of the old bore in a way. Deep in her heart, though, she would like to grease the stairs and watch him totter to his doom.

He knows it, but he needs her. The old curmudgeon keeps his choicest secrets from her, and watches her craftily as she gossips to the neighbors. The two settle into a conditional, often fairly genial, truce. They cling together when they must, waiting for the end.

With President Reagan, this has a literal as well as a figurative application.

The throng of reporters that trails him to no-news places like his Santa Barbara ranch is known rather morbidly as the Death Watch.

In the event of assassination or sudden seizure, they want to be there and become famous.

Reagan is keenly aware of this. One of these days, he tells friends, while riding horseback under the relentless telephoto eye of the newsbringers, he will clutch his chest and fake a tumble from his horse, just to see what they'll do.

Administrations that handle the peculiar marriage best always retain their courtly manners toward the hellion bride, no matter how unseemly her behavior. Most important, they retain good humor. They jut do as much business as they can *behind her back*.

Kennedy understood this utterly. Johnson knew that a combination of moist-eyed, gallant attention and the occasional quick crack to the side of the head would keep the lady in order; Nixon could simply not sustain politesse toward a bride who so openly loathed and despised him; Ford—at an advantage because he replaced the loathesome and despicable one—observed a plodding, mannerly tolerance. The Georgians never understood what they were doing at all.

*"Everybody has their cross to bear. I'm yours, and you're mine."*
        —JODY POWELL TO PRESSPERSONS, JANUARY 7, 1980

It takes amazingly little civility to keep the press at bay.

Avoid insulting it openly. Attend its little fiestas a couple of times a year.

Carter consistently skipped events dear to the hearts of the men and women he most sorely needed. He actually forwent the Gridiron Club dinner to run off and do something political in Oklahoma one year.

Oklahoma! The press was cut to the quick. Could anyone prefer anything in *Oklahoma* to its witty satire of presidential foibles?

It was to get worse. He avoided Washington Press Club banquets. Horrors, where was he at the White House Correspondents' dinners?

To be frank, the most exciting thing that happened at the latter was when Carl Bernstein tipped a basket of rolls and a bottle of wine into the lap of Zbigniew Brzezinski. But a president does not attend for pleasure. It is only to grant a brief, cheap but treasured massage to the ego of the media.

The press, you see, in spite of its sophisticated *moue* of indifference, adores the presidency. It is, beneath its flinty rat-a-tat-tat shower of hostile questioning, awed by the office. It is in love with the bigtime of it all.

It is pleased and flattered by its own proximity to the mountaintop. It is anxious to grip its toehold on history and carve its name on the vacant face of time. No reporter, for example, has ever sent back to the White House a photograph of himself with a president.

Eight top correspondents, besotted with nostalgia when they flew west on Air Force One with Jerry and Betty Ford for the last time, stripped the plane bare of memorabilia—pillowcases, ashtrays, tumblers, coffee cups—anything that indicated They Were There.

Obviously, to the press, little things mean a lot. One day, Jerry Rafshoon, Carter's erstwhile image man, actually cancelled a luncheon with Walter Cronkite.

"Like cancelling lunch with the Pope," breathed the anguished acolytes of truth.

Press Secretary Powell did worse. He stood scribes up at big, organized breakfasts. He not turn up for a news talk show; he was churlish and rude to no apparent purpose.

He told *Playgirl* magazine at one point that he'd like to punch Sally Quinn "right in the mouth." He added, "Since I can't punch Sally Quinn, maybe I could punch Ben Bradlee and see if she cared."

After reporters candidly noted that the president's translator in Poland had told the Poles that the president "desired them carnally," Powell observed cloddishly: "Most of the American press was drunk on well-chilled Polish vodka . . . It was the most successful job of flacking the American press under the influence of vodka that I have ever seen."

He installed ropes at the White House exit so reporters could not approach visiting dignitaries to question them, but had to shout each other down. "Confined like cattle, required to act like Australians,"

growled one indignant grand old man of journalism, nursing
wounded *amour propre.*

Powell did not realize that a press secretary must be like a dentist:
disliked but essential, abhorred but respected.

Some administrations have shown disapproval of writers or organs
by leaking to a more favorable and constant friend. Some ignored the
slings and arrows, to their sorrow.

*"They're like kids—unless you whack them across their*
*ass once a day they'll run all over you. They're slanted*
*as an old cowshed, but where they really get their rocks*
*off is on that editorial page . . . and those smart-ass*
*columnists are as whorish as the high-blown Washington*
*lawyers and bankers. I could have their peckers in my*
*pocket any time—if I cared. But who wants them? Give*
*me the headline writer, the photo editor and the*
*cartoonist, and you can have all the editors and*
*columnists you want."*
        —LBJ, QUOTED BY EDGAR BERMAN IN *HUBERT*

The Carter people conspicuously did not invite the offenders to
news briefings. Stu Eizenstat cordially uninvited the the New York
*Times* to White House backgrounders; Zbig Brzezinski uninvited
*Time* to the newsweeklies' security briefings; on it went. The press
corps finally became like a conspiracy of children in a cruel Dicken-
sian orphanage. It was quite a badge of honor to be uninvited.

*"MORE MUSH FROM THE WIMP"*
        —HEADLINE ON AN EDITORIAL IN THE BOSTON
        *GLOBE* OVER A THOUGHTFUL EDITORIAL ON THE
        CARTER BUDGET PLANS IN 1980. THE WRITER
        HAD DASHED IT OFF AS A "DUMMY." IT RAN IN
        THE FIRST 140,000 COPIES.

Where the hostility can be held at bay between the two sides, the intimacy of the arranged marriage settles in.

In the Carter culture, where rock music and drug use tended to separate free-swingers from old fogies, there was a brief dropping of traditional barriers.

A Carter White Houser announced loudly at a Georgetown dinner party—one of the few attended by the Carterites—that a new shipment of grass had just arrived. And was anybody interested? (Several were, but would not have said so for the world.)

Later, young journalists and young Carter staffers revelled in the mutual trust of dope, companionably and rather briefly.

Wrote James Wooten, of the New York *Times,* in the summer of 1978: "Reporters—including at least two employed by the New York *Times*—have smoked marijuana in the presence of and with members of the White House staff and other federal employees." The paragraph was cut from his story.)

When the square media began to focus on the possiblity of drug use by some White Housers, rumors surfaced of a Dope List. It purportedly gave thirty-five journalists' names, lovingly collected by the White House. All thirty-five were known to have been On Something.

"Oh, God. Suppose they release the list, and I'm not on it?" fretted one reporter.

Meanwhile, the corps was evenly divided between the weary old seen-it-all set and the young. Even in the White House press office, they huddled in different corners of the room, watching different soap operas on television in the afternoon.

Both youth and age eager awaited the end of the daily briefing eagerly. Traditionally, it is signalled by the dean of the corps, its oldest member. (He is also the one who pops the first question at all presidential press conferences.) He says, "Thank you." The press secretary pipes down. It is over, and everyone shambles back to his soap opera or a game of gin rummy. One terrible day, as Powell droned endlessly on about the economy, the "Thank you" never came. Notes and nudges through the ranks did no good.

"The dean's dead," word buzzed around. Not this time. He was just sleeping.


*"CAN'T BELIEVE YOU'RE 45. YOU DON'T ACT A DAY OVER 14."*
  —BIRTHDAY GREETING TO ABC CORRESPONDENT
  SAM DONALDSON FROM THE CARTER WHITE
  HOUSE, 1979


In some administrations, the intimacy between coverer and co-veree is so symbiotic that it's incestuous.

Reporters, as constants on the Washington scene, find themselves in curious semiofficial positions.

Society reporter Betty Beale has been seen completely taking over the protocol of a party when a frosh administration wife foundered on the fine points—guiding introductions, supervising cake-cuttings, directing toasts—an elegant referee among the chandeliers and oriental rugs she knows better than her hosts.

It was White House (now *Time*) photographer David Kennerly who talked Ford and Kissinger out of bombing Cambodia in the wake of the *Mayaguez* incident. It was from Walter Cronkite that the Nationalist Chinese Embassy first heard about the recognition of Mainland China. No one official had bothered to tell them.

The press becomes, in some cases, the grease that keeps the wheels rolling or stops them.

At Christmas 1975, powerful Sens. Hugh Scott and Mike Mansfield stewed impatiently in Scott's office. They were waiting for official word from the president that it was time to adjourn for the Christmas break. No call came.

Finally, Scott rang the White House.

"Scott," eavesdroppers heard him snap. "Hugh *Scott!* Senator, of Pennsylvania. It's very important that I talk to the president."

"Required by law, in fact," piped up Mansfield, testily.

The operator said she'd try to get President Ford on the line. Vain hope. He was in the Green Room, attending the annual press party, yukking it up with reporters as two butlers chased a gate-crashing White House mouse around with a broom.

The Senate cooled its heels.

Finally, Sam Donaldson, then covering the Senate, came to the rescue. He called the Congressional Liaison Office at the White House. It sent word to the scene of all the jollity. Mr. Ford, chortling, came to the phone. The wheels of the United States government squealed, slightly slower than usual, to their annual halt.

The intertwinings of media and might often don't unravel for all to see until they are over.

When James Fallows left a job as Carter's speechwriter in the winter of 1978, it turned out he had during his tenure written four pieces for the *Washington Monthly* magazine under phoney bylines: "How Jimmy Carter Can Find Out What Government Is Doing," "The American Class System and How to End It," "China, India and Me," and "How to Stop Masturbating."

At Carter's first—and almost lone—major media event, the installation of the chief of the White House correspondents, the President's speech was very funny. And so was the speech of the new chief, Paul Healy. The reason: both speeches were written by the same people—old Kennedy hand Dick Drayne, columnist Art Buchwald, Frank Mankiewicz and Al Spivak.

The consanguineous entanglement sometimes bears strange mooncalves. During an American-Iranian contretemps in 1979, London *Daily Telegraph* reporter Stephen Barber frantically sought comment from State Department spokesman Tom Reston.

He telephoned Reston at home.

"Mr. Reston?"

"Yes . . ."

"What do you think about Iran rejecting the new American ambassador?"

"Did they? I didn't know. I've been sitting here watching the Bullets game . . . What does it matter? There's hardly a government there anyway . . . I don't really think it makes very much difference . . ."

Titillated and aghast, the scribe filed his report. Hours after the London papers had gone to press, it dawned on New York *Times* columnist James Reston—father of State Department spokesman Tom—that he had been roused from the Bullets game for a purpose. In fact, his words of wisdom were being bandied all over Europe as the official State Department line.

The media-administration incest has a baroque charm in many of its manifestations. The *Washington Journalism Review,* a slightly absurd publication, is now owned by Jessica Catto. She is the wife of the State Department spokesman Henry Catto.

(Upon their joint acquisition of the *Review,* Henry wrote a hard-hitting editorial about how wonderful the Pope and the queen of England are, and how we need many more like them. He has since officially detached himself from the charade.)

Jessica's mother owns the Houston *Post.* WJR's editor is Katherine Winton Evans. *Her* husband is the Evans of Evans and Novak, whose column, of course, appears in both Jessica's mummy's paper, the Houston *Post,* and the Evans' local mealticket, the Washington *Post.*

One delicious issue of WJR included a letter from National Public Radio chief Frank Mankiewicz. It also contained a book review by Frank. Then, there was a toadying little takeout on something new at his network. Finally, proudly listed up front among the magazine's board of advisers, was—surprise! Frank Mankiewicz.


## "JOURNALISTS DO IT DAILY"
## "FORGIVE US OUR PRESS PASSES"
### —WASHINGTON PRESS CORPS BUMPER STICKERS


The press that covers official Washington has a problem. It is boredom, boredom that gnaws like a rat.

Yes, the constant pressures of deadlines lead to alcoholism, hardened arteries, triple-bypasses, irregular haircuts, bitten fingernails, ulcers, hypertension, acne, fat, ugly clothes, piles, swelled heads, shrunken incomes, broken marriages, unacceptable triglyceride levels and nervous twitches.

But the boredom is what gets them—the trival, repetitive grind. At the "pinnacle," as Rona Barrett so ingenuously dubbed the peak of power, the pedestrian and the predictable stroll on endless hand-in-hand promenades through the empty hours.

This is particularly true aboard campaign planes. There, on the campaign trail, the gray monotony is dotted lightly with the candidates' stifling, all-alike speeches in wretched, barren halls in the ugliest towns in America. Days run together like slop. Any diversion is welcome. Reporters covering the last Reagan campaign trail were enraptured when Roy Rogers and Dale Evans boarded Reagan's Dallas-to-Houston plane. Roy sang "Happy Trails." World-weary old columnists tumbled over each other to get his autograph "for the kids."

Aboard the Reagans' press plane, too, in a brave effort to amuse the scribes, stewardesses began to make little pastries shaped like sex organs, and engaged in risqué banter with the scribes.

United Airlines caught wind of the doings. The offending stews were yanked from press-plane duty, and replaced with males.

The press, deprived of its only certain sensory stimulus—besides the daily prospect of watching Nancy bowl an orange down the aisle at takeoff—raised such a stink that a kind-hearted Reagan staffer phoned the airline. He urged strongly that the young women be allowed back on the plane, pastries and all. The male stewards lingered on as serfs; the bantering belles were welcomed back aboard with cheers and rechristened "Public Relations Personnel."

Meanwhile, on the Carter campaign plane, reporters amused themselves like adolescent prisoners, with food- and pillow-fights. Even the most ardent Democrats among them wished they were among the fun set aboard the Reagan plane, singing along with "Happy Trails." Here was the long Reagan honeymoon born.


*"May I speak to the prime minister, please?"*
*"No, you may not. It's three o'clock in the morning."*

*"But this is the Washington Post."*
*"And this is the prime minister's husband. Good night."*
    —TELEPHONE CONVERSATION REPORTED BY
    ARNE OLAY BRUNDTLAND, HUSBAND OF THE
    PRIME MINISTER OF NORWAY


A certain arrogance goes with being media. It is also an important part of being an elected official. The opponents are well-matched.

Of course, there are clashes.

Even in the midst of a genteel "photo opportunity" at the White House—a magic moment when photographers and reporters swarm into the Oval Office to goggle at the president and another head of state—they will not be stilled.

"Whattaya gonna do about the air control strike?" trumpeted a voice, during one tea-party smooth photo op with the late Anwar Sadat. It was UPI's Helen Thomas, bête noire of a half-dozen press secretaries. (Jerry Ford's Ron Nessen calls her a "rude, raucous, ill-informed, pushy witch." She and ABC's Sam Donaldson are the only people with the guts to ask exactly what readers and viewers are wondering about.)

Reagan aide Michael Deaver turned mauve. Press spokesman Larry Speakes blanched. And a memo appeared on the bulletin board ordering no more questions at photo ops, or reporters would be banned forever from the moments. Temporarily, the voice was stilled. Fitfully, it rises again.


*"Competence and humor are no longer sufficient to deal*
*with the job of being the president's chief spokesman.*
*You need a hide of steel . . . I wouldn't want Jody*
*Powell's job for a million dollars."*
    —PIERRE SALINGER, WHO WAS JFK'S PRESS
    SECRETARY, IN 1976

The press works hard. It prides itself on getting it fast and right. It wants to beat the competition. Its journalists would sell their Saabs to win awards—the Pulitzer Prize, the George Polk Memorial Award, the Headliners' Award, the Overseas Press Club, the Penney-Missouri—countless proud certificates dangle in countless rec rooms around the country, witness to the lust for recognition of tight deadlines and loose lips.

The *Wall Street Journal* was proud to win something grandly called the Herbert Bayard Swope Memorial Awards one year. Then somebody revealed: the awards were actually given by a kind gentleman named Robert Juran. He was an ad salesman from Missoula, Montana. He charged newspapers $18 a head to enter. Mr. Juran himself chose the winner. (It was an excellent choice, by the way, all about the meat racket.)

Meanwhile behind the bright patchwork of the television screen, life as an observer of politics is not easy.

Countless statistics must be juggled, places known, names memorized. Well, almost.

Computers and teleprompters ease the strain. Teleprompters—those lettered scrolls that most television newsmen are reading as they gaze sincerely into the camera—do not always work. They flip-flop, roll too fast, vanish from view. Computers, especially at election time, are all-powerful and treacherous.

Viewers wondered what on earth had happened during the 1978 election, in which the entire Congress and one-third of the Senate ran.

Suddenly Walter Cronkite could not find South Dakota; David Brinkley was way behind; Howard Smith and Barbara Walters babbled; Gordon Peterson kept trying to track down strange small counties no one had heard of. Even Eric Sevareid, temporarily down from Olympus—the CBS cameraman has standing instructions to "focus on his ears," so as not to show the wrinkles—wrung his hands like a launderer and couldn't finger a trend.

The reason: ABC, CBS, NBC, AP and UPI all subscribed to the same computer service. On the night of nights, the computers zonked out. ("Certain interruptions in the systems" was how the president of the comnany explained it to me.) The entire hard news establishment was left floating on its wits alone for ninety-minute stretches. It was a poignant sight.

What makes media biggies run? Is it power lust?

They have a kind of power—the power of a ghost in the ballroom, who can trip up the dancers as they waltz by.

They have fame, especially on television, where their faces are more familiar to the average American than the people they talk about.

They have adventure. A reporter covering a presidential trip to Helsinki, who sought *amour* with a pretty young Finn, returned to Washington with three stitches, a bandage and a sock covering the place where she had bitten him.

They have money—the fabled $500,000-a-year to a million-a-year salaries that let them live like princelings and buy houses on Martha's Vineyard, near Walter Cronkite.

People know them everywhere. Hi, Sam. Hi, David.

Perhaps this will end as the era of cable television sets in. Dan Schorr, who runs Ted Turner's Cable Network News in Washington, thinks it will.

"It is not likely that there will be superstars . . . As anchor persons replace each other every couple of hours, inevitably you will come to see the anchor for what the anchor really is—a necessary part of the process, not a demigod," he said once, gazing into the new starless age with a certain smugness.

Some members of the press make the hunt for the unrevealed their lives' missions.

Jay Gourley, the *National Enquirer* reporter who stole Henry Kissinger's garbage back when it counted, once confided that he had tripled his income since reading Evelyn Waugh's satire of cheap journalism, *Scoop,* and applying its techniques to Washington.

Doing a television piece on perquisites of the Senate one day, he barged into the Senate gym with a cameraman. Within the hallowed hall, the nude and near-nude mighty were being pummelled by masseurs and whirlpooled to serenity.

Furiously protesting staffers raced to stop the intrepid intruder.

"Who's in charge?" Jay kept shouting, as his cameramen whirled about recording the sybaritic scene. Naked senators leapt from their tables and ran. Three enormous masseurs finally wrestled the cameraman to the floor and stuffed towels into his lens.

"My God, what's going on?" cried Sen. John Warner, walking in on the frantic scene.

"Is Senator Warner in charge?" shouted Jay, scribbling away in his little notepad.

"No, no! No!" bawled a masseur. As he was bundled out, Jay kept shouting, "Who's in charge? Who's in charge?"

"It's not my worry," John Warner explained graciously.

"You bet it's not," said one of the nude stars later. "John had his clothes on."

Not only for image, but for spy control, leak-stoppage is a constant war. The first rule laid down by Richard Allen, Reagan's ill-starred intelligence expert, was that no National Security Agency staffers may take phone calls from members of the press without specific permission from Allen. The exception: "social calls." Instantly, "social calling" became a by-word.

The job of the press officer, then Phyllis Kaminski, was simply to say to scribes, "No, Mr. So-and-So will not speak to you."

"Not ever?" inquired one reporter.

"No, not ever."

Later, Allen's star fell over the $1,000 honorarium Japanese journalists gave for an interview with Nancy Reagan. No newspaperman leaped to his defense. Would they have reacted differently to soft soap?

The Reagan Administration is very spy-aware. It fears strongly that material "off the record" to the press can end up on the tape recorder of other interested parties.

(Such bugging is difficult on interoffice government phone calls. Something called Federal Secure Telephone Service "minimizes vulnerability" to unwelcome eavesdroppers. In early 1982, the comptroller general agreed that the government could install the service in some officials' private residences, too, to be used only "for official government business of a sensitive nature." Of course it is a great, if maddeningly secret, status symbol.)

The fact is, the press is unlikely to deliberately let loose a security secret on the world.

It is sensitive to the point of sycophancy when it can identify with a subject.

At one newspaper, when caricaturist David Levine provided a conventionally cruel caricature of a friend of the editor—Joe Califano, as it happens—it was kindly touched up: multiple chins and the belly given by God and the artist were removed.

Did you see photographs of Nancy Reagan being bowled topknot over teakettle over by Liberty, the Reagans' golden retriever, at the ranch, right after the Reagan victory? Certainly not. Editors empathized. Suppose it was their wife . . .

The poignant truth is that the partners in this odd marriage cannot live without each other.

Richard Nixon, wherever he is, maintains a mail subscription to the Washington *Post*.

# Nancy Through the Looking Glass

*"There is no greater happiness for a man than approaching a door at the end of the day knowing someone on the other side of the door is waiting for the sound of his footsteps."*
—RONALD REAGAN IN A LETTER TO HIS SON, ABOUT TO MARRY

NANCY REAGAN believes in romance.

One of her favorite stories is about her faithful quarterhorse, No Strings.

"When we were in Sacramento I put No Strings on the ranch of a friend of ours," she says.

"As you know, horses have a pecking order and No Strings became the head man. There was a little old mare there the other horses treated badly. They wouldn't let her get to the feed.

"No Strings took this little mare under his wing, and when it was feeding time and the others would try to get her out of the way, he would get them out of the way, to let her eat. When she had finished, they could come in.

"Well, she was very old, and eventually they had to put her to sleep. When it was feeding time that day, No Strings couldn't find her. So he took off into the hills, neighing and looking for her everywhere. I have never heard of a horse doing that."

Nancy's eyes "puddle up," as she says, at stories of love or loyalty, like this one, told to Betty Beale.

Mrs. Reagan is a tender-hearted woman.

In fact, she is the type of woman who for centuries has been man's ideal mate. She is the complete wife-as-mistress. She is careful guardian of her own beauty; chatelaine of her husband's house; believer in goodness, God, home and country; prettily turned out (the Secret Service codenames her "Rainbow"); fierce defender of her man (he is "Rawhide" to the same Secret Servicemen); and a loyal friend to her own kind.

Her husband would do anything for her. Nancy does not like snakes. So the president performs a regular St. Patrick-type ceremony during the warm months at the Reagans' Santa Barbara ranch. He tugs on his swimming trunks and wades into their pond, carrying a large burlap sack. He scoops up all the water snakes he can find and stuffs them into the sack. Then he carefully transports them to a neighbor's pond—presumably the neighbor's wife likes snakes—or tosses them onto the bank, where they are on their own.

Plainly, Ronnie adores Nancy.

Why, then, is she the most controversial First Lady since Eleanor Roosevelt? Who declared her looking-glass war with the media? And why?

The fact is none of the above qualities are what reporters ask about, when contemplating their president's wife. Here are the questions most commonly asked of Sheila Tate, Nancy Reagan's press secretary:

"What is Nancy wearing?"

"How much does that cost?"

"Who is paying for it?"

"Will Frank Sinatra be there?"

"What kind of bed do the Reagans sleep in?"

"What brand of jelly beans do they prefer?"

"Does the president snore?"

"What size shirt does he wear?"

"Does Nancy wear a bulletproof vest?"

"What do the Reagans eat?"

"And on what dishes?"

When reporters are not asking questions, somebody else is.

"How many people are there who can afford to go out and buy a $1,000 dress?" sniped Joan Mondale, wife of the former vice-president.

Objectively, as "Joan of Art"—her flattering nickname during the Carter years as an urger-on of the fine arts—Mrs. Mondale might have inquired how many people can really afford to go out and buy a $1,000 painting?

Washington, however, does not think objectively. It thinks politically.

The answer is, at least nine people can easily afford a $1,000 dress.

They are the women in Nancy Reagans' Group.

A $1,000 dress is what they wear to meet hubby back from a rough day tumbling around among his millions.

Dressing up—along with beating back the encroachments of cruel time upon their beauty—is a full-time job for the Group's ladies.

It encompasses both duty and virtue. Ugly is a sin. Fat is a sin. Tacky is a sin.

The entire constellation of elderly starlets in Nancy's Group will greet the grim reaper, should he drop by, with unchipped manicures, faultless coifs, full-toothed smiles, good jewelry, a suitable outfit—maybe the Oscar de la Renta tiered silk taffeta skirt ("I've had it for *years*") with dyed-to-match pumps—and the firm but chilly handshake usually reserved for reporters.


*"Superficiality, vulgarity, especially in women, untidiness*
*of mind and person, and cigars!"*
      —NANCY REAGAN'S DISLIKES, LISTED IN 1949 ON
      HER BIOGRAPHICAL INFORMATION FORM FOR
      MGM


Most prominent in the Group, of course, is the fluffily exquisite Betsy, mate of Alfred Bloomingdale. Alfred founded Diner's Club.

Betsy, an habitué of the best-dressed list, is vivacious, charming, and a favorite subject for the photographers of *W,* the bible of high-priced consumption. She was also, on April 14, 1975, unlucky enough to be caught "concealing an invoice" for two Christian Dior dresses, valued at $3,880, into Los Angeles International Airport.

Both dresses were forfeited and auctioned off later by Customs. Upon pleading guilty in 1976, poor Mrs. B. was also fined $5,000.

"She has paid her debt to society," a friend observes reverently.

There is blonde and *soignee* Mary Jane Wick. Charles Wick, her husband, is Reagan's chief of the United States Information Agency (as it is to be renamed) and once produced a movie called *Snow White and the Three Stooges.*

Ronnie and Nancy spent their first Christmas eve in Washington at the Wicks' Watergate apartment.

Next is Leonore Annenberg. Lee was Nancy's first chief of protocol. Her husband, Walter, is the publishing mogul. As long as anyone can remember, Nancy and Ronnie see in the new year at the Annenbergs' Palm Springs place, with old pals like Efrem Zimbalist, Jr. and Jimmy Stewart swarming around.

Then there's Betty Wilson. Betty is an heiress in her own right, and William is a ranch developer. You can count on Betty to throw Nancy's birthday party every year. For the first one in Washington, she had frozen chili from Chasen's, the Group's favorite Los Angeles restaurant, flown in, for a picnic at the beautiful old Woodlawn Plantation in Virginia.

Surely you know Bunny? Bunny was the actress Bonita Granville who married showbiz-rich Jack Wrather. Virginia, the next member, is married to Holmes Tuttle—he's Ronald's close auto dealer friend.

Jean spends a lot of time with Nancy because she is married to William French Smith—he, of course, was Reagan's lawyer. Now he is his attorney general.

"No one told me what was expected of me on the job, so I've been reading *Martha,* the biography of Martha Mitchell," Jean told *W.*

There have been no symptoms yet.

Then there are Jane Bryan Dart and Justin Dart. Jane was an actress—which is why she is one of the few Group gals to hang on to her own name in the middle there—and Justin owns Dart Industries. Marion and Earle Jorgensen are the kind of pals who always pitch in to help celebrate Nancy's birthday in some special way. Earle is a steel magnate, so there is no need to skimp.

And to each of the women, her persona is her art.

Their celebration of womanly wiles, even at sixty, from coif and makeup to manicure, from muscle tone to *ligne,* from hemline to jewels, is not, of course, a Washington art. It is a Hollywood art. Worse—and this is so bizarre to the prudish, macho Washington mind that hard-boiled reporters gulp when it sinks in—at their age, yes, *all* the Group women still believe, à la Hollywood, in romance.

At Christmas 1981, Nancy mentioned to reporters that, after the unveiling of the White House tree, her husband had kissed her under the mistletoe.

"What happened after that?" Sam Donaldson, ABC's bad boy, asked saucily.

"If you can't figure it out, I'll never tell," said Nancy with a twinkle.

Hollywood would never have asked such a Washington question. Washington would never have expected such a Hollywood answer.

Jingle the sleigh bells and fade out, please.

*"I have to wonder how much sour grapes resides in that critical chant? I wonder how many women, with their great brains and empty beds, would not wish to exchange places with Nancy? To have, at the age of sixty, her handsome husband, who is all man and not some wimpish wet macaroni, a husband who has been successful at anything he tried . . . Nancy Reagan a dismal failure? Who is kidding whom?"*
    —SVETLANA, THE ASTROLOGY COLUMNIST FOR
    THE WASHINGTON *POST,* DECEMBER 1981

*"A woman, I would hope, would be a help to her
husband no matter what he does. Of course, the more
successful he is, the more important her role becomes."*
        —NANCY REAGAN, IN INTERVIEW FOR SMITH
        COLLEGE ALUMNAE IN 1971

Women who do not subscribe to the values of her art do not like
Nancy Reagan.

And Nancy's relationship with women—any women—outside the
Group has been grist for the gossip mill for years.

She is interpreted as being . . . well, jealous. Why else, ask foes,
would she have omitted any mention at all of Ronald Reagan's first
wife, Jane Wyman, from her autobiography?

One socialite told a writer of boarding an elevator occupied by
Nancy after a Republican fundraiser with actress Ruta Lee.

"Then all of a sudden she was saying, 'Oh, no, you can't come in
here.' Well, we got off but just then Ronnie showed up and said,
'Sure, they can ride with us.' I couldn't figure out what had happened
until a friend of theirs later told me that Nancy simply didn't want
two good-looking women in the same elevator with her husband.
Honestly, I couldn't believe it."

It probably wasn't true.

Nancy's foes are not legion. They are chosen with care, for specific
offenses against her art.

She will never, ever forgive writer Judy Bachrach for describing
her legs as "piano."

She will never forgive Lyn Nofziger, her husband's former aide,
for leaking a little something about her way back in the beginning
of their campaign, or for looking slobby in Daffy Duck ties and then
dribbling Bombay gin all over them.

She will never forgive Betty Ford for her cavalier treatment
throughout their joint history as fellow Republicans and fellow wives
in pursuit of the same niche.

Her treatment at the 1976 convention still rankles in the early
eighties. Nancy tells friends that she never had a decent box at the

Republican Convention, until they *had* to get one.

"They have always tucked us away in the back," she claims, stuck beyond the view of the cameras in a box on the very highest tier. Blocking them was a glass shield that would reflect the lights, blind the cameras and conceal her art.

At the time, Nancy told close friends, she believed that Betty Ford was on drugs. She "wasn't responding" to the people around her in the Ford box.

Nancy, who wished to respond, could barely snatch a glimpse of what was happening on the convention floor at all from her eyrie. She had to "change badges with alternates in a delegation so the children and I could sit in the delegate section"; and when Reagan was nominated and the shouting and flag-waving began the only way she could acknowledge the cheers was to stand up and lean dangerously over the glass.

Nancy believed that Betty tried to hog the limelight, at her expense, at the 1980 Convention, too.

In return, Betty likes to get a poke in whenever she can, to please the apposing army in Nancy's Looking-glass war. She likes to say she is "disappointed" in Nancy's ERA stand, abortion stand, or whatever. There are many excuses given at various Republican fundraising events where it would be logical to see the two women together. I have not seen them.

But Nancy Reagan came to Washington determined to make allies as her predecessors had not.

She is friendly to Cabinet wives. She invited them all to lunch in the Blue Room after a year in office, apologizing for the lateness of the invitation and describing the past year as "an emotional rollercoaster, so many highs and lows." (The day before, on a visit to the Washington Hospital Center, she had described it as "a kaleidoscope of highs and lows." A little metaphorical counseling had clearly intervened.)

She is more popular than most with the tightly knit, embattled Congressional wives.

"Rosalynn Carter never came to this building once," cried the club's president, the wife of Rep. Bob Lagomarsino, when Nancy

came a-calling, by invitation. She added the words that must have
bound her to Nancy with hoops of steel: *"Because no one ever asked
her."*

The quest for compatible women friends for Nancy in Washington
goes on, as her basic Group drifts westward again.

The now-famed Washington Ladies' Luncheons for Six, arranged
at first through Tish Baldridge, who was Jackie Kennedy's aide, and
then through Nancy's social secretary, Muffie Brandon, are designed
to pump new blood into the stream.

*"I am not an instant-friendship girl and I am reserved.*
*Maybe some people have taken that as being aloof."*
    —NANCY REAGAN

The luncheon campaign started unadventurously with tried-and-
true Old Line Established Washington: Evangeline Bruce, Ethel
Garrett, Susan Mary Alsop, Oatsie Leiter Charles. For reasons described elsewhere (see chapter, "Is There Life After Washington?")
Old Line Established Washington's permanent village is Democratic
in its leanings. Muffie and Tish themselves were too, before. This
meant Nancy was trotted out among somewhat insincerely chummy
elders of the village.

By February of 1982, Nancy's social headhunters were casting
further afield. Buffy Cafritz, a best-dressed wife of a local rich builder
(and niece-in-law to Gwen Cafritz, who vied for Washington's hostess-with-the-mostes' crown in the Eisenhower years,) trundled out a
new group including Ann Hand, wife of LBJ's brief chief of protocol
Lloyd Hand, Mrs. John Kluge, wife of the Metromedia mogul, Mrs.
Jack Kent Cooke, wife of the Redskins owner.

Each Nancy hostess, of course, tries to provide a smorgasbord of
women to whom, she hopes, Mrs. Reagan will take a fancy—but not
too much of a fancy.

Balancing the Nancy's fancy factor against being overshadowed,

against repetition, against close friends mortally offended at not
being included, requires very swift footwork. It was already getting
tricky by September 1981.

That was when Selwa "Lucky" Roosevelt gave her momentous
Nancy Lunch.

Lucky was a double threat. She is a free-lance writer, who has
often writes for glossy *Town & Country,* and she is the wife of Archie
Roosevelt, who is David Rockefeller's international aide for Chase
Manhattan Bank. She offered something refreshingly new: a literary
angle. She invited Cynthia Helms, the wife of the former CIA director, who was ambassador to Iran. Mrs. Helms had recently written
a book, *An Ambassador's Wife in Iran.* She invited Sylvia Morris,
who had written *Portrait of a First Lady,* about another Mrs. Roosevelt; and Arianne Stassinopoulos, who wrote *Callas.*

The chatter waxed happily about the written word. Nancy, who
enjoys biographies, had read two of the books. Lucky made a fast
friend. Ironically, the written word would soon bond the hostess and
her guest of honor closer as the media war waxed fiercer.

Soon after Lucky's Nancy Lunch, Washington *Post* reporter Judy
Mann lobbed a grenade into Nancy's camp. She wrote a column
attacking Nancy for her obsession with trivial and expensive things
—"fundamentally unimportant" tasks like decorating the White
House and buying china. Besides, wrote Ms. Mann, Nancy's favorite
cause, Foster Grandparents, was hardly a substantive issue.

A few days later, a ringing counter-attack called "Give the First
Lady a Break" was written by Lucky Roosevelt and published in the
*Post* under the heading "Taking Exception."

"Dear Fellow Presspersons: Fun's fun, but the pummeling of
Nancy Reagan has gone on long enough," she wrote. ". . . Only
yesterday you were making fun of Bess Truman's avoirdupois and
Mamie Eisenhower's bangs. You laughed at their dowdy clothes and
pedestrian friends. Along came Jackie Kennedy, and you extolled in
her the very things you now deplore in Nancy Reagan. . . ." At last,
someone was looking into the glass from Nancy's angle.

No worthy charities enjoyed the benefit of Jackie Kennedy's pa-

tronage, Lucky pointed out acerbically. The press did not mind Lady
Bird primping up the Mall while the poor suffered in the ghetto.
Nobody asked the price of *her* clothes. Besides that, Pat Nixon was
maligned for being "determinedly middle class" and Betty Ford,
while favored for her candor and her guts, and for being an out-
spoken defender of the ERA, often "shocked the less sophisticated
hinterland with remarks" unbefitting a First Lady. Even Rosalynn
Carter—nicknamed the Iron Magnolia—was chewed out by the
press for her weekly how-to-run-the-country lunches with Jimmy.

"Most First Ladies can't win, whatever they do," Lucky protested.
Mrs. Reagan is shy, sensitive, vulnerable; she cannot dissemble; is
apprehensive and defensive with the press because bewildered by
their hostility; she's a "real lady and a loyal friend . . . fun, relaxed,
and excellent conversationalist . . . eager to listen and learn," and had
simply dedicated her life to Ronald Reagan.

The blitz for justice won several female hearts, most notably con-
firmed Mrs. Reagan's. Ere long, Lucky Roosevelt was nominated as
Nancy's second chief of protocol.

Older friends agree that Nancy Reagan is "fun and relaxed" under
the right circumstances.

They also enjoy some fun at her expense. One California tradition
holds that her most endearing trait is what is called the Nancified
joke.

A naughty joke is told to Nancy.

"What's the definition of a nymphomaniac?" asks the jokester.
The answer is, "A woman who gets screwed an hour after she gets
her hair done."

Retold by Nancy later, the whole thing is Nancified. This means
it gains a flavor both genteel and surreal: "What do you call a woman
who makes love right after she's had her hair done?"

"A hypochondriac."

*"The latest word in Washington is that the prince is
absolutely cuckoo-nuts about Nancy Reagan."*
—BETSY BLOOMINGDALE, JUNE 1981

*"When am I ever going to see anything like this again?*
*I've never been to a polo match. I've never been to*
*Buckingham Palace—well, the whole thing. I've never*
*been to a royal wedding!"*
   —NANCY REAGAN, FLYING TO LONDON, JULY,
   1981

The most Hollywoodish skirmish in Nancy's Washington war actually happened in London. It was, of course, the wedding of Prince Charles to Lady Diana Spencer. This provided a chance for the international press to get its potshots in, too.

There had been talk beforehand that she would not go at all, because her seat in Saint Paul's Cathedral was so poor.

Her husband's convalescence, after the March attempt on his life, precluded his attendance. This meant she would have the stage to herself, not a disagreeable prospect.

British newspapers had reported with horror that she had demanded to be seated in the front row, along with royal relations.

As it turned out, Nancy's three-piece salmon Galanos—loaned, of course—and smart straw hat with chiffon scarf sat, with her inside them, in the sixth row, halfway across the cathedral. She was only two rows behind Raine Spencer, known as Lady Di's wicked stepmother.

The British thought this a great coup for Nancy.

They were not universally charmed, however. The British press giggled at the American's six-car, and sometimes eight-car, motorcade. The gigantic, glittering black Yankee limousines lumbered through the scattering of little English Rovers like elephants at a dog show.

The press marvelled at her entourage—hairdresser Julius Bengtsson, a nurse, and, of course, First Friend Betsy Bloomingdale, who was mistaken by some of the English media for a bodyguard. The Secret Servicemen swarming fore and after had them nudging and twittering.

The *Guardian,* a fashionable British newspaper, sniffed that the "restrictions imposed on her behalf were more regal than anything attempted by Buckingham Palace in recent memory." (Being parlor-pinkish in politics, of course, the *Guardian* is far more snobbish than its right-wing peers. It enjoyed calling Nancy "The one-time starlet of such B-films as 'The Next Voice You Hear' (1950) and 'Hellcats of the Navy' (1957)," and hooted with scorn when she accidentally called the queen and Prince Philip "the king and queen.")

Even the *Guardian*'s snide attentions could not squash Nancy's high spirits. Her art was on display. It was looking very good. She was gracious to the press.

Peter McCoy, then her chief of staff, ordered photographers to stop snapping her with Princess Grace of Monaco and Douglas Fairbanks, Jr. No! She chided that he hadn't given them nearly enough time to capture the moment.

British television viewers were tickled at her approval of their monarchy. ("I think it's wonderful. I think it's wonderful, I would hate to see it ever disappear.")

She watched polo from the royal box, with Prince Philip at her elbow explaining the subtleties of the game.

She had the satisfaction of having bought the bride and groom a $75,000 Steuben glass bowl at the bargain price of $8,000. (Harry Truman had given the queen, then Princess Elizabeth, a somewhat similar Steuben bowl called "The Merry-Go-Round" at her marriage to Prince Philip in 1947. The Windsors must by now, if they have been careful, be fairly well equipped with Steuben bowls.)

"Oh, my husband *would* be jealous if he knew what a good time I've been having here!" cried the First Lady.

Indeed, in one week, Nancy took in, in addition to the royal wedding itself, five dinner parties, five luncheons, two receptions, a ball, the polo match ("It seemed to me as if they were all going to kill themselves"), a wreath-laying, a fireworks display (again seated in the royal box) and a social service stop.

On the last occasion, Lord Snowden, Princess Margaret's ex, spoke to her earnestly and at terrible length about the Spastics Society. She retaliated with information on her favorite Foster Grandparents program. Apparently neither understood a word the other was saying.

One single day in London embraced a luncheon with Princess Margaret, the Queen's naughty sister, at Kensington Palace; a performance of the Dance Theater of Harlem at Covent Garden; a quick trip back to Winfield House to change from theater gown to ball gown; and then—off to the grandest event of them all, apart from the wedding itself: the Queen's Ball at Buckingham Palace.

Theoretically, this last tiara-starred event was exclusively for European royalty and British aristocracy.

Other mere heads of state and their wives were not invited. Betsy Bloomingdale, the First Friend, tripped in with Nancy and later described the experience to reporters: "Beautiful, stunning and divine!" she squealed. She added, "All the kings and people had their decorations on."

Nancy's decorations were a beaded white Galanos gown—another of the famous "loans"—and enormous, blindingly beautiful diamond earrings. American reporters, dogging her steps as she glittered her way into the ball, shouted at her: "Are they real?"

"I'll never tell!" she replied merrily.

Somebody, however, did. They were.

They had been loaned, too—by Harry Winston of New York. Winston intends for the White House to keep these jewels, as an "ongoing" collection for first ladies; but Mrs. Reagan plans to return them.) More interesting were other jewels she took along for her London social splash. These were a dazzling Bulgari *pareur*—a set of necklace, earrings and rings—of diamonds and rubies.

There is something of a mystery about these jewels. Supposedly, they were borrowed for the wedding. Yet Susan Meyer, a Bulgari spokeswoman, told reporter Maxine Cheshire that they were completed at the time of the inauguration, but not delivered to the White House until "forty-eight hours before the attempted assassination of President Reagan," in March.

Besides that, Mrs. Reagan had been seen wearing at least part of the *pareur* with a red Bill Blass dress in Washington at a private party well before the wedding.

"There's no timetable for her to give it back," Miss Meyer said, before clamming up.

The Bulgari-Reagan relationship is a warm one. In 1977, Nicola Bulgari, who runs the North American operation, met Mrs. Reagan in her Pacific Palisades home. Nancy emerged as the owner of one of the famed Bulgari gold coin necklaces—the type that Frank Sinatra has bought for many of his woman friends—and a Bulgari watch.

Indeed, some mutual friends believe that Frank Sinatra either bought, or tried to buy, that particular *pareur* for his friend Nancy when she became First Lady. That precise *pareur* had been shown in a splendid full-color Bulgari ad in one of the glossiest social magazines. It has been whispered that Nancy leaves such illustrations "lying around" where they might be seen by generous friends.

With all the publicity, the *pareur* was, supposedly, returned to the shop. "Bulgari: Jewelry (assorted)" was listed as "made available" on loan to the First Family in their financial statement in May 1982.


*"The real reason Nancy didn't curtsy to Queen
Elizabeth was that she was under the impression that it
was supposed to be the other way around."*
—JOHNNY CARSON, JULY 1981


That was a minor battle.

Life has has held battles on several scales for Nancy Reagan.

Although born in New York, she was, in effect, a Washingtonian before most current Washingtonians were. As a child she was sent to live in suburban Bethesda, Maryland, with an aunt and uncle.

Her mother, actress Edith Luckett, had separated from her husband immediately after Nancy's birth. He had been a car salesman named Kenneth Robbins. At two, Nancy went to Bethesda while her adored mother carried on her acting career.

One hateful aspect of her young life were the visits with her natural father. On one occasion, when little Nancy took exception to a remark he made about her mother, he locked her in a bathroom.

Nancy still cannot bear locked doors.

Five formative years were spent in Bethesda, with occasional trips to New York to see her mother.

"She used to live in residential hotels or in brownstone apartments," Nancy has said. "To this day, I can't pass this type of building without getting a terrible sinking feeling in my stomach."

When her mother was preparing to remarry, to Dr. Loyal Davis, she came to tell seven-year-old Nancy that now they could all live together in Chicago.

Nancy was fourteen before she allowed Davis to adopt her legally. By then, she was ensconced on fashionable Lake Shore Drive, a student at the excellent Girls' Latin School, and preparing for Smith College.

While at Smith, her first fiancé was killed when hit by a train. There, too, her second engagement was broken.

*"At Smith I learned that life is not always easy, and romances do not have romantic endings. I went through difficult changes and emotional experiences, and I learned that you have to take life as it comes and be prepared for sudden twists of fate. But I have always been a romantic; I almost feel I was fated to meet Ronnie."*
  —NANCY REAGAN

*"Sometimes he comes home and he is so tired, he just doesn't want to talk, no, about anything. And so we don't talk. I mean about anything."*
  —NANCY, OF RONALD REAGAN, TO MIKE
  DOUGLAS, AUGUST, 1981

The assassination attempt on her husband in March 1981 outside the Washington Hilton Hotel was like a stone of grief dropped into

the serene pond of the couple's extremely happy and mutually sup-
portive marriage.

It affected Nancy profoundly. It was, of course, far more nearly
lethal than the public was to know for some time.

She had always feared it might happen, she said: "I've learned to
live with the thought and the possibility of danger for a long time
now."

But the reality of her changed life was not to dawn immediately.

"I think once you've had an experience like we had, possibly extra
precautions are taken. It's always on your mind," she told British
interviewer who asked, in essence, if her security measures were not
a bit much.

There was a minor uproar when *Newsweek* reported that beneath
the First Figure's Adolfos nowadays rustled a "bulletproof slip."

Outraged denials were issued from the White House; manufacturers of such apparel said coyly that if such a garment existed, it
wouldn't be a slip anyway, but a sort of bodice.

But worse than increasing Nancy's fears, the attempt thwarted the
easy movements about the city which she and the president had
adopted as their Washington way of life. Just a few days before the
shooting, the couple had mingled freely at a party in Gerogetown for
Jim Brady, the White House press secretary.

There, press friends of Brady had remarked on the unceremonial
security. A couple of advance Secret Servicemen just slipped in,
cased the crowd, then stood to await the presidential arrival, her-
alded by the magical words over their earpieces: "Arrive, arrive—
we have an arrive."

Now, risk hangs in the Washington air like the smell of the Potomac in high summer. The Secret Service's SWAT team and all its
trimmings (see chapter "Some Enchanted Evenings") are standard
on every trip to every party.

Nancy gave up Christmas shopping that winter. Where is the joy,
even for a passionate shopper, of trudging with a pack of fidgeting
Secret Servicemen through the handbag department at I. Magnin's?

Instead, she asked friends to buy her gifts for her. Spy-style secrecy
surrounds her luncheon forays.

She remains opposed to gun control, preferring the threat of harsher punishment as a deterrent to violent crime.

"I agree with the death penalty," she told Susan Granger, the daughter of her friends, the Armand Deutsches, whom she allowed to interview her for *Redbook* magazine. "I think that people would be alive today if there were a death penalty."

*"There's nobody who likes everybody, but there are people who do like me. But they [reporters] seem to find a person who has something nasty to say and that's the one they quote."*
—NANCY REAGAN

Television interviewer Barbara Walters once asked Nancy, "If you were a tree, what kind would you be?"

Her guest's startled reply—perhaps because it was the only tree she could think of in a hurry—was "an oak."

Friends say no, she is not an oak. She is a willow or aspen— sometimes weepy or shaky, but supple enough to bend, tougher than she looks and rooted firmly in her convictions.

There is only one axe she fears, and one woodsman: the Washington media.

The media did not become more generous toward the First Lady with passing time. If anything, throughout the first fifteen months of her husband's administration, they became harsher and harsher.

"I *wish* I knew how to develop a thick skin," she sighed.

Nancy got off on the wrong foot. In fact, she got off on several wrong feet.

Washington's first real introduction to her was a widely publicized remark that slipped out unbidden in Chicago, as she gazed over a sea of Republicans. It reflected her joy at the sight of "all these beautiful white faces." "Beautiful black faces" were hastily added, but too late.

Although you rarely glimpse a beautiful black face at the Georgetown dinners where the remark was re-heated as the tastiest course, the media were appropriately horrified.

Then, as quickly as possible after the election, a Washington newspaper reprinted an intimately revealing series from the Los Angeles *Herald-Examiner*. This repeated all the bitchiest things anyone in California could be persuaded to say about Nancy.

"She's had it with all the gossip about how she bore her first child only seven and one half months after her wedding date . . . And she's just plain mad about how everyone says she and her stepfather caused Ronnie's switch in party affiliation, not to mention influencing every blessed political thought he's ever had . . ."

One of her few original allies, Betty Beale of the late Washington *Star,* rose to welcome the new Nancy Era: "It could be that we have at last outgrown the era when it was considered a must to have some ill-clad activist present to indicate broadmindedness. Uncombed hairdos, messy beards, raggedy jeans are hopefully a thing of the past."

Fits of giggles rocked the rest of the media.

Even *Time* magazine, picking Ronald Reagan as its "Man of the Year", perplexed her with its negative remarks about her.

How could *Time* say she didn't like the Reagan ranch? she implored.

"We worked on it ourselves. We painted it ourselves. We tiled the floors. I decorated it. It's part of ourselves. I love it."

She could not understand. How could a story call her a good mother and a loyal friend—mention her work with hospitals and how she puddled up around retarded children— how could it report all those things, and yet not find her "nice?"

To *Family Circle,* she revealed her ancient magic for exorcising the devils: "I do my bathtub routine—get into the tub and have long, imaginary conversations with whoever's said what's bothering me. And I am absolutely sensational! Really, just wonderful! All the right words come to me and I say exactly what I think and no one can answer me back. I never shout or raise my voice, but I'm very firm."

Washington referred to the rite as her Babble Bath.

She is unperturbed by the ordinary push of "hard" news. When

Michael Reagan, the president's son, used his father's name on a letter soliciting business from the military, Nancy came out and told the New York *Daily News* her views: "He made a mistake in writing the letter, I don't think he should have written it. I think he realizes that."

It is the other type of news—the kind that amounts to cold criticism of her art, that freezes her in misery.

Her husband leaps to her defense, loyal as the faithful quarterhorse No Strings.

"There's been an awful lot of false image building that has gone on about her," Ronald Reagan complained during their first December in office.

It still stuck in his craw in late January 1982: "She's warm and generous," he insisted to the rows of reporters' cold fish-eyes at a press conference, "and vulnerable to the kind of unjust criticism that comes this way." The media, he said, gave his wife a "bum rap" for doing nothing that Jacqueline Kennedy Onassis did not do in trying to make the White House "the prettiest house in America."

Meanwhile, the polls tracking Nancy's war zigzagged wildly. At the end of 1981, a *Newsweek* poll found that 57 percent of respondents approved the way Nancy handled responsibilites, 62 percent thought she stressed elegance too much during the time of federal budget cuts, and 61 percent found her less concerned about the poor and underprivileged than the past five First Ladies.

The same month, a Gallup poll found Nancy topping the International List of Most Admired Women. Lo, her name led over that of Margaret Thatcher, prime minister of Great Britain, and Supreme Court Justice Sandra Day O'Connor, over Mother Theresa, Betty Ford—ah—Jacqueline Onassis and Rosalynn Carter, over Barbara Walters, Queen Elizabeth II and, finally, Jane Fonda herself.

A Washington *Post*-ABC poll around the same time found that 51 percent had a "favorable" impression of the First Lady, but more people disapproved of her than of others at that stage of their First Ladyhood. The annual *People* magazine poll in April 1981 had found two-thirds of the respondents defending Nancy; by April 1982, one-half declared her "too fancy."

*"Will Nancy Reagan ever become enough of a phoney to
ingratiate herself to cheap minds? All available evidence
suggests that she will not!"*
     —COLUMNIST E. EMMETT TYRELL, DECEMBER
     1981

*"Now that's silly. I'd never wear a crown, it would mess
up my hair."*
     —NANCY REAGAN AT THE ALFRED E. SMITH
     MEMORIAL DINNER, COMMENTING ON THE
     POSTCARD THAT SHOWS HER IN QUEEN
     ELIZABETH'S CROWN AND ERMINE, AS "QUEEN
     NANCY"

A fresh wave of hostilities broke with the decorating *crise.*

"High Decorator Traditional" is how Sarah Booth Conroy of the
Washington *Post* described Nancy's controversial redo of the living
quarters in the White House.

In all, $730,000 was spent. Two hundred or so private donors had
raised $822,640. They ranged from twelve-year-old Michelle Booth
of suburban Alexandria, Virginia, who sent a dollar from her allowance to the cause—as did eleven-year-old Barbara Abernethy of
Steubensville, Ohio—to several Texas and Oklahoma oilmen. They,
solicited by Mr. Reagan's auto-dealer friend Holmes Tuttle, had
given sums of around $10,000 apiece.

Both children and all millionaires were invited to view the results.

It was plain that the First Decorator, Ted Graber, had concen-
trated on the bedroom.

There, a handsome king-sized bed faces a gilded mirror. The
wallpaper is hand-painted with Chinese birds and vines, airily scat-
tered on a pearly-white ground. It picks up delicate hues from the
other furnishings—Empire chairs upholstered in needlepoint, a comfortable white sofa, and Nancy's little collection of Battersea boxes,
which are displayed on an inlaid octagonal table.

The family living rooms are warmly dressed in pale yellows, from lemon to ochre hues. A yellow-based blossom-sprigged Aubusson-type carpet sets the scheme. There are gilt sconces on the soft yellow walls. Pale lemon brocade chairs and yellow curtains with gold-swagged drapery around the tops set the scene for, say, visits by Prince Charles—that is the room in which Nancy's friends chose to bob or not to bob. Gossips with Jerry Zipkin, Nancy's homely but witty best male friend, are in the similarly hued West Sitting Hall.

Nancy's dressing room, where she prepares for such events, is papered and carpeted in various flattering shades of salmon pink.

The president's private study is in sunny dark reds and warm gold.

The central hall, which *Architectural Digest,* called "bare and awkward," now has its space filled properly according to the same organ.

Nancy had made a few "art-type acquisitions," Sheila Tate acknowledged. But, on the whole, she had chosen to display objects like her mother's fine Chinese blue-and-white vases, bowls and urns.

Decorator Graber had been quite sickened at the state of the living quarters' plumbing and electrical wiring, he said. (Some of the plumbing fixtures had to be custom-made to fit the ancient piping.) The draperies had been simply falling into rags. There were mahogany doors that hadn't been "attended to" since President Truman had marched through them shouting for Bess.

No new furniture or chandeliers had been bought for the dramatic transformation, he claimed. A few old things had been dragged over from the White House warehouse and repaired, tightened-up, re-gilded or re-covered, along with some of the Reagans' own furniture from home.

"This house belongs to all Americans, and I want it to be something of which they can be proud!" said Nancy, after the great redecorating ordeal was over.

Unfortunately, she said that to *Architectural Digest,* the magazine that a relatively few Americans, very rich and very picky, read.

In fact, no photos of the redo of the private quarters were allowed to be released to the ordinary media—which were absolutely furious

—until the *Digest* had had its day.

As it is the publication whose pages every decorator dreams of gracing, and also the one that refuses to permit between its glossy covers pictures that have appeared in lowlier organs—and since he received no payment for his toil—one must presume that the exposure was Graber's reward. The *Digest* ran twenty-seven color photographs on eighteen pages.

Some leftover monies from the drive went to paint White House public rooms—the East Room, the State Dining Room and the Cross Hall. Downstairs floors were refinished; marble on the ground floor was cleaned to a glistening finish by acid-etching; the grand staircase was repainted; the fireplaces were cleaned.

Even after this, an embarrassment of riches was left over from the project.

In June 1981, Nancy announced that $25,000 of the money left would be donated to Wolf Trap Park for the Performing Arts, in nearby Virginia, for its birthday.

The media happily noted that the White House Historical Association had a fit. What about its antiques fund?

But Mrs. Jouett Shouse, the founder of Wolf Trap became yet another ally in the sniping war.

The following February, when the storm broke over Nancy's head about her unusual clothing arrangements, the *grande dame* of the arts leaped to her defense with an impassioned letter to the Washington *Post*.

"Do not these writers know that Mrs. Reagan is doing for the American designers' profile what costs the French government millions of dollars?" she wrote. "The French *couturier,* so widely subsidized, is kept alive by sizeable government subsidies!"

(Sadly for this mutually beneficial alliance, in April 1982, Mrs. Shouse's Wolf Trap burned to the ground.)

The press had sharpened its spears, too, when the private White House just-for-Nancy hairdressing parlor, with several thousand dollars' worth of panelling and disappearing dryers and worktables, was completed, courtesy of the National Hairdressers and Cosmetologists Association and their donations.

Sheila Tate, Nancy's press secretary, won this round. The whole salon had been originally planned for and approved by Rosalynn Carter.

"It was *allowed* to be finished by the Reagans," said she, graciously.

*"Mr. President, the style of your administration is being called 'millionaires on parade.' Do you feel you are being sensitive enough to the symbolism of Republican mink coats, limousines, thousand-dollar-a-plate china at the White House when ghetto kids are being told they can eat ketchup as a vegetable?"*

*"Let's set that straight once and for all, because Nancy's taken a bit of a bum rap on that. There has been no new china for the White House since the Truman Administration. Some partial augmentation under Lyndon Johnson, but not a full set of china. Now, breakage occurs even in the White House. I know that everyone's supposed to be walking around on feathers and that doesn't happen, but it does. And the truth of the matter is at a state dinner, we can't set the tables with dishes that match. We have to have them mixed, so don't look too closely at the other tables in there. And this was the result of an anonymous contribution and the company making the china made it at cost. So there was nothing out of the taxpayers."*

—FROM A PRESIDENTIAL PRESS CONFERENCE, OCTOBER 1981

Nancy's "china policy" brought on a new wave of enmity.

In all, 4,372 pieces of official china were to be made by Lenox of Pomona, New Jersey, at a cost of $209,508.

The Reagan china is said by frequent diners at the White House to give a more pleasing effect than, for example, Lady Bird Johnson's

china. (That, although it boasts a bright display of handsome wildflowers, also has, squatting in the middle, a naturalistic and extremely ugly brown eagle, "like a dirty old duck.")

Nancy's set was financed by the tax-exempt Knapp Foundation,
which usually goes in for the preservation of nature. Luckily, nature
was kept off the china. It is of ivory hue, very fine, with scarlet and
twenty-four-carat gold border. In the middle, the presidential seal is
emblazoned in gold.

The set boasts nineteen pieces for each place setting.

There is the serving plate, which is just to sit there stylishly filling
a hole until the food comes on; there are the salad plate, the dinner
plate, the fish plate, and the dessert plate, as well as the demitasse
cup and saucer. All of these made their grand debut at the Reagans'
dinner for Premier Mubarak of Egypt.

Mr. Mubarak missed some of the choicer pieces: the soup plate,
the fingerbowl plate, the butter plate, the teacup and its attendant
saucer, the bouillon cup, the cream soup cup and stand, the berry
bowl, the ramekin and the cocktail cup. Also included, unaccountably, is a cereal bowl, perhaps for elderly heads of state who crave a
simple serving of All-Bran with prunes.

Naturally, the news that this set of china was about to be launched
set the china makers of the world off on a flurry of charity. One
manufacturer threatened to send the china-weary Nancy a complete
set designed by Salvador Dali. Carleton Varney, a designer who had
helped the previous First Lady, tactlessly offered a service of stone-
ware named "Rosalynn."

Helen Boehm, the irrepressible woman responsible for countless
china birds roosting in dusty corners of foreign palaces as gifts from
our presidents, jumped in immediately.

She offered a $6,000, 120-piece service for 24, for Nancy's private
pleasure, to be called, modestly, "Nancy."

Mrs. Reagan was "thrilled" with the new design, according to
Mrs. Boehm, who quickly sent along several china birds for display
in the White House lobby along with a few pieces of the set.

Nancy, perhaps having heard enough about china, decided not to
nibble. She did not buy nor did she accept it.

*Q: Is it true that Nancy Reagan has a recurring
nightmare where she is abducted from the White House,
taken to a Sears store and forced to buy a dress off the
rack?"*
—C.H., GLENDALE, CAL.


*A: The First Lady has no such recurring nightmare.
Neither did Jacqueline Kennedy, Lady Bird Johnson,
Pat Nixon, Betty Ford or Rosalynn Carter."*
—"WALTER SCOTT" PARADE MAGAZINE
FEBRUARY 14, 1982


The clothes lost the next battle. In February 1982, Nancy Reagan mournfully told her favorite designers, Galanos and Adolfo, that she would no longer accept their free suits and gowns.

Outfit trouble had been brewing for some time.

Limousine drivers had regaled each other for months with tales of being sent to the airport to pick up dresses with nobody inside them.

Clerks, delivery people and designers' aides low on the totem poles had, from the beginning, nudged to friends that Nancy's wardrobe was mostly provided gratis. The gallant designer fraternity—at least those involved—had closed ranks and refused to gossip. Those who were not involved gossiped splendidly.

The truth squeaked out embarrassingly.

In mid-January 1982, a grand announcement was made that the First Lady would give some of her designer clothes to museums, "to encourage the American fashion industry, which she feels is the best in the world."

A White House source whispered to a reporter that the museum project was designed to limit the PR damage that would be wrought when it emerged irrefutably that Nancy had not . . . well, paid for her clothes at all.

National Security Adviser Richard Allen had just been hung up to dry after accepting some decidedly minor freebies from *Shufu no*

*Tomo,* the Japanese *Housewives' Companion* magazine. He had accepted a couple of Seiko watches and tucked a thousand dollars in an office safe, and then forgotten it. Nancy's wardrobe value was obviously in the tens if not the hundreds of thousands of dollars. Her heart must have plummeted into her color-keyed shoes as she pondered for the first time the media's forthcoming rain of fire over her garb.

"She felt the practice was being misunderstood," explained Sheila Tate.

It would certainly have been misunderstood by the Internal Revenue Service. Tax experts pointed out the entire wardrobe's retail value might have to be declared as taxable income. Its charitable disposal, and its hasty baptism as "loans," just might save the day.

The inspiration to pass on the outfits to museums was a natural one. The past year, Nancy had given the splendidly beaded, one-shouldered Galanos she wore to the inaugural ball to the Smithsonian.

The Smithsonian had been pleased to receive so handsome a gift, especially seeing it is a perfect size six. Bess Truman's original inaugural gown, a large, limp gray number that dangled on its form like a tarpaulin, had been exchanged for another quite recently, in response to tourists' unpleasant observations on Bess's taste and girth.

The news of the hasty defensive action was received with rare pleasure in several quarters.

Betty Furness, who had been LBJ's consumer adviser, threw up her hands with horror and dubbed Nancy "a woman who doesn't even wear her own clothes."

Mary Hoyt, who had been Rosalynn Carter's press secretary, delightedly told Nina Hyde of the *Post* that "the emphasis on the unusual acquisition and disposition of her clothes could be perceived as a cold and inappropriate priority in these times."

Geoffrey Beene, clearly not among the blessed selected to garb the First Form, indignantly summoned up the ghosts of Eleanor Roosevelt and Bess Truman. "Great First Ladies, and their appearance was secondary!"

With much fanfare, Mrs. Reagan sent back birthday presents she had received five months earlier, including a $1,600 alligator purse and belt from designer Judith Leiber.

Everyone was not against Nancy. Goodwill Industries had planned to give her one of its dresses—a deep purple floral print dress worth $3. It changed its mind after phone calls from the populace suggested that Goodwill was poking fun at their First Lady, and they didn't like it.

Neither was everyone upset by her emphasis on the outer woman. A Ronnie and Nancy paper doll book produced by Dial Press was a bestseller.

The First Dolls sported starred-and-striped underwear. Paper props included a hotline, a hair dryer, jelly beans, Bonzo, inaugural ballgown and white tie, kickaround clothes for the ranch, and neat suits for the campaign trail.

They were very popular. When students at the Corcoran School of Art created gigantic Alice In Wonderland figures, based on Sir John Tenniel's illustrations, to decorate the 1982 White House Easter Egg Roll, they also, very quietly, produced ten-foot copies of the Ronnie and Nancy paper dolls. These were to be nailed up—"crucified," somebody said—close to the White House at a later date.

As it was her clothes and her act that dragged her into the war with the press, it was to be her clothes and her act that were to turn the tide of battle.

The miracle happened in late March 1982—almost a year after her husband had been shot.

It happened at the Gridiron Club's ninety-seventh annual dinner and show.

The satirical show is put on by the cream of the Washington press corps for themselves and Washington's most powerful movers-and-shakers. Its stated aim is to "singe but not burn" the White House and the out-of-power party.

One year, the Carters created a sensation by briefly jitterbugging onstage for the scribes. Usually more fearful of the barbs than grateful for the diplomatic openings, they ignored the event.

Nancy's miracle began halfway through the 1982 show. There had been a satirical number about Nancy's clothes, sung with gusto, to the tune of "Secondhand Rose."

Suddenly, from behind a rack of clothes onstage, peeped Nancy herself.

"Let me see that score!" she cried.

The audience craned. It could not believe its ears, nor its eyes. On she swept, dressed in bag-lady finery—feathered hat, dangling beads, pantaloons and yellow boots, clutching a plate painted to look like the new White House china. The assemblage stood to applaud the sheer courage of her presence.

She threaded her way on stage, swung into motion, and warbled in a smoky voice:

*"Secondhand clothes, I'm wearing secondhand clothes,*
*They're all the thing in the spring fashion shows.*
*Even my new trench coat with fur collar Ronnie bought*
*for ten cents on the dollar!*
*The china is the only thing that's new . . .*
*Even though they tell me that I'm no longer queen*
*Did Ronnie have to buy me that new sewing machine?*
*Secondhand clothes, secondhand clothes*
*I sure hope Ed Meese sews."*

And then she smashed the plate.

It was masterful. The assembly rose to roar its approval.

Her husband, caught completely unawares, declared himself a stage-door Johnny.

The miracle was, so was the Washington Establishment.

"I have never seen anyone given such an ovation!" raved Judge John Sirica, the Iceman of Watergate, writing to Mrs. Reagan's press secretary. "I wish every American could have seen it."

Librarian of Congress Daniel Boorstin wrote to congratulate Nancy on her "brilliant and delightful performance," and likened it to "William Jennings Bryan's "Cross of Gold" speech—one of the most brilliant events in American political history."

Even the press tossed aside its spears, and left with thin smiles. They had caught the act. They knew that few among their own number would have dared risk failure among foes. Nancy had risked, and won.

She had shown she could make fun of herself. Now the press was willing to take her seriously.

*"I wouldn't mind the clothes, if she was only doing something when she goes around in them."*
      —A FRIEND QUOTED BY COLUMNIST DOROTHY
      GILLIAM

*"NANCY REAGAN: IS SAVING CHILDREN IN FASHION?"*
      —SIGN CARRIED BY DEMONSTRATOR IN DALLAS,
      WHERE NANCY WAS TOURING IN THE INTERESTS
      OF DRUG ABUSE IN FEBRUARY 1982

When Nancy Reagan decided to take on drug abuse as her crusade, she did not know what awaited her.

As late as the fall of 1981, on a visit to New York to watch son Ron junior dance with the Joffrey Ballet, she stopped at Phoenix House, a 24-hour drug treatment center. (It was about to face a 25 percent cut in federal funding, thanks to the Reagan budget.) Her distress was evident, but unfocused. She told five young drug addicts of her fear that America would lose a whole generation, as "brains are going to be mush."

While dutifully continuing to address groups like the National Federation of Parents for Drug Free Youth, she remained emotionally detached.

"Kids have picked up quickly on the broad sanction 'social' drug use now enjoys," she recited. "They get the word through music and much of today's humor, through publications for drug users and the widespread sale of drug paraphernalia."

It was not until her tour in February 1982 that reporters noted that her emotions were now engaged. Donnie Radcliffe of the Washington *Post* reported an extraordinary scene at a Florida drug center.

For two and one-half hours, kids in a free-floating rap session told what their lives on drugs were really like. The accounts of how they had lied, cheated, stolen, fought, hated and run away—how they had overdosed; how they had smoked and popped and sniffed and mainlined pot, cocaine, uppers, downers, PCP, acid, THC, hash, hash oil, mushrooms, insecticides, D-Con powder, gasoline—formed a moving and horrifying litany.

Nancy was stirred beyond anything she had expected.

She "puddled up." Her voice trembling, she looked around at the group and said that her heart was full—"So many things I'd like to say to you, if I can only get through them . . . We only make this trip once and that one you ought to make as wonderful, as full, as interesting as you possibly can."

(The choice of words was unfortunate; that was doubtless what they had tried to accomplish chemically. But the emotion, powerful and genuine, was undeniable.)

In Dallas, she called drug abuse "the most democratic of diseases" —certainly intending a small "d" on the adjective.

"There's nothing as awful for a parent as having something happen to their child, nothing as hurtful," she said at one stop.

She became interested in the clinical effects of drugs. Back at Children's Hospital in Washington, she revealed that as a child she had gone to Northwestern University, "where my father was a professor of neurosurgery, and watched him cut a brain." (Nancy is not squeamish. In fact, she was a nurse's aide during World War II. As she told a group of nurses in California, "My first patient died in the middle of the bed bath.")

The doctors had her rapt attention.

Computers can now measure the effects of popular drugs on the brains of children after about six months, they told her, but "a dramatic way" to spread the word around was required.

Say, something like the White House's public backing.

By now, Nancy was hooked.

The following month, the White House, which has seen some strange sights, saw one of its strangest. For a meeting there of the Drug Use Prevention Program, a dazzling display just outside the elegant Blue Room showed visitors an awesome array of forbidden substances—cocaine, heroin, uppers, downers, and several different breeds, colors and classes of marijuana.

These were backed up with an impressive jumble of bongs, cutting equipment and other paraphernalia usually seen in murkier surroundings.

As the final fillip, there was a show of drug-hiding and smuggling equipment, ranging from Frisbees with secret compartments to toy dope trucks and shoes with special smuggle-a-hit heels.

"I hope it doesn't give Nancy ideas," grinned one Washington scribe, no stranger to the substances on parade.

Nancy, clearly, is already getting ideas.

They are not the sort he's thinking of.

Watch that space.

# Talking on the Town; or, Does the Subject Matter?

*"To be is to do."—Plato*
*"To see is to do."—Socrates*
*"Scoobie doobie do."—Frank Sinatra*
*"Yabba Dabba Do."—Fred Flintstone*
—WASHINGTON GRAFFITI. VARIATIONS HAVE
APPEARED IN THE NATIONAL PRESS BUILDING,
THE PENTAGON, AND AT THE UNIVERSITY CLUB.

PERHAPS YOU feel you do not yet have enough ammunition to plunge into the sophisticated world of Washington conversation?

You have nothing to fear but fear itself.

Even Franklin Delano Roosevelt decided that, on the whole, it did not much matter what words were exchanged on Washington's social front. He would boast to friends of how, after greeting dozens of guests at White House functions with the "Very kind of you to come" and "How good to see you," he would, just to alleviate the boredom, occasionally lapse into murmuring, "I murdered my grandmother this morning."

The response was usually "Wonderful, Mr. President," or "Marvelous job, thank you so much, sir."

The only man to actually listen, said FDR, was a diplomat. He nodded gravely and replied, "I'm sure she had it coming to her."

278

Do not feel you must read Oscar Wilde, or practice swift witticims, unless you plan to spend a lot of time in the local gay bars, the only places where repartee is valued.

On the whole, Washington does not approve of talk that isn't going somewhere, promoting someone, or nailing down a deal.

*"I suppose all the food in Israel is kosher?"*
*"Not necessarily. Everyone who eats there's not Jewish.*
*Why, we even had butts for dinner." "You mean pork*
*butts?" "No, I mean Earl Butz. He was our secretary of*
*Agriculture."*
        —CONVERSATION BETWEEN AN AMERICAN
        AMBASSADOR TO ISRAEL, AND A SWEET YOUNG
        THING, AT A WASHINGTON LUNCHEON FOR AN
        ISRAELI PRIME MINISTER

*"Mr. Ali, please fasten your seat belt, we're coming into*
*Washington."*
*"Superman don't need no seatbelt."*
*"Superman don't need no plane, either."*
        —CONVERSATION BETWEEN AN EASTERN
        AIRLINES STEWARDESS AND MUHAMMAD ALI
        (THIS IS NOT WHAT YOU'D CALL A *WASHINGTON*
        WASHINGTON CONVERSATION, BUT WE ALL NEED
        TO COME DOWN TO EARTH SOMETIMES.)

Don't go to a lot of trouble to memorize the names of all the nice new people you meet. The city will be astonished and rather shocked if you do, and will certainly wonder what you're up to. If you don't know immediately who someone is, it doesn't matter.

When Tennessee Rep. Bill Boner first came to town, he strapped a tiny tape recorder beneath his jacket. As he met each new acquaintance and shook hands, he made them all say their names twice and give their addresses. If they mumbled, he waited until they walked away, flapped open his coat and hissed to his chest, "That was Sidney Bumpforth, a lawyer whose grandfather came from Nashville."

On the whole, almost everybody on the circuit says his or her name clearly upon meeting for even the twentieth time. An exception might be if you have within the last week spent an entire day or night together, alone; sometimes, out of habit, Washingtonians employ the name exchange even then. This is both a courtesy and a face-saver. Too many Washingtonians have heard too often the humbling whisper behind them as they left a rapt two-hour conversation, "Who the hell was *that?*"

The very famous, like Teddy Kennedy, say "Good to see you" to all comers. Then, if worried he's met you before, he'll add "again."

After that, it is on with the topic.

Genuine Washington topics, of course, change with the era. Gossip is always delightful; name-dropping, sometimes. (See chapter, "Mind Your Manners, Please.") Exactly where the President stands in the public perception out there, meaning not in Washington, is an ever-refreshing spring for speculation.

For several years, real estate values and how they'd soared filled the aching hush around many tables. Prices and percentages, interest rates and equity figures peppered the air like shot at a duck shoot.

Now, this is generally superceded among the numbers-minded by the Reagan budget.

At one typical Washington early-eighties, on-the-ball cocktail party, topics that bobbed to the top of the babble included the following: had anybody actually tasted the free surplus cheese distributed in the cheese line? (Nobody had.) Speculation on the sex life of Washington's mayor; Ronald Reagan's return to radio as an image tool; the weather; what Jimmy Carter's support of Mario Cuomo over Ed Koch as mayor of New York would do (several Koch supporters had cheekily urged mailing Cuomo his airfare to New York); the virtues of a Jacuzzi whirlpool bath, and why they do not install one in Blair House, the president's guest house (foreign dignitaries presume they will be electrocuted); how the Ikards' Jacuzzi—named the Walter Cronkite Memorial Jacuzzi after their in-law—

overlooks the Washington Monument; and why somebody puts apricot juice in his or her Jacuzzi. Then, the fact that, as vice-president, Walter Mondale had had to have a haircut every week because his hair sprouted so fast, and what that meant; Ronald Reagan's hairline, and what that meant; Tip O'Neill's hair, and what that meant; why elderly Rep. Claude Pepper started wearing a wig, and why he stopped; who had written a book and how much money he was making; the fortune to be made in television script-writing.

*"I see you wear a hearing aid too, senator."*
*"Oh, well, yes. But it's not because I'm hard of hearing, it just helps filter out background noise in the hearing rooms."*
*"Oh, really? What kind is it?"*
*"Let's see. Exactly 4:30."*
    —CONVERSATION REPORTED BETWEEN SEN.
    CHARLES PERCY AND A CONSTITUENT, IN
    WASHINGTON

Some former high-ranking officials claim that the only intelligent conversations they had in years in Washington were with strangers —cab drivers, someone bumped into at an art gallery, the man at the next barstool at the Class Reunion or the bar at Charlie's nightclub in Georgetown—perhaps because, the Who You Are syndrome does not enter into these exchanges.

They are not as reliable as, say, Agriculture Department budget briefings.

President Reagan's beloved press secretary Jim Brady—who was wounded in the assassination attempt on the president outside the Washington Hilton Hotel—was always one of Washington's best barroom blarneymongers.

"That's an interesting book you've got there!" he cried in the Class Reunion bar to a stranger perched on the next stool one day, before he was famous. "*Seven Games in October* by Charles Brady, is it?

That was written by my uncle, you know. Great guy. Boy, does he
drink a helluva lot. Still, the family puts up with him. We're kind
of proud of him."

The book-clutcher looked doubtful.

"Don't believe me? Here's my I.D.! See the name? Jim Brady!"

"Interesting," said the stranger. "I'm Charles Brady. I wrote the
book."

Back on the social treadmill, Washingtonians are still tramping
around talking about What They Do, or being pleased with whatever
is playing at the Kennedy Center. Almost all the Washington jokes
you hear were first made by Mark Russell, the splendid political
comedian. ("Jerry Brown took a vow when he went into the priest-
hood: poverty, chastity, and expediency.")

On the conservative side, there is a distinct weakness for puns
("Some say that Alexander Solzhenitsyn is a prophet; but this is a
non-prophet organization," popped out at an Ethics and Public Policy Center dinner); others favor aphorisms.

Some people go to a lot of trouble to make quotable remarks;
sadly, those that get quoted usually slip out before the talker has time
to clamp on his Washington inner censor, a skill that sometimes
takes as long as six months to polish.

If you plan to be in places where you might be quoted, you'll
probably want to practice Washingtonian observations first. Here are
a few random remarks from different eras of recent history to get you
in the mood. Take them slowly at first. Some may be sung in the
bathtub, or murmured softly over your first shad roe of spring at Le
Lion d'Or restaurant.

Gradually, you can increase your dose. After a couple of weeks,
your Washington mind-set should be good enough to take out on the
town:


*"Two wrongs don't make a right. But they make a heck
of a good conference report."*
    —EX-REPRESENTATIVE BOB ECKHARDT

*"One of the ways I save energy is by asking my servants not to turn on the self-cleaning oven until after seven in the evening."*
    —BETSY BLOOMINGDALE, NANCY REAGAN'S FIRST FRIEND.


*"Na noon han kook salam ib-nida."*
    —REPRESENTATIVE JOHN M. MURPHY (D-NY), MARKING THE TWENTY-FIFTH ANNIVERSARY OF THE KOREAN WAR (IT MEANS "I AM A KOREAN.")


*"There is nothing the rich and powerful like better than to have someone spend money on them."*
    —AUTHOR WILLIAM WRIGHT


*"Well, as I told Nancy Reagan, follow Kennedy's advice: 'Don't get mad; get even.' "*
    —CLARE BOOTHE LUCE


*"Democrats give away their old clothes; Republicans wear theirs. Republicans employ exterminators; Democrats step on the bugs. Democrats eat the fish they catch; Republicans stuff 'em and hang 'em on the wall. Republican boys date Democratic girls. (They plan, of course, to marry Republican girls but feel they're entitled to a little fun first.) Republicans tend to keep their shades drawn, although there is seldom any reason why they should. Democrats ought to but don't."*
    —SEAN DONLON (HE WAS AMBASSADOR FROM IRELAND.)

*"It was stupid—like General Motors breaking in to steal Edsel plans."*
   —FORMER SECRETARY OF AGRICULTURE EARL
   BUTZ, ABOUT THE WATERGATE BURGLARY


*"Practically* no one *will be having live-in servants. We'll all have to be more self-reliant and use more caterers, which is dreary."*
   —SUSAN MARY ALSOP, PREDICTING CHANGES FOR
   THE EIGHTIES.


*"Simple virtue is more powerful than arrogance. Let your verdict tell us that none shall raise his head too high in defiance of our common standards."*
   —RICHARD M. NIXON, AS A PROSECUTING
   ATTORNEY IN AN AMATEUR PLAY IN WHICH HE
   STARRED WITH THELMA CATHERINE RYAN, HIS
   WIFE-TO-BE, IN 1938


*"Making foreign policy is a little bit like making pornographic movies. It's more fun doing it than watching it."*
   —WILLIAM D. ROGERS, WHEN HE WAS SWORN IN
   AS UNDERSECRETARY OF STATE FOR ECONOMIC
   AFFAIRS


*"The life of a government flack is like a mushroom's. You're kept in the dark, they shovel crap on you, and you end up getting canned."*
   —AN UNDERSECRETARY FOR PUBLIC
   INFORMATION

*"Chez, you put together a great meal."*
—MAYOR MARION BARRY, LEAVING A
RESTAURANT CALLED CHEZ BROWN


*"It's Boy Scouts, beauty queens, high school bands and
ferries that make this country great!"*
—NORTH CAROLINA'S REP. WALTER JONES


*"Pete Rose—isn't he the congressman from North
Carolina that was on the House Administration
Committee with Wayne?"*
—LIZ RAY, WHEN THE CINCINNATI REDS THIRD
BASEMAN POPPED BY THE CAPITOL


*"It is the party of big business, the party that does not
care at all about the working people."*
—RONALD REAGAN, SPEAKING OF THE
REPUBLICANS, IN 1948 (A TAPE OF THIS IS
SOMETIMES PLAYED AT DEMOCRATIC
FUNDRAISERS IN CALIFORNIA.)


*"Give the MX missile to Amtrak, give the schedule to
the Russians, and they'll never be able to find it."*
—SENATOR ED ZORINSKY, AT A SALT HEARING


*"Helen and I were talking over drinks. If there's one
person in the country we'd pick as a son, it's Hamilton
Jordan."*
—BOB STRAUSS, AT A MEDIA BREAKFAST

*"You know, Frank, we both have the same problem. The press is always misquoting us."*
    —MISS LILLIAN TO FRANK SINATRA


*"It's the fifth leg of the tripod!"*
    —SENATOR CHARLES PERCY, DESCRIBING THE
    ENERGY TAX BILL AS THE NINETY-FIFTH
    CONGRESS WOUND DOWN


*"Women have gone about as far as they ought to go now."*
    —JIMMY CARTER, AT THE FIRST BAPTIST CHURCH
    BIBLE CLASS


*"The only* real *secret in Washington is the recipe for lobster rolls at the annual Cathedral Flower Mart."*
    —A STATE DEPARTMENT WIFE


*"By the way, you appear to be taking a picture of your breasts. Would you send me a copy?"*
    —ROBERT REDFORD, TO A FLUSTERED FEMALE
    FAN AT THE WASHINGTON PRESS CLUB


*"Into each life a little tacky must fall, and I've been tackied out of town."*
    —FORMER WASHINGTONIAN BARBARA HOWAR,
    LEAVING WASHINGTON, PERHAPS FOREVER


*"I got a mama who joined the Peace Corps when she was sixty-eight. I got one sister who's a Holy Roller*

*preacher. Another wears a helmet and rides a*
*motorcycle. And my brother thinks he's going to be*
*president. So that makes me the only sane one in the*
*family.*"
                —BILLY CARTER


That will do for a start.

You may not be required to talk at all. If you are very important, every word you say will be greeted with most agreeable attention, and every joke with uproarious laughter; you will realize what a very witty fellow you really were all this time, and wonder why nobody noticed before. If you are not important, well, perhaps you can offer useful information like the name of a good dry cleaner or furniture refinisher.

Luckily, there are ways of setting up social situations so that guests or hosts cannot get a word in edgewise. These are very popular in D.C., where conversation, as understood in a Paris outdoor cafe or a Mayfair drawing room, is regarded as a dangerous sign of flakiness, unreliability and, probably, homosexuality.

The less chattering the better, is the Washington rule. A group of Carter White House Georgians, for example, was invited to the Soviet Embassy to meet their peers from the Kremlin for mutually beneficial discussions over dinner. They counteroffered, and took the puzzled Russians to a Willie Nelson concert at the Capital Center.

The Reagans throw screenings of movies at the White House for friends and to repay social debts; large bowls of popcorn are served to keep mouths busy; the stars are often invited, and there is as little talk as possible.

Ronald Reagan, famed as both an "easy" host and guest, is relaxed, sociable, conversational and, like most Washingtonians, very attached indeed to jokes, although not, to the disappointment of some, Washington jokes.

While you probably will not need too many Washington jokes for this administration, you should understand the phenomenon so that you know what it is when it happens, like appendicitis.

Connoiseurs thought that inept Jimmy Carter jokes were the cruelest, and therefore the most pleasurable to Washingtonians: "Hey, come on. Don't criticize Carter, he's doing the job of two men—Laurel and Hardy."

"Why does everyone in Washington run when they see Carter coming toward them with a pin in his hand?" "Because it means he's got a grenade in his mouth."

"Why is Jimmy Carter like Christopher Columbus?" "He didn't know where he was going when he set out; he didn't know where he was when he got there; he didn't know where he'd been when he got back; and he did it all on government time and money."

After the election, as Reagan's inauguration drew nigh, and Carter's Iranian hostage debacle remained unresolved, Bob Hope phoned Sinatra to pass on his contribution to Washington humor: "What's flat and sandy and glows at night?"

"Iran, after the inauguration."

(Sinatra spread it quickly. A man fond of a vivid image, he once likened *People* magazine's relationship to accurate journalism to that of "Preparation H to advanced medicine.")

He is much valued for his humor by the present administration. The day after the attempt on Ronald Reagan's life in March 1981, he rushed to Washington to visit his friend and president.

That evening at Pisces, the Georgetown club, he proudly quoted Nancy Reagan's first words to him: "Frank! Thank God you're here. There's finally someone I can tell my dirty stories to!" (See chapter, "Nancy Through the Looking Glass" for Nancy's idea of such a story.)

*"The Reagan Cabinet are the kind of guys who come home exhausted from a white tie affair and slip into black tie."*
—MARK RUSSELL

Reagan's own favorite one-liner serves all sorts of purposes. He turned around to murmur it to Tip O'Neill during his first address to the Congress on the budget: "If I'd gotten applause like this in Hollywood, I never would have left."

A similar remark, "If I'd gotten all this attention in Hollywood, I never would have left" was reported from his lips after his shooting, as he lay in George Washington Hospital.

So have variations of the (rather flattering) remark, "Sometimes I think that Washington is just one gigantic Ear," which has been heard on a Westinghouse interview, an ABC interview, and at a press conference or two.

Standard Washington circuit jokes, chuckled over near the black-tie buffets at places like the F Street Club or along Embassy Row, are often crisis-engendered and youthfully ebullient rather than waspishly sophisticated:

"I have some good and bad news for you, Mr. President. First, the bad: the Martians have landed in California."

"That's terrible. What's the good news?"

"They're eating oilmen, peeing oil, and heading East."

Zbigniew Brzezinski's own Polish joke was born during the hostage crisis in Iran:

"Q: What would the Polish government do with the current Iranian situation?"

"A: Exactly the same as the present American government."

A visiting Chinese made a big splash on Embassy Row with his definition of the American businessman, which was hailed at several gatherings with hysterical laughter: "One wife, two children, three pets, four cars, five suits, six acres, seven credit cards, and fortunate to have eight cents in pocket."

Long before each election, Washingtonians gather in corners of places like the Class Reunion or the Capitol Hill Club and replace conversation completely with jokes called ticket toppers.

These are the Washington equivalent of Japanese haiku in their economy of expression and breadth of allusion, and refer, of course, to proposals for viable presidential and vice-presidential running teams.

Examples:

"Herman Talmadge and Teddy Kennedy: The Drink and Drive Ticket."

"Jerry Brown and [National Organization of Women president] Eleanor Smeal: The Zen and NOW Ticket."

"Abzug and Reigle: The Bella-Donald Ticket."

"John D. Rockefeller and Robert Bauman: The You Can Call Me Jay or You Can Call Me Gay Ticket."

In duller times, it is trickier to focus on a good topic. One Washingtonian with a superb reputation for good Washington conversation and penetrating insights once revealed his secret: before going to a party, he glanced at all three of the Establishment newspapers —the Washington *Post,* the New York *Times* and the *Wall Street Journal.* But then, while his wife lay on the bed with witch-hazel pads on her eyes before dressing, he lay on his bed and devoured Washington news as reported in the most vulgar New York tabloid he could lay his hands on.

He never cited his source, and he bowled 'em over, every time.

# TAPS

# Is There Life After Washington? Food for Thought in the Sunset of Each Era

*"HI! I USED TO BE SOMEBODY WHO WAS RECOG-*
*NIZED WHEN SHE WALKED DOWN THE STREET*
*BUT NOW NOBODY KNOWS ME."*
>     —WRITTEN ON A STICKUM BADGE AT A CARTER
>     STAFF REUNION

ONE DAY it is all over. An election has changed Washington.

The New People of four years back become the Old People.

The elders of Washington's Permanent Village settle back to watch as the torch is passed.

Who among the Old People is going on to greater glory in the private sector? Who will sink from sight? Who will become a Washington media sage? Who will skip lightly across that shallow stream that divides government from industry, on the felicitous stepping stones of good bureaucratic contacts laid during the past four years?

And who will join the Permanent Village?

The last is viewed with the most fascinated attention. Washington's Permanent Village, essentially, is made up of people who can't go home again.

In some cases, the Villagers are descendants of those people. So many generations have passed since that decision that they have forgotten where home was. (These permanent children of the transient decision-makers, usually from old WASP families, form part of Washington's so-called cave dwellers; the other part is the old local country gentry, who scrape the mud from their boots and swing into town periodically for tribal rites like weddings and funerals.)

In other cases, the Villagers are simply recent additions to the ranks of the out-of-power.

Their children are in Washington schools; their lives are set in the Washington pattern. They cannot bear to leave Washington newspapers, Washington standards, Washington gossip behind. The curious provincial sport known as Washington life has become addictive.

These tend to be Democrats. Perhaps this is because Washington often means a pay boost for newly arrived Democrats; their eyes are suddenly opened to enriching (read "lobbying") possibilities unthought-of before their arrival. Republicans often leave better-paying jobs in industry to go to Washington, and can't wait to get back to Grosse Pointe or New York or Los Angeles. They regard their romance with Washington as one of the shipboard variety—love it, then disembark before it gets embarrassing.

With each administration change from one party to another, the jostling begins.

The newly Old People, remnants of the just-past administration, naturally cannot hope to play any role in the plans of the New People. At best they must try to leapfrog to something glitteringly better than, if not so powerful as, their lost administration role; at worst, they must lie fallow for four years.

Unless they have taken pains to ingratiate themselves with the Permanent Village they discover, to their horror, that the leapfrogging is harder than it looks.

This was the case with many Carter people. Who cared about an exciting administration that had not gone to pains to endear itself to the Village? Everyone wished it to sail into the sunset as swiftly as possible so that the new romance could begin.

*"Nancy Reagan is counting the days 'til she becomes
First Lady of the house on Pennsylvania Avenue. She
thinks she's got to wait seven days too long. Mrs.
Reagan wonders why the Carters don't just move into
Blair House the week before the inauguration, so she
can have the White House ready for Ronnie as soon as
he takes the oath of office."*
        —JANE PAULEY, DECEMBER II, 1980

Profitable positions await most high-powered former office holders
on the boards of large corporations. Some corporations battle for the
honor of impressing their stockholders with big names. This will cost
them a great deal of money for very little work, but they get respect.

Right after the Reagan election, perhaps with thoughts of the new
Hollywood-Washington axis buzzing in their brains, Columbia Pictures hauled former Vice-President Walter Mondale onto their
board. Promptly, Twentieth Century Fox's Marvin Davis added to
*his* board former President Jerry Ford and Henry Kissinger.

Could it go any further?

A joke memo appeared, to giggles, at the Fox offices one day in
1981: "Former French Prime Minister Charles De Gaulle's body was
exhumed and stretched out on the Fox board this week. 'The addition of M. De Gaulle's remains will bring an international perspective to my ultimate goal, which is to provide a haven for all washed-
up government personages,' Fox President Marvin Davis
proclaimed. M. De Gaulle could not be raised for comment."

Some entertainment media actually expect their money's worth in
personalities. Rosalynn Carter was seriously weighed as a possible
television performer by at least one television network after the Fall.
Generally, it is the former presidential and vice-presidential press
secretaries who find a working niche in that medium.

The field is getting quite crowded. One fine summer morning
during the Reagan Administration, on Lafayette Park, right across
the street from the White House, as bag ladies fed the pigeons and
winos slurped from paper bags, onto the scene walked Ron Nessen,

once Jerry Ford's press secretary. He was talking to the veterinarian son of famed Marine General Chesty Puller for NBC's cameras, with the White House as his backdrop. Under the trees with his ABC camera crew in tow strolled Pierre Salinger, once JFK's press secretary. He clutched the script for his major in-front-of-the-White House takeout on the Berlin Wall's twenty-fifth anniversary.

Meanwhile, new White House people bustled by, giggling and shouting over their shoulders: "Anybody seen Bill Moyers (LBJ's press secretary) and the CBS gang?" and "Where's (Carter press secretary) Jody? Anybody seen Vic?"

(Jody Powell, Jimmy Carter's press secretary who hated the Washington press, now writes a Washington-based column for a Texas paper and "consults" for ABC. Victor Gold, once Vice-President Spiro Agnew's press secretary, authors a sophisticated and curmudgeonly column for *Washingtonian* magazine under the nom de plume "Fantod," which means "restless anxiety.")

Other former stars of administrations' media circuses jump into more profitable rings. Ron Ziegler, Richard Nixon's former press secretary, has leapfrogged into the business world as president of the National Truck Stop Operators Association; Jerry terHorst, who was Ford's, is now a vice-president of the Ford Motor Company. Former Federal Trade Commission press head, Frank Pollock, now tills the soil of his grandfather's farm in Pennsylvania and markets cow manure in custom-printed bags labelled "Moo Magic."

Yes, there is life after Washington, for those who know how to exploit their position.

There is even life for those who did not leave with the cheers of a grateful nation ringing in their ears. John Dean, Nixon's aide and a star at the Watergate hearings, was a while back trying to market a television sitcom about a group of prostitutes who hoped to form a labor union. Since then, he has taken to the profitable lecture circuit.

Donald Rumsfeld, a top staffer in both the Nixon and Ford White Houses and Ford's Defense secretary, is at the helm of G.D. Searle & Co. and also chairman of the board of trustees of the right-wing think tank called the Rand Corporation.

Hamilton Jordan left the White House telling friends, rather touchingly, "There's a lot of people in this town I'm gonna get." He neglected to say with what, but went on to teach at Emory University in Atlanta—which is endowed by Coca-Cola—make speeches and toil on a "personalistic account" of his role in the Iranian fiasco.

Carter's original secretary of Health, Education and Welfare, Joe Califano, slipped back into citizenship of the Permanent Village after he was prematurely uprooted.

Shortly thereafter, he rode in a Washington cab.

"Say," cried the cabbie, also a Villager. "Aren't you Joe Califano, who used to be secretary of HEW?"

Modestly, Joe allowed as he was.

"I really don't see much difference between Carter and Kennedy," mused the driver. "But ya know who ought to run for president? You and [Atlanta mayor] Andy Young."

Joe suppressed a flattered smirk.

"Yeah," said the driver. "You'd make a terrific vice-president."

*"Do not go gentle into that good night.*
*Rage, rage, against the dying of the light."*
    —DYLAN THOMAS

The pain of making an exit from the world of the Washington In to the world of the Washington Out can be devastating.

It is cruel, sudden, and completely unexpected. Out of the blue, White House telephone operators do not recognize the names of the people still working in the White House. ("Jody who? I'm sorry, she's busy.")

Suddenly, the hometown newspaper disappears from the newsstand on the street corner near the White House—the Atlanta *Constitution* is replaced by the Los Angeles *Times.*

Henry Kissinger, calling Washington barber Milton Pitts about a haircut after his exit from power was told, "Please be on time. I have a V.I.P. coming fifteen minutes later."

Many people just creep quietly from office when the votes are in and the writing is clearly on the wall.

Experienced Washingtonians know they may as well make a scene on the way out.

Eleanor Holmes Norton, Chair of the Equal Opportunity Employment Commission in the last administration, did herself proud. She sent out a press release on her (inevitable) resignation, along with a copy of her resignation letter, which read rather like a job application.

She lingered at her Equal Employment Opportunity Commission headquarters, meanwhile, long enough to see a display mounted in a prominent spot in honor of Black History Month. Of course, it saluted Eleanor Holmes Norton. Glossy photographs showed Ms. Norton being sworn in, Ms. Norton getting her honorary doctorate, and high points of Ms. Norton's three-year EOEC career. (No mention, friends noted, of the fact that her Guyanese housekeeper was at that time suing her for $18,663 in back wages.) She has since gone on to glory as a Senior Fellow at the Urban Institute in Washington.

*"Hooray! Your victory is a high spot in a dismal scene. Let me help in any way I can! Sincerely, Esther Peterson."*
> —LETTER FROM MS. PETERSON, CARTER'S AIDE
> FOR CONSUMER AFFAIRS, TO SEN. JOHN DURKIN
> OF NEW HAMPSHIRE. UNFORTUNATELY, THE
> SENATOR HAD LOST HIS SEAT BY TWELVE
> THOUSAND VOTES.

The end of an administration presents the last chance for a grateful departing president to do small favors for his staff. Carter permitted Vice-President Fritz Mondale to bring his wife and spend the night in the Lincoln bedroom at the White House. Clearly, he thought he'd done his duty. Fritz's friends could not help noticing that Carter grandly presented the Medal of Freedom to people like his consumer aide Esther Peterson and National Security Council chief Zbigniew Brzezinski, but did not give it to Fritz.

A certain bitterness sometimes colors the proceedings. The Carters' last Christmas press party ended with the hard core singing carols round the piano, tears, and Jody Powell crooning "Amazing Grace" and "Goodnight Irene." He gasped at the end of the latter, "Ah want you to know this is the last time that song will be sung in this house for four years—damn their eyes!"

The unwilling exit takes its toll. One recently existing administration member, shortly after the loss of the election, inexplicably treated himself to a vasectomy. A Ford staffer, before leaving, tiptoed into the Rose Garden and planted marijuana seeds. The seedlings, spotted that spring by sharp-eyed White House gardeners, were uprooted before they could do any harm—or good.

Some Carter White Housers, it was rumored, saved the right wings from their Thanksgiving turkeys to leave in their desk drawers for the incoming Reaganites.

Unaccountably—or perhaps accountably—the very mice left the White House with the Carters. By that February, the First Lady's press office reported that the mousetraps were suddenly yawning empty every day.

Not only in the White House but throughout the Washington bureaucracy, the tide of change swells high. Some gleeful Permanent Villagers rise early on transition mornings to stretch black ribbons across the doors of presidential appointees who must leave.

At the Labor Department last time, the change was more dramatic. There, Carterites had exhumed for conspicuous display several old Works Project Administration paintings of the hod-carrier-and-tractor school, showing the Dignity of Labor in Action.

These, of course, had been created by government-employed artists in the thirties. They reflected an unmistakable political viewpoint.

The Reagan team walked in, eyed the people's heroes in their revolutionary poses, decided they did not precisely reflect the *nou-*

*veau* elegance of the Reagan Age and promptly bundled them back into mothballs until such day as Dame Fashion turns the tide. Labor knew precisely where it stood.

At the Interior Department, the little buffalo on the letterhead's seal suddenly turned from facing the sunrise on its left to facing the sunrise on its right.

For exiting congressmen voted out of office, life after Washington is ripe with promise.

Yes, they are Out. But for them, unless they are notoriously wicked, the life after Washington is life *in* Washington.

Ex-congressmen may continue to use the House gym and the House dining room. Pensions are fairly generous. (The rule of thumb is that each retiring congressman receives, as his annual pension, 2½ percent of his annual salary *for each year he has served his government;* that service includes not only his time in the Congress, but any time he has spent in the military, or working in such facilities as a post office.) Most important of all, he has complete freedom of access to the House floor at any time at all. This means he can mingle very profitably with his former peers as a lobbyist or "consultant."

Some congressmen become addicted to Hill life per se.

North Carolina Congressman Lamar Gudger, for example, became Legal Counsel to the House Merchant Marine and Fisheries Committee. Bob Bauman, the unfortunate Maryland congressman whose alcohol and sexual problems led to his untimely departure, is so skilled a parliamentarian that he was retained on the Hill as an adviser on Procedures to the Republican freshmen, and also worked behind the scenes for three of his former brethren of the right wing.

A few go home. They stray into familiar fields. Representative Ed Beard of Rhode Island, who had been a house painter and then headed the Blue Collar Caucus on the Hill, went home to run a bar in Central Falls, Rhode Island. Utah's Gunn McKay became mission president of the Church of Jesus Christ of the Latter Day Saints, in Scotland. John Anderson, who had run for president as a congressman, went on to teach at Stanford, talk on Chicago television and brood about another presidential plunge.

Every two years, as the congressional elections roll around, Capitol Hill bars brace for wakes and extended mourning drunks, as a sizable part of their clientele moseys to the clover.

One pub, the Man in the Green Hat, offers Lame Duck Libation-Pink Slip Specials after congressional elections.

These include, for deposed congressmen and their staffs, a free drink, a lending library of books on How to Write a Resume, a new copy of the so-called Plum Book if the election has been presidential (this lists vacant presidential appointments), plenty of sharp pencils, and the phone number of the "Ear" column, so the out-of-office can announce when they get something.

As always, what comes as a shock to a lame-duck congressman is the suddenness of the whisking away from beneath his feet of that magic carpet of power.

After their defeat, exiting Reps. Bob Carr of Michigan and Andy Maguire pleaded vainly with rock critics, friends, promotors—even the box office—for tickets to a Bruce Springsteen concert; they were even willing to pay. Too late. The door of privilege had been slammed shut.

Author Warren Adler wrote a short story for *Dossier,* the glossy local social magazine, about a former high-voltage Washingtonian being uninvited to a classic Washington dinner party. Adler's telephone rang a dozen times. Twelve former public figures on Washington's social scene inquired piteously: "Is that Out person based on me?"

*"Always remember that your time is short in the sweep of history, so take time to smell the roses and nod to the portraits of those who were privileged also to be here."*
—NOTE FROM MARY HOYT, ROSALYNN CARTER'S PRESS SECRETARY, TO SHEILA PATTON (LATER TATE), NANCY REAGAN'S PRESS SECRETARY. IT ARRIVED WITH FLOWERS, NOTABLE AS ONE OF THE FEW CIVIL GESTURES OF THE LAST TRANSITION.

The Permanent Village sees them come and go.

It adapts its preferences to fit reality.

For instance, anyone of any party who can go to the incoming people's inaugural ball without making a complete laughingstock of himself will try to do so.

Old People who have said really terrible things about the New People, of course, cannot; they must make their own fun.

Bob Squier, the political consultant to so many Democrats from New York's Liz Holtzman to Kentucky governor John Y. Brown, rose to the occasion for his gloomy Permanent Village Democratic friends.

As the Reagan inaugural balls rolled underway all over the city and country, he quietly held a black-tie screening for friends of the movie *Bedtime for Bonzo.*

"What I had to do to get hold of a print of the movie would not be considered illegal or immoral by Al Haig," he said darkly. Indeed, Reagan's Hollywood connections have whisked every possible copy of the movie down the Orwellian memory hole.

Out-of-office presidents hurry away as quickly as possible for some well deserved self-indulgence. Jimmy Carter headed for his favorite Pennsylvania trout stream, Spruce Creek, in a camper, with several Secret Servicemen and little Amy in tow. He wrote a charming account of the adventure for *Fly Fisherman* magazine, which bodes well for his memoirs.

("Everyone was in good spirits, dampened only by a fly hook embedded in the lip of Wayne's six-year-old daughter Heidi, who had walked too closely behind daughter Amy on one of her backcasts . . .")

Then he went to China.

China is very big with ex-presidents. Richard Nixon, equally fond of *choses chinoises,* keeps a live-in Chinese couple to cook for him at his Saddle Creek house. His relaxation is small stag dinner parties for six, at which he shakes the martinis himself. One party will be, for example, all first-term congressmen; another, all journalists. Authors like George Gilder, who dreamed up supply-side economics, and Joseph Sobrin, the editor of William F. Buckley's *National*

*Review,* have supped happily with the former president. Although disliked and rejected by many of his countrymen, particularly in Washington, Nixon maintains high popularity abroad. In Paris, he is accorded as much as $120,000 for a single television interview; on one trip, former President Valery Giscard d'Estaing sent a gigantic bouquet to his room at the Ritz.

There are things men can do when the great gate of power crashes shut behind them. For Washington women who have stooped to folly, there is a different kind of Life Hereafter.

Rita Jenrette, estranged wife of John Jenrette, enjoys a present as checkered as her past: since calling the marriage quits, she has been invited to gossip professionally on a television show, offered $200,000 for a television story from her memoirs and diaries, gained and lost a movie role (as a newswoman with Morgan Fairchild in *Seduction* —Ms. Fairchild reportedly did not want her on the show) been featured in a television soap opera and "Fantasy Island;" and offered some juicy television "special" roles.

Paula Parkinson, the lady lobbyist who tattled about her romantic involvement with various congressmen and created a tremblor on the Hill, hurried off to Dallas. There, Paula preserves as her proudest possession a framed letter from Jerry Ford thanking her for her help during the 1976 campaign. And she worries about smaller issues, like a photograph of her in a Washington newspaper, puffing a cigarette.

"I just hate for my mother to see that. She gets very upset when she sees me smoking," she said. "I got a lot of fond memories," she told a Dallas paper. "And the men I was with do. When they think of me they're going to smile."

Washington wives who find themselves suddenly detached from power—either because their husbands are elected out, or because *they* have elected their husbands out—do not smile much.

The former wife of another congressman who was later caught in the Abscam web, Republican Richard Kelly of Florida, went to work for Ethel Kennedy—a member of the Democratic Permanent Village —as a housekeeper. After that, Lorraine Kelly, knowing she was equal to anything, began to think of running for her ex-husband's seat herself.

Some seek amusement by lending their still-lustrous names to various affairs. Both Joan Kennedy, after her estrangement from Ted, and Nancy Kissinger, after Henry's estrangement from power, for example, chaired Washington's very swank Opera Ball.

Meanwhile, the Permanent Village's most entrenched inhabitants —its journalists—settle ever deeper into their roles as bardic record keepers.

With each quadrennial chorus of "All change!" the Tom Bradens, the Evanses and Novaks, the Germonds and Witcovers, the Jack Andersons, the David Broders and the Mary McGrorys treasure more their inimitable and unique repositories of myth and anecdote.

They watch with slightly bloodshot eyes as the new arrivals pour in, radiating passion, ideals and ideas, stirring the stale and sultry Washington air like a cool wind on a sweltering summer evening.

The new kids think they are just in town for two or four or six years. The Permanent Village knows that, for a lot of them, that isn't true at all.

Yes, there's life after Washington.

But for a Washingtonian, it's either in Washington. Or it ain't much.